Navigate to Freedom

Will natural law free humanity and change the course of human history?

Kenneth E. Bartle

aotf publishing

ISBN: 978-06455837-2-4 (sc)
ISBN: 978-06455837-3-1(e)

For rights and permissions, please contact:
Kenneth E. Bartle

bartle@iinet.net.au — http://aotf.site

Disclaimer

This book is written and formatted in Australian English, but uses indent paragraphs for economy in keeping with most published works.

Natural law is markedly different from positive law and everyday use of the word Law. Moreover, Lex Naturale is substantially different from Ius Naturale, although both refer to natural law as commonly understood.

Positive law dominates today's world, that in most cases, is Maritime or Admiralty Law. Within this compass, virtually every English word denoting a member of the Homo sapiens species attaches legally to some form of body politic, i.e., to a legal or judicial entity having that status and obligation. Juristic systems at large deem many words innocently used in everyday speech to have an overriding legal meaning. These include but are not limited to the terms person, a natural person (versus robot), individual, he, she, and citizen. In the Maritime or Admiralty Law system, nothing remains for any judge to address a living man or woman. The word human in legal terminology is not a man or a woman, but rather an animal or a monster. Commonly said, man, is a social animal.

As a result, this book's content writing and grammar editing have proven highly challenging, specifically concerning the term human being? Additionally, use of the terms man, mankind, person, individual, people, humanity, or humankind. More than politically correct, or gender-equal, the correct term must also refer to each living being singularly yet allowing for plurality. Refer to the Definitions given in the Appendix.

Because this book disavows the subjects of legal positivism, statute laws, and the government itself, it does not infer, offer or give any legal advice whatsoever. This book does not need the legalese of lawyers, attorneys or (legal) practitioners. Its focus is the study of Man and the orderliness of his activities, rights, respect, and responsibilities. Altogether these provide a lawful, moral, just, expansive, life-sustaining, and enjoyable objective framework for Man's free will to embrace. All diagrams are for illustration of ideas only.

Given examples portend potential outcomes, not actual results. They do not represent or guarantee that anyone will achieve the same or similar results since each individual's success depends on their intent, application, valued desire, and motivation.

Table of Contents

Table of Diagrams

Introduction

Powerful globalists, sociopaths and psychopaths are hell-bent on decimating the human population to create a new world order of domination and control, altogether a heinous crime that makes Communism look like a kid's party. People are slowly awakening to a tragic global disaster, but few have any inkling of its solution. But no more!

This book goes straight for the jugular. It describes the root cause of tyranny and how to stop it in its tracks. It reveals why all socio-political structures fail, even in stable countries having robust legal and security systems and firmly instituted law-and-order. This book smashes through damnable ignorance that holds the people in check and how criminal arrogance prospers.

These pages show how free organic societies can prosper and how they must, henceforth and forever. If you want to live in a free, peaceable community and want the same for your children and grandchildren, this book leaves no stone unturned. It describes twenty governing laws encrypted within the nature of every man, woman and child. They are Creator's model for social freedom par excellence, yet never taught!

Albert Einstein said, *"No problem can be solved from the same level of consciousness that created it."* Buckminster Fuller picked up on that thread, *"You never change things by fighting the existing reality. To change something, build a new model that makes the existing model obsolete."*

This book does both. My book *'Conscious Ascendance'* revealed the truth about human consciousness about which Einstein spoke. This book builds on that irrefutable foundation and goes further. It introduces the new model that Fuller referred which overturns 'natural law theory and replaces it with 'natural existential law.' As a result, authenticity and potency multiply many-fold, whereby the gate to societal freedom swings wide open as no one has dreamt possible. The old models of 'positive law,' admiralty law, common law, and democracy vanish. You will learn the true origins of the word 'law' and how 'lawful' is rightfully divorced from 'legal.'

Like dominoes in a line falling one after the other, political theories and bogus social ideologies are laid flat. Ethics, morality and natural justice now properly emerge from millennia of concealment. Unalienable and inalienable rights have new meaning thereby. Unique ID for each of us as 'living beings' completely excludes dead and fictional entities legally referred to as citizens or persons.

In sum, the whole of today's legal/politico/social structure is rendered obsolete and sent packing, just as Fuller nominated it should. The replacement model is a *'Protectorate.'* Its demonstrable joys are immutably based on self-governance, as Creator consented. These enable a charter of individual rights offering freedoms, comforts, and security for every human being, now and hereafter. Such societal freedom has never existed in human history.

Around 2012 I began researching how the government in Australia could repurpose, but neither law, common law, nor natural law offered any answers. Undeterred, I turned to human consciousness, where my efforts smashed headlong into a wall of blind ignorance. No one explains what consciousness is or how it works. But, having already clocked up forty-five years of study and practice of Objectivist philosophy, I pressed on. Pieces of the conscious puzzle slowly fell into place until the whole picture emerged with unmistakable clarity. The word 'gobsmacked' does not do justice to that one key piece. Tears of compassion for the human race streamed for several weeks, which led to my publishing *'Law from Within'* in 2017.

That book described human consciousness as never before taught. I separated the subject of consciousness from its natural laws for further study. In 2022 I published (part one) *'Conscious Ascendance',* which explains the story of consciousness more powerfully and beneficially. This book follows from that. It applies the same logic, method, and irrefutable laws to societal matters applicable worldwide. It puts natural law and freedom on the world map, impossible to erase. Whereas nothing in the past has dealt with sociological issues as human nature impels we should, that circumstance now reverses entirely. This book is humanity's lawful remedy.

What benefits result? *Conscious Ascendance* describes personal benefits as 'ramping off the charts.' This book explains how social benefits do likewise. Imagine every cell in your body as a society of fifty-trillion individuals. Everyone thrives according to natural governing laws and their precise nature, independently yet cooperatively. Outcomes result from the consequences of their actions, for better or worse. That form of cooperative self-governance is no less than Creator's model for free organic societies on earth.

Bingo! If we replaced all forms of manufactured law with this new model, the result would mimic precisely what Einstein and Fuller hailed should be. Then all your benefits are protected in full, plus societal benefits ramp up the charts as never before witnessed.

The fact that you prosper from nutritious food, but suffer otherwise, is ample proof that natural law governs the consequences of your behaviour. Thoughts prescribe your ethics, which then defines your morality or its lack. As you determine your path, so you choose the outcome. Natural law governs the consequences. You are the living proof of natural governing laws, amply sufficient to demolish tyrannical rule forever, thereby preserving your freedom and all generations following in your footsteps.

Every success in your life is proof of your ability to self-govern. Who can deny it? None can, which means you've already established how to navigate your freedom. All you need now is a navigation chart — which is this book. It highlights all the hazards and illuminates your passage to freedom. You win with no contest because the natural governing laws of your being are innate and immutable. No one can remove them. If you transmute them into society as this book describes, you become a radar beacon for humanity.

Just think what happens when morality is struck from the public domain and reinstated where it privately belongs. What happens when your free choice is protected absolutely? What happens when those who choose to violate your life are apprehended? Are they free to choose you as their victim, or have they sacrificed their right to make such choices by choosing to be an outlaw? Try wrestling that idea in today's courtrooms, and you'll grasp how far-reaching the compass of this book is. Forget any ideas about fixing what went wrong. It could not have been otherwise because its premises were evil. Render them such, and the problem vanishes while freedom prevails.

Buckminster Fuller's suggestion of a new model is what this book delivers. It is revolutionary in concept, uncompromising in its promise, and demonstrably empowering for everyone. And it is all based on exactly what and who you are, in full accord with Creator's intention concerning how we should live. Put these principles into practice, and you win.

Any outlaws who stand in your way self-confess their guilt through their actions, their supposed power self–destroyed. Switching from legal to lawful is radical. Nothing compares, nor can it.

If you prefer repeated secrecy, injuries, usurpations, corruption, theft, malpractice, and despotism when you are the rightful master of your life, best you put this book back on the shelf. If not so mind controlled, then grasp hold of natural law and navigate to freedom, thus becoming a founder of the most significant social revolution the world will ever witness. If you've not already grasped this urgency, you soon will. If you have, you'll be among the first achievers.

> *"Never underestimate the power of a few committed people to change the world. Indeed, it is the only thing that ever has."*
> *—Margaret Meade*

As this book unveils Creator's truths, you will see through today's rhetoric and nightly news with crystal clarity. You will avoid all debate as futile. Your heart will sing as you navigate freedom. The secret lies in knowing your nature and how to employ it.

This book and *Conscious Ascendance* are the only books that explain full consciousness and the natural governing laws encrypted in your character. Please read this book and practice its principles; your rewards are highly compelling — beyond measure — nothing excels. You will never look back.

Chapter 1

1. Law it is not

Despite all claims of benefit, governments harm people in every country and nation. Escape from authoritarian dictatorship is impossible, yet since burden and distress prevail, the law is dysfunctional. Flip this atrocity on its head using natural law, and a glorious future for humanity opens to view. My purpose in this first chapter is to show, without exception, every aspect of the enormous task that natural law must overcome. Our blessing is that these laws are innately encrypted within each of us. All we need do is discover and practice these twenty natural governing laws encrypted in the nature of every man, woman, and child.

As a radical alternative to every artificial law ever written, they offer the prospect of free societies never before witnessed. My task is to assist you in resoundingly proving them for yourself, for your freedom. After that, no one will convince you otherwise. Then, you will live freely as your Creator intended.

Law, as people know it, is not law. Written' statutes' are erroneously called law. All artificial, so-called law, including common law, is referred to as 'Positive Law' or 'Legal Positivism.' Positive law ostensibly upholds and preserves society, but more customarily today, it serves to maintain the state as an entity in its own right, to your detriment.

Natural law is vastly different, indeed the exact opposite. It is the (unwritten) governing laws of nature itself, also called God's, Creator's, or Divine law. I speak not of the laws of physics, such as gravity, conservation of energy, or the law of thermodynamics. Instead, identity, respect, integrity, causality, free will and independence all pertain to upholding and maintaining human life.

Removal of Divine law is impossible, but statutes can overrule as though it never existed. Ruling emperors, kings, queens, dictatorships and governments have maintained that condition throughout humanity's history. To make rules for managing government, the word 'person,' which we all think means you and me, is usurped and construed to have a 'legal' meaning. Your natural (flesh and blood) nature is legally stolen at birth, and a 'body politic' is attached, whereby you are thereafter treated as a dead, fictional, legal entity, not unlike a pawn on a chess board. After that, your name in ALL CAPS refers to you as a 'citizen' or 'person.' That word derives from 'persona,' a mask. In practice, therefore, you are a fraudulently created, fictional, LEGAL ENTITY having legal obligations to the state. Different states and types of states fall under the umbrella of 'society by company,' as distinct from 'society by symbiosis,' or 'symbiotic society' that we would call free societies.

Government's must-have you believe their fictional identity is the real you, and their legally contrived laws are all there is. Your passport, a driver's license, and ID cards are your legal ID. But they are not your ID as a conscious living being born of nature. Those instruments identify the legal persona of the government's corporate slave. So you are recognised only as that LEGAL ENTITY, a citizen by NAME, subservient to the (legal) (society by company) government, to be ruled and regulated, as a servant; all non-compliance with their statutes punished. All of that is taught as necessary for your benefit, as though no alternative existed and never could it. This fraudulent scam traps us all. Every time we show their ID upon request, we agree to be their servant while fully believing it is our ID. So they claim 'consent of the governed.' That is false because the fraud occurred when you were only hours old. You had no means, no words to 'consent,' much less to know what the word 'approval' means.

Most people commonly use the word 'person' in colloquial everyday speech; in that sense, we are 'natural.' However, governments blended our (live birth) nature with the fictional 'person,' as if that were possible, to create the 'legal term' of 'natural person.' Their express intent was to have multitudes not recognise this impossible merger. Thus we are fraudulently deceived in that we agree or consent that we are a Legal Entity, not a living being. Unbeknownst, therefore, our individual rights are trampled as though they never existed. With natural law rejected, statute laws reign supreme, all backed with deadly force.

You have no natural born rights today as a (flesh and blood) breathing individual. Nonetheless, government entirely depends on your flesh and blood body, participating and acting in the capacity of the (fictional) legal entity, known by your citizen NAME, as though that is your sentient living being. All such citizens are dead, however. Legal entities are fictional inventions. Your (upper case) NAME is a fiction. Constitutional usurpation of your born name, and the process that makes it your LEGAL NAME, is a fraud. All fraud is void ab initio, a Latin term meaning invalid from the beginning. It cannot be amended or fixed.

Most people are entirely ignorant that we function in positive law, as and for a counterfeit legal entity stolen from our born name without our consent. Consent of the governed prevails to the great delight of sociopaths who rule us. Governments are the (legal) monopolists of terror, the very thing they purport to despise. Although claiming their purpose is your protection, your wellbeing is sufficient only to maintain their slave labour force. Without your forced contributions, governments would collapse.

> *We are fast approaching the stage of the ultimate inversion: the stage where the government is free to do anything it pleases, while the citizens may act only by permission; which is the stage of the darkest periods of human history, the stage of rule by brute force. —Ayn Rand*

If we are to build a new societal model, as Buckminster Fuller suggested, the whole fraudulent legal construct must be trashed and replaced with what is lawful according to nature.

Few people perceive any means to overcome legal oppression, slavery, tyranny and unceasing war? So-called leaders know this well. Yet, they do all possible to ensure natural law remains concealed, which explains the occulted concealment of full consciousness throughout our history.

As a result, government violence and coercion increase in quantity and severity. We vote for its continuance out of ignorance, thereby granting the government the right to protect its legal status vigorously. Censorship, propaganda, state schooling, licensing and registration, political correctness, and media control serve that purpose. Governments assume the moral right to use force and coercion to preserve and protect the state. Your unalienable right to life is denied thereby.

History repeatedly shows the foolish irrationality of majorities, proudly and loudly proclaiming the virtue of democracy. Corporate political power is nothing but a state-run monopoly, using methods that enforce its continuity at the expense of the people thereby enslaved. The notion that authority is a benefactor, and protector, is a monstrous lie. Authoritarian rule permits neither. No truly moral, honest, individual man or woman can participate in or endorse the (initiated) coercing of others. Because no amendment is possible, truth must now replace the lie.

Man is not his brother's keeper. We are keepers in the sense that we do not violate other people. But we are not keepers such as to command others, even for their supposed benefit. Force-backed authority is an act of violence, antithetical to all it upholds as moral.

The three primary sources of positive (artificial) law are constitutional, statutory, and case law, all ranked in that order.

Constitutional law is the body of rules, doctrines, and practices that govern the operation of political societies; the state. Constitutional law defines the fundamental principles that enable governments to exercise their authority, and to define the relationship between the various branches of government within the state.

Statutory law is the body of law resulting from statutes. A statute is a legislated command; thus rules, or statutory laws, are also referred to as legislation. Whether federal or state law, a statute is a written law that you can read at a law library or online. Human rights, also known as civil liberties, form a crucial part of a country's constitution. These purportedly uphold the individual's rights against the state, but seldom do they.

Common law (Case Law) is a body of unwritten laws based on legal court precedents. In practice, judges make legal rules in issuing rulings on court cases instead of endorsing legislated regulations or official statutes. For any new case, consistency requires that a judge abides by the same logic and reasoning used in similar past cases, hence the name 'case law'. Here, judges actively shape the law, and a court decision becomes a precedent for future cases.

The term 'Society as Company' applies to all social systems governed through a system of invented rules. These include sporting clubs, charitable and educational institutions, corporations, and incorporated governments, they being corporations masquerading as governments.

1. Law it is not

Although society is commonly considered an aggregation of people living and freely interacting in an atmosphere of liberty, strictly speaking, that is misleading. Tribes, far removed from what we think of as a society, may indeed be socially acclimated yet live as free individuals having no authoritarian governments.

It remains that societies (by company) such as clubs, institutions, corporations, and corporate governments, rely on and demand that their subjects give exclusive attention to the societal structure and its nature, especially its preservation. Thus we all are bound to its social rules. A rule-bound company is what the word society means. Loyalty to its members and leaders is foremost. Members, constituents, and its citizens, highly prize the fairness of its governance — its government. All consider themselves beneficiaries.

Rules governing these societies' management are neither law within their original meaning nor a science. Instead, they are artificial orders of artificial persons whose legal systems attach legal rights, duties, and obligations, to different organisational positions.

Artificial order is an order of artificial persons. Artificial persons are not living human beings. Instead, they are positions, roles or functions within a particular game, social system or society, governed through a system of (invented) rules intended to facilitate their (respective) functioning. Think of artificial persons, for example, as white and black pieces in a game of chess, including the governing rules of the King, Queen, Knights, Pawns, etcetera. Other examples include Rector, Dean, Student or Faculty member in a university, or King, Government, Parliament, Minister and Citizen in a nation-state. Such legal artifice does not attach to the actual living beings elected or appointed to occupy those positions. Indeed, legal separation removes any misdeeds or personal liability from public accountability. It thereby excuses and forgives those who serve those organisational roles, save for censure(s) within the company itself. E.g. Susan didn't do it; the branch manager did. No living individual is legally accountable; only the position. Notice how an office bearer signs off all government documents, not a living being.

Collectivism is the notion that Man is an 'animal,' a creature to be herded like sheep or cattle. A subservient victim of force or mental onslaught to every conceivable form of domination and control ever invented until, stripped of mind and soul, all that remains is a writhing carcass of flesh, pleading food and deliverance. Our entire history has been, and still is, premised on the 'collective,' never a man, woman, or child as unique individual beings of creation.

Regardless, most people have some understanding of their biological processes, bone structure, nervous and digestive systems and so forth. Further, outstanding individual achievements witness even sparks of genius in literature, public speaking, art, music, science, and many other disciplines.

Had we studied our mental processes as attendant upon themselves, marking precisely that which they serve, just as we learn our breathing and digestive functions, we would have known the natural laws of our consciousness centuries ago. We might then have grasped Creator's gifts for mastering our lives, thus not become beholden to oppressive, dictated conformity.

We failed that test. We ignored our independence, one from another. Instead, we used the 'collective' of humanity, race, humanism, politics and sociology as our baseline benchmark. Having trashed our individuality, we've suffered almost never-ending tyranny and bloodshed for millennia, all believed for the good of the country, society, race, religion, empire, or some other 'collective.'

Authoritarians welcome human crises. Governments are thereby permitted to deceptively conceal freedom-killing plots and initiatives necessary to resolve purported problems. A pandemic will create turmoil and anxiety, whereby disproportionate responses seemingly appear inevitable and therefore acceptable. Using the same strategy on such things as climate change, gender equality, crime and justice systems, education, and the Critical Race Theory helps ensure the complete fragmentation of society, as is now happening.

We enthusiastically vote for these 'programs,' fully believing that we're expressing our will and deciding our future 'democratically,' when in truth, our flawed belief in the morality of 'democracy' is used to manipulate our minds so that we surrender our 'rights' to 'permissions.'

Legal positivism has provided law schools with a dismissive yet comforting notion that law belongs in what lawyers know and practise. Positive law, or Legal positivism, is a school of 'Jurisprudence' whose advocates believe that the only legitimate sources of law are written rules, regulations, and principles. Governmental entities and political institutions, including administrative, executive, legislative, and judicial bodies, recognise these laws, adopt them and expressly enact them.

1. Law it is not

Legal positivism does not base its laws on divine commandments, reason, or human rights. Instead, it consistently adheres to 'positive norms,' that is, patterns of legislated social order or what is considered common law or case law. Legal positivism neither suggests nor implies ethical justification for the law, for or against the obedience to the law. To explain, positivists do not judge laws based on questions of justice for humanity but on how laws are created and upheld. Positive law, loosely speaking, is any express written command of the government.

Law's study and practice are separate from considering justice by equating 'lawful' with' legal.' Accordingly, justice is enabled and indeed is wrongly converted into expertise in legality, answering to no law yet vehemently positing that it is the law.

Who then decides the law? It can be anything. Because it is not defined, everyone is ignorant of it, yet *'ignorance of the law is no excuse.'* Not surprisingly, the law is now a decreed social order for our complicit agreement and compliance, all disagreement regarded as *'breaking the law.'*

How then does justice relate to you and me? It does not and never will while its sole purpose is to uphold the state.

Today's legal systems apply to government, corporate governance, and any societal body such as corporations, sporting clubs, libraries, galleries and workers' unions. Once grasped that government is 'Lord over all,' so too is incorporated government, which means we all are corporate ruled, not government ruled. It remains that rules and procedures of Society as Company have respect and applicability only within their enterprise.

It became essential, therefore, to make all citizens a 'legal' part of the (government) corporation so that everyone will adhere to, obey and comply with authoritarian prescriptions, legislations, rules and procedures. Clubs, institutions, transport systems, food processing, construction processes, and even emergency services fall under this umbrella of prescription and forced compliance.

Consequently, all Legal positivists must employ means to enforce their invented rules politically. Threatened violence, including financial theft (fines) and even organised violence, upholds the legal system of politically organised rule enforcement, ensuring compliance.

Statute law is legislation passed in Congress in the United States and Parliament in the United Kingdom and Australia. Its origins, at least in countries with an English legal heritage, are the royal proclamations from the King or Queen, later replaced with Parliamentary Acts as the source of Statute Law. In the United Kingdom and Australia, statute law still technically gets its authority from the Crown, but nowadays a rubber-stamp. In brief, Statute law, also known as statutory law, refers to the written and legislated statute (laws) of a country, state, or nation.

Today, most people believe that their 'rights' fall into various categories such as human rights, civil and political rights, economic, cultural and social rights, and, more recently, environmental rights. Within countries, or according to international law, all of those so-called 'rights' are subject to (state upheld) rules of law. However, rights, supposedly state-protected, do not protect one's right to act at all. Instead, they regulate and control specific actions purportedly to curb abuse. Governments wielding authoritarian control deny every individual's (unalienable) right to life. Believed right to force, coerce, enslave, rob, and murder others is 'statism.' All statist doctrines are the same. The frequency of force, its extent, victims, purpose, or benefit are considered irrelevant questions. Regulations purportedly exist for people's best interests and the good of all; force is thereby essential. Accordingly, all productive activities and financial management are subject to government management, that being statism.

Thus in practice and principle, statism is gang warfare brutally devoted to looting the productive efforts of the people of its own country. Statism survives through looting, pillage and theft. A free country survives and thrives through creativity and production.

> *STATISM: The most dangerous religion in the world. Those who believe that "Authority" is necessary and that it MUST continue have actually been duped into believing that human SLAVERY is necessary and MUST continue in order to prevent chaos.*
> *STATISM: The brilliant idea that we give a small group of people the right to kidnap, imprison, harass, steal from and kill people so that we can be protected from people who kidnap, harass, steal and kill people. Violence and slavery cannot prevent chaos. Violence and slavery ARE chaos. —Mark Passio; Extrapolation from his video work*

The belief that any state has the moral right to initiate the use of physical force against any one of its people is to believe that the political doctrine of control cannot be averted. It is to agree that some men have the right to force, coerce, enslave, rob, and murder others. Yet, insensibly, most people are today convinced that the 'political doctrine of state control' is necessary since that is what guarantees their freedom. They suffer in silence, unwilling to relinquish nanny state coddling that frees them of personal responsibility.

Worse yet, once conceded that state acts or statutes guarantee 'liberty,' no need exists to protect one's freedom.' After that, the 'state' has complete liberty to trash your free will, whence it is free to deny your unalienable rights and means of self-protection.

Understand that your freedom to appoint the state as the regulator of others' freedom to protect yours was the day you granted the state unlimited free license to overrule your freedom and that of all others. To uphold that condition is to maintain the denial of freedom.

Many groups of people promote the idea of overthrowing oligarchs who control nations, stupidly referred to as 'leaders.' They believe that socialism is the answer to oligarchy, even though socialism has never toppled power-hungry sociopaths. Oligarchs promote socialism as their stock in trade. As a result, people and groups who press for a better world through socialism are unwittingly doing the oligarchs bidding. Authoritarian rule is the goal of socialism.

Socialism's core doctrine is that no man has no right to exist for his own sake and that his life and work do not belong to him. Instead, they belong to society, that he exists solely to serve the community, which is the only justification for his existence. Consequently, society may dispose of him and his efforts as it pleases for the sake of whatever it considers its collective good.

Socialism alleges that it abolishes poverty and achieves general prosperity, progress, peace and human brotherhood. Yet the result has paralysed or collapsed every country that tried it, every resultant disaster proportional to the degree of socialisation. The principles, policies and practical consequences of socialism today are akin to any historical or prehistorical tyranny.

Force-backed authority is an act of violence, antithetical to all benefits it purportedly upholds, yet this violation of our life is declared legal and deliberately misconstrued as moral. The scam is skillfully hidden in plain sight so that the masses approve its perpetuity at the polling booth — natural laws and knowledge of full consciousness are thereby occulted. Nothing will change until we awaken to this crime against humanity and eliminate it.

Before William the Conqueror invaded England, local communities would decide disputes based on custom. Thus law derived its authority from long-standing tradition. However, William set about creating a common law for his kingdom, whereby Legal decision-makers were supposed to have regard for precedents from across the country. Accordingly, Common Law, also known as case law, is based on custom and general principles, which serve as a precedent or are applied to situations that statutes do not cover.

Common Law lays its foundation in natural law, which is natural law theory. However, my book, Conscious Ascendance, convincingly showed that natural law is not a theory; instead, factually encrypted in our human nature. Therefore, I refer to it as 'natural existential law.' As an existential fact, it founds the content of this book, whereby the (believed) theory has no place.

If common law and natural law theorists accept the principle of authoritarian rule, statute law is certified legitimate, and nothing changes. People have no knowledge that natural law even exists. Witness that today no 'common law' advocate points to natural law as its foundation.

Should it surprise that very few people perceive any means to overcome legal oppression, slavery, tyranny and unceasing war? So-called leaders know this well. They happily occult this knowledge to conceal natural laws that would end their rule. Censorship, propaganda, state schooling, licensing, legal registration, political correctness, and media control serve the government's purpose. Thus implemented and provisioned through our labours, governments take unto themselves the right to use force and coercion for their protection. Consequently, government violence and coercion increase in quantity and severity, and we ignorantly vote for its continuance.

Because common law, also known as 'unwritten law,' and 'case law,' is not written as legislation, no legislation prescribes it, nor can it be read at a law library or online. Human rights in common law countries fundamentally derive from legal precedent in the court's interpretation of constitutional law. In contrast, for civil law countries, rights are almost exclusively composed of codified law, constitutional or otherwise. In other words, rights are legal permissions, not divinely endowed.

Sadly, many people firmly believe the idea 'we' can enjoy a revolution, yet none have grasped that there is no 'we' to make the breakthrough collectively. Others think that Citizen Initiated Referendums (CIR) are the answer. A referendum is a general vote of the electorate concerning a single political question expressly referred for a direct (majority decided) decision from the people. In other words, a referendum validates or rejects a law after publication.

Conversely, plebiscites (referenda) are a people's vote to decide on some issue proactively. Thus plebiscites are called before the enactment of a law. For example, the British decided if they wanted the UK to be part of the EU Brexit. The majority voted for leaving, albeit a tight margin, whereby the parliament negotiated the terms and began enacting the outgoing departure.

Letting the people manifest their will and decide about something that directly impacts them may seem 'good,' a sign of a healthy democracy. However, history testifies a margin for abuse and results of these processes, which denies that simple acceptance. The merits of different options, democratically debated forever, defeat the goal entirely. The acute risk is that one's constitutional rights may be put up for grabs through a questionable process, having questionable results. Polarisation of the electorate inevitably results in purportedly justifying authoritarian legislation.

Small margins of victory put the whole process in question, notably since the minority's rights have been cancelled, not upheld and protected. Moreover, that condition may last the life of the electorate.

Worse happens when governments accrue even more power while the population is weakened, in the most part due to their own choice. Depreciative results are immediate.

In sum, democracy is a form of collectivism that denies individual rights. As a totalitarian manifestation and not freedom, democratic governments are all-powerful. They thrive on the 'collectivist' doctrine of unlimited majority rule.

Just think. If we are pressed into crime to avoid becoming its victim, mob rule and gang warfare are more certain than sunrise tomorrow. But, on the other hand, if we become more willing to accept, comply and conform despite our cries for deliverance, what future do your children have?

For evidence, look at the power-grabbing script now crippling former bastions of independence and freedom in Australia, Austria, New Zealand, Canada, Germany, the US, the UK and many others.

Democracy, or 'system of parliamentary democracy,' is described or considered a system of government in which the whole population or all the eligible members of a state express their preferences, typically through elected representatives. It all sounds so innocent but beware.

> *"Democratic" in its original meaning [refers to] unlimited majority rule. a social system in which one's work, one's property, one's mind, and one's life are at the mercy of any gang that may muster the vote of a majority at any moment for any purpose. —Ayn Rand* [2]

Governments take power through brute force in countries with weak and unstable institutions and populations. Elsewhere, power-grabbing schemes use a more sophisticated script to gain moral acceptance, best known as democracy. Authorities looking to increase their power have successfully used this method many times throughout history. In practice, 'rights' are taken through sleight of hand, one bite at a time, through Machiavellian manipulations that successfully divide the population while claiming to have enrolled full support. The method is simple. Problem — Reaction — Solution.

- Create a problem and stoke fear among the population.
- Measure the reaction and throw in measures to test the waters.
- Politicise issues to promote divisiveness.
- Offer a previously crafted solution to solidify the polarisation, thereby obtaining civil approval to initiate the authoritarian initiatives politically desired from the beginning.

Democracy has given us the most brutal period of human history. Like Common law and Statute law, Civil Law, Case Law, and Admiralty Law all comprise of Man-made Laws having nothing in origin to do with (existent) Natural Law. Inevitably they run roughshod over it. Collectively they are referred to as 'political law' and in the legal context, 'positive law,' or Positivist Law with some differences,

If, as previously described, the law means order, then law and order is a nonsensical phrase. Yet practitioners of (so-called) law (legalities) will trot out platitudes such as social order, or justice, trusting that those who hear will feel comfortable that law serves their interests. Such sayings intend to engender a feeling of comfort, or more wickedly perhaps, seduce people into believing that LEGAL practice is LAW. Natural Law does not abide by any such escape clause because it immutably exists independent of any opinion about what law is or ought to be.

1. Law it is not

Positive Law is a product of our human invention, a fabrication expressed as an opinion of human interests. If we accept the law as it is from a legal viewpoint, then we agree that Law is Legality. Therefore, justifiably it would seem, but stupidly, science should properly abandon all research and leave the world as it is.

Law is not a human fabrication. It emanates outwardly from Man's nature, fundamentally expressing itself as what Man ought to do, according to what ought to be his reason for so doing. Thus every Man-made prescription is in complete opposition, in principle if not in measure. What we ought do, and why, is trampled.

There is no court of appeal for this criminal injustice. Natural Law is the reality of our nature, indelible within the truth of our existence. The science of justice may be misinterpreted as any science can, but that does not alter the reality of our existence one iota. Error in our thinking should initiate correction, not new laws.

Governments do not have to force peoples compliance when they volunteer for slavery. Governments know that to maintain power and control, they must continually create fear and chaos while continually offering themselves and their programs as a solution to the chaos they create, despite that solutions rarely eventuate. Centralised and concentrated power is, by far, the most dangerous and destructive thing our planet has ever seen, and will ever see.

When government no longer serves us, it controls us for service to itself. It presumes the right or entitlement to take private wealth and property by which we are servant and not master. That switch is unlawful since it abrogates our rights. Accordingly, we each have the lawful right as individuals to reclaim our right to life. We may refuse, revoke and breach any contract imposed by force or coercion or without full disclosure and our consent.

Social equity is properly served by private voluntary charity and personal compassion than by any collectivist bureaucratic static dogma issued by threat of law and force.

What we believe is today protecting our freedom is murdering it! The insane, criminal immorality of this inversion is complete. Our free will to choose has become the government's uncontrolled will to rule. Humankind has approved its slavery. Our unalienable rights have vanished, and today, nothing protects them.

It should now be evident that what our Creator decreed as (existent) law in nature and what Man passes as law are vastly different. I'm indebted to Frank van Dun[8], philosopher of law, for one of his many astute observations because it has profound implications-

"Without the hypothesis of a divine legislator, who for some unfathomable reason prefers to encrypt his commands in nature, theories of 'Leges naturales' (natural law) get nowhere–and with that hypothesis, non-believers can only conclude that they are conjured up out of thin air."

With profound respect and gratitude for van Dun's offerings, the (very fathomable) reason, I submit, why a 'divine legislator' would encrypt his commands in nature is precisely so that no other legislator could ever override His legislation. (Never lose sight of our free will.)

Humanity has attempted to override natural law for centuries, producing mayhem, war, carnage and endless bloodshed as a result. The most vicious criminal contrivance ever perpetrated on Mankind was to replace 'who' (living) with 'what' (non-living).

The most damming sin we have ever committed and continue is apathetic acceptance of criminal fraud without question, allowing legions to *"conclude natural law is conjured up out of thin air,"* all because no law library describes it.

'Rights' presently fall into various categories such as human rights, civil and political rights, economic, cultural and social rights, and, more recently, environmental rights; individual rights are never mentioned. The unstated premise is that government must force some people to perform particular actions or force them not to so that others are free to act as they see fit. The whole of it is a sham based on initiated force.

"No one, individually or as a group, can give consent for something to be done to someone else. That is simply not what 'consent' means. It defies logic to say, I give my consent for you to be robbed. Yet that is the basis of the cult of 'democracy': the notion that a majority can give consent on behalf of a minority. That is not 'consent of the governed,' it is forcible control of the governed, with the 'consent' of a third party." —Larken Rose [3]

The insanity is obvious. Freedom depends on physical coercion of others, which immorally denies every individuals unalienable 'right to action. Personal freedom is abolished thereby.

1. Law it is not

While today's justice systems are almost universally perceived to uphold one's rights as a living being, the truth is very different. No reconciliation or compromise is possible, between natural and artificial, now or ever! Meanwhile, incomprehensibly, thousands, if not millions, daily fight in courts in every country, attempting to reconcile the natural law of living beings with the positive law for artificial beings, as though some conciliation or meeting ground is humanly possible. It's not!

'Positive law' courts, bound to their jurisdiction and structure, must banish natural law as incompatible precisely because it is. Evidence is not given by a man or woman but by a concocted artificial legal entity called a natural person within a legal jurisdiction. They must submit to that court's jurisdiction, which action automatically admits that fake law will legally preside. The court must dismiss all natural law presentments because none accord with its non-natural jurisdiction.

Fortunately, we now have the remedy. Natural order, being natural law, is not a commandment, nor can it ever be. On the contrary, the orderliness of process within our nature confirms that natural governing laws are Creator's endowment to secure life, comforts, efficiency and security. We each are complete in all respects. No more thing is needed, given our free choice, commitment, and our respect for the lives of all others. Nothing could be more simple. Nothing could better serve justice.

Will Society by Company ever be done away? Not while it writes the legally claimed (moral) rule book that enforces compliance through gunpowder laws! Neither will authoritarian force and coercion vanish while human sciences ignore the natural laws of our being as though non-existent.

Overt control and dominion will remain while Creator's invitation to live remains deliberately hidden through religious or secular contrivance. Tyranny will continue to thrive while political authority violates Man's right to life, most notably when (polling booth) billions endorse those conditions, utterly ignorant of a free organic society perfectly modeled in their very nature. Governments will always survive while we each disavow, indeed refuse our endowed independent nature, preferring to be herded, branded, and corralled as a social animal.

I promised to paint a picture of law as it operates today. Although only a sketched outline, still it is not a pretty picture. I've shown capitalism as the light at the end of the tunnel. It resides in that befitting place because it underwrites the value of life itself. My task now is to walk you along this path of value as it pertains to life as lawful. The course is natural law. The remainder of this book will aid your discovery of what you should have learned during childhood.

Chapter 2

2. Ruled or free societies?

Freedom and protection go hand in glove. When initiated force arrests freedom, then protection demands. Initiated force and correctional force are opposites, the difference being respect and responsibility versus their lack. This chapter explores all these matters, their relationships and morality.

For too long, humanity has depended on theologies, philosophy, and political ideology, all absent conscious understanding, which academia freely admits today. Philosophers have long ignored human nature and recommended invented fictions. The following examples are still taught in today's universities.

> *"Plato (and a long line of political thinkers after him) argued that likeness (equality) was a fact, but that people ought to be taught that it was not, lest they refuse to accept the different benefits and burdens that come with different positions in a politically organised society. Aristotle, on the other hand, argued that likeness is but a superficial illusion. Thus, he taught that there is no true likeness between Greeks and barbarians and that consequently there was nothing wrong with the superior Greeks holding other inferior people as slaves.*
>
> *Rousseau (and many socialists after him) maintained that human freedom was a fact of nature but that people should be taught to*

believe that it is dangerous and that they ought to renounce their human nature in favour of the artificial condition of citizenship. In that condition, everybody is supposed to be a creature, not of nature, but of the laws (leges) enacted by the state (which is but name of the collectivity of citizens). In short, natural persons should become artificial persons, that is citizens -- wittingly or unwittingly, willingly or by legal compulsion.

Marx, on the other hand, appealed to the much more radical idea of universal socialism. He claimed that no human being is free but that only the human species can be free. As far as individuals are concerned, freedom is an illusion. Hence, it cannot justify any claim. However, those who identify themselves with humanity as a whole are universal individuals. As 'species-beings', who know themselves to be identical with the human race, they are the true communists. As such, they represent a superior evolution of mankind. They should not be deterred by the illusions of morality and justice of those who still are mired in the false consciousness of their particular individuality. —Frank van Dun

Given these teachings, it should not surprise 'We the People' have for centuries been socially corralled, denied our independence and subjected to domination, control, and tyranny. Mentally deceived and with scant knowledge of consciousness, we have allowed authorities to become tyrants. When stripped of our unalienable right to life, panic, irrationality, and fear run our minds and societies, in which we gladly hand over precious rights and freedoms. The words of Rousseau, Plato, and Marx are now daily practice. Socialism has brought communism to our doorstep.

Unable to think clearly, we accept house arrest, virtual martial law and denial of our intrinsic, inherent, individual rights, precisely as those insane philosophies have long taught. Moreover, former (de-jure) governments are now service corporations restricting our ability to gather, assemble, move, trade, work, shop, and live everyday lives. So, we must question whether invention rules reality or vice versa.

The positivists may object that the opinions that make up the law as they define it are not opinions about matters of fact, but about what ought or ought not to be the case, about what is good or bad, better or worse. The point of the objection is, of course, that such opinions about norms and values may not be the sort of opinions of which we can sensibly ask whether they are true or not; or that, if there is some sense in asking this, we have no agreed on procedure for deciding such issues other than the appeal to effective authority. But this objection misses the point. Natural law theory, properly understood, is not some sort of normative moral theory. It does not seek to make moral judgements. It seeks to identify the principles of social order, to judge human actions as either lawful or unlawful, depending on their relation to such principles. The question "What is law?" is logically distinct from, and prior to, the question "Should we live according to law?" Frank van Dun [4]

In my book *'Conscious Ascendance,'* I answered both questions by showing that natural laws govern our biology and conscious processes. We cannot live without those laws. In the same article van Dun writes—

"Laws are patterns of order, hence Natural Laws are patterns of natural order, Natural Law is the natural order of persons; human beings that are capable of rational, purposive action, speech and thought."

Conscious process is confirmed once again. Natural law exhibits as irrefutable, which explains why all forms of positive law must deny its existence.

"The doctrines of legal positivism have provided the law schools with the comforting notion that law is to be found in the things lawyers know and practise. Consequently, to study these things, to familiarise oneself with them, to acquire the necessary skills to use and apply them in a wide range of real life (or: court) situations, should suffice as the proper aims of an education in the law. It is little wonder, that the "education in the law" these schools provide resembles nothing so much as an initiation in the rites and customs of a particular profession, its dogmas, doctrines and prejudices, especially concerning the so-called "sources of law": legislative, judicial and administrative rulings, treaties, and the main currents of opinion among the members of the profession. Positivism has rationalised the idea of "law" having its source in the decisions of

designated political and professional authorities. By equating the lawful with the legal, it has helped to push the study and practice of law away from considerations of justice into a mere expertise in legality." — Frank van Dun[4]

Let's see how that is accomplished. Wikipedia states...

"Natural law (Latin: ius naturale, lex naturalis) is a system of law based on a close observation of human nature, and based on values intrinsic to human nature that can be deduced and applied independent of positive law (the enacted laws of a state or society)."

That sounds plausible, but the Latin derivation phrases, ius naturalis and lex naturalis, are grossly misleading when associated as though one. As explained, 'law' was first derived from the Latin word 'Lex,' arising from the mobilisation of armies and organising military campaigns. Thus *"Lex was a command, which came to mean any general directive, rule, or law issued from the highest political authorities." Confusion arose because the word 'law,' also translated from the Latin word 'Ius', refers to "a bond or obligation that arises out of a personal commitment made in solemn speech."*

The word 'lex' later became 'Lex Naturalis,' ostensibly to give moral legitimacy to statute laws and commandments, especially those arising from the *'natural law theory of positive law.'* Accordingly, Wikipedia's use of 'ius naturale' and 'lex naturalis' respectively refers to the *natural law theory of law* and, differently, the *natural law theory of morality*, both discussed later.

Statutes, commandments, or edicts intended to secure orderliness are not law. Law is orderliness. Either the phrase 'law and order' is an oxymoron or the deliberate intent to plunder the natural order of the human world. The vital difference between statute law and natural law is clear. Statutes are invented rules applied to fictional (legal) entities. Natural law is the modus operandi of nature itself. Neither is compatible with the other, therefore. They cannot be blended and treated as one. Van Dun uses the term *'natural persons'* as we should use it to denote flesh and blood living beings. That done, subsequently, the term 'natural persons' does not and cannot ever mean artificial persons or legal entities as governments prescribe.

2. Ruled or free societies?

Force is one of two kinds—

- Initiated force violates one's life. It is unlawful, unjust and immoral, criminal.
- The defensive arrest of such unlawful and destructive force is legitimate. The resistive or corrective force that restores the natural order is lawful, just, and moral.

That last was to have been the role of government, but none in history have done so. No state has entirely barred initiated force, although America came closest. The tragic, if not insane truth, is that most if not all governments consider it necessary to launch harm to preserve the peace. Victimless crimes like speeding tickets are a prime example.

While ever authoritarians rule it morally wrong to rape, pillage and plunder, so their rules that rape, pillage and plunder are upheld as legally right.

That diabolical circumstance arises from failing to understand Creator's 'natural law of no trespass,' modeled within us.

Neither our heart nor lungs can trespass the other, nor can our conscious mind trespass our subconscious mind. Those boundaries source the 'non-aggression principle (NAP). Sadly, voluntarists champion it but do not understand the 'natural law of No Trespass' or its encryption within our nature.

Aggression, for this purpose, is defined as using (or threatening) forcible interference with an individual's life or property. For this, the non-aggression principle admits that force used for self-defence is morally lawful, which it is.

The NAP is fundamentally sound in principle. Force initiated against another is anti-life, whereby arrest of that force is rightfully pro-life. Notice the switch in focus, however. The primary lawful and moral issue is not the arrest of aggression or violence but the living of life! Our primary concern and focus is properly our unalienable right to live. Until that condition holds supremacy, all discussion concerning the cessation of violence puts the cart before the horse.

As described in my book, *'Conscious Ascendance,'* the subconscious mind protects our conscious mind and vice versa. In like fashion, the *'natural law of No Trespass'* morally protects society and reciprocally protects our individual life choices. Accordingly, the *'non-aggression principle'* is no longer a theory or moral proposal, left open to debate or consensus agreement. The *'natural law of No Trespass'* is an immutable scientific fact of self that has existed since the advent of man, and nothing can erase it. That law endorses the NAP principles with the punch and power of factual existence. Natural law is not a theory.

Our failure to grasp these immutable principles has allowed despotic rulers to compel us to adapt to the state's artificiality. It is as though invented rules were nature herself; therefore, we must adapt ourselves to that artificiality, bound to a state of servitude like a herd of farm animals, just as animals must adjust to nature. But we are not animals and are not equipped to act that way! Therefore, conflict, aggression and wars are the only possible outcome to which human history amply testifies.

Physical force is well understood, including rape, bodily harm, detention, torture, and murder. Also included are theft, legal or otherwise, blackmail, fraud, overt mind control and debilitating threats of violence. Ayn Rand cut through centuries of confusion concerning 'rights,' stating that violating one's rights compels us to act against our judgement. That is serfdom, not freedom.

Freedom means protecting one's life and property from interference or trespass, specifically through physical force or coercion. Such is well understood, including rape, bodily harm, detention, torture, and murder. Physical force arrests one's choice to do other than is forcibly commanded.

The basic principle of morality and justice is that no man may initiate the use of physical force against others. Rand also points out "no man may initiate (start) the use of physical force against others." Physical force is moral and lawful only in retaliation to arrest those who initiate force.

Creator's Natural Law of NoTrespass forbids physical force initiated against others. Therefore, in practice, no Man, group, society or government may assume the criminal right to initiate the use of physical compulsion against any man, woman, or child.

Freedom means protecting one's life and property from interference or trespass, specifically through physical force or coercion. For example, Rand pointed out, *"a holdup man seeks to gain a value, wealth, by killing his victim. But the victim does not grow richer by killing a holdup man."* The principle is unequivocal, namely that no one may obtain any values from others through physical force. Two primary principles are crystal clear.

1. No one may initiate or start the use of physical force against others. This act of evil may not be sanctioned or forgiven.

2. We each have the right to use physical force, only in retaliation against those who initiate its use. As Rand clarified, 'the ethical principle involved is the difference between murder and self-defence.'

These two principles in the natural law of no trespass and the natural law of just consequence come together in the law of natural justice. The principle is unavoidable, not subject to differences of opinion, majority decision, or the arbitrary decree of society. To deny those principles is to refute one's nature, which automatically annuls all such authority. Those who step outside natural law are outlaws, period!

Willingness to accept that we are social animals has crippled our minds to accept centuries of authoritative harm blindly. We should have busted the herd mentality millennia ago, yet today its truth remains unknown to all but very few. I invite you to search 'physical force' at http://aynrandlexicon.com. It explains that initiated force that violates one's life is unlawful, unjust and immoral. Conversely, defensive arrest of destructive force is lawful, just, and moral.

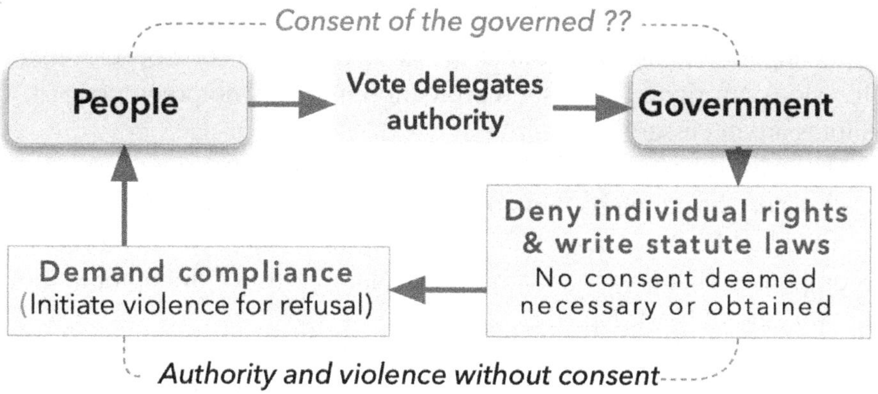

1. Ruled societies

Those who step outside natural law are outlaws! They can choose differently. Every aggressor is responsible and accountable for their actions, thus predetermining the extent and degree of necessary remediation or compensation. That is the fundamental of Natural Justice, inherent in the Natural Law of No Trespass.

Observe the fundamental difference between diagrams 1 and 2. An educated organic society replaces an indoctrinated (ruled) society. Freedom, protection and natural justice for all replace the organ of corruption.

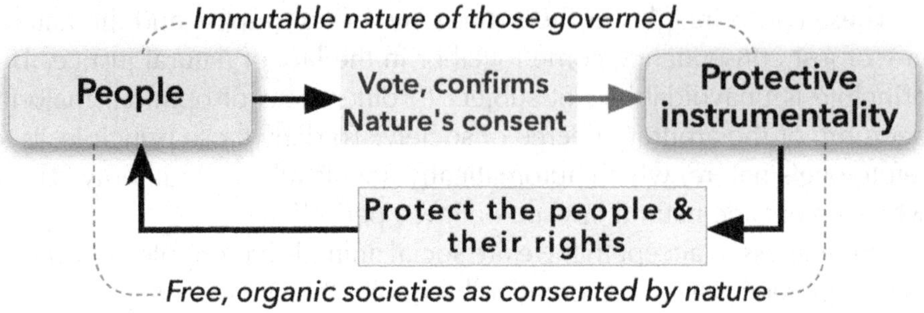

2. Free societies

Now, the difference between morality as a social convention, and its proper place within each (individual) living being, becomes vibrantly clear. Every cell, tissue, organ, system, and our conscious and subconscious minds point to morality as that which sustains life. That condition has existed since Man's inception, and life demands that we protect it. What's needed is an institution constitutionally charged with protecting individual rights under the same objective code of rules that provisions our rights. With such protection in place, no preemptive statutes are necessary

That was to have been the role of government. Not one government in all history has done so. No government has fully upheld the concept of Individual Rights. America came closest. necessary remediation or recompense. That is the fundamental of Natural Justice, inherent in the Natural Law of No Trespass.

> *"You cannot see too clearly that force and reason—which last is the essence of the moral act—are at the two opposite poles. When you act by reason you are not acting under the compulsion of other men; when you act under compulsion you are not acting under the guidance of reason. The one is a force within you and the other a force without. Moreover, physical force in a man's hand is an instrument of such a brutal character that its very nature destroys and excludes the kindlier or better qualities of human nature. The man who compels his neighbour is not the man who reasons with*

and convinces him, who seeks to influence him by example, who rouses him to make exertions to save himself. He takes upon himself to treat him, not as a being with reason, but as an animal in whom reason is not."Auberon Herbert[11]

Each man and woman is a unique and precious being wherein the natural laws of their nature govern their actions. Their right to live is exclusively independent and immutable. Their life is what they are. Their singularity, beautiful uniqueness, and the natural order of their life ordains boundaries that separate each of us from others; their rights, words, deeds, works, and property, from ours, and from other things.

- Accordingly; no trespass of any other living being's right to life is permissible under natural law.
- No claim of right may negate, usurp, or overrule the unalienable rights of other living human beings.
- Independent rights of Man preside over all other life forms.
- Our right to act, so to live, fully accepts the reciprocal right of all others, equally so to do.
- Trespassing another's rights self-cancels our (individual) rights, respective of that particular action.

"Bureaucrats protect the establishment. Leaders protect individual rights." — Charlie Kirk.

Integrity, honesty, commitment, truth, and self-preservation are inherent in the natural laws that govern all our faculties, systems, and processes, without which life would cease. Thus, values, ethics, and morality emanate from within individual men and women regardless of country and culture, corresponding with everyone's right to choose. Natural law grants no permission or authority for one to trespass upon another's life. The precedent is unmistakable. Neither of our two minds can overrule the other. Furthermore, independent human lives cannot fuse into one unified entity without sacrificing their singular unalienable right to life and the means to live it. Accordingly —

Natural law refuses all authority. It denies all orders and all authority save its own, regardless of source or claimed authority.

Natural law refuses initiated force in all forms, whereby the right to exercise the muscle to arrest such assaults is morally justifiable. Murder and self-defence are opposites.

First, it must be understood that we do not need to extract ourselves from maritime law and its statutes. Why not? Because those juristic practitioners and their political allies have voluntarily separated themselves from those who truly live already. They walked out on life willingly. Neither are we obligated to prove natural law since we cannot exist without it. Those who refuse it already use it and cannot escape it. They can only step outside its boundaries, which actions confess outlaw behaviour. They choose to violate natural law using their invented dead, fictional entities. Voluntarily refusing to recognise the integrity and authenticity of their flesh and blood, they renounce their nature, thus denying their legal statutes any lawful foundation. All are null and void from inception; their authoritarian proclamations are inventions of demented minds. To legalise a fiction as though real instantly invalidates it. Fantasy has no power! Denial of one's in-built natural law is a matter for the Creator, not for a courtroom to decide.

The affirmation to protect against foreign and domestic enemies is our human nature, and so is the right to bear arms. Witness how the bodily immune system protects against all enemies; 'foreign' being ingested toxins, 'domestic' being diseased cells. Similarly, feelings and emotions serve to protect our conscious process from enemies; 'foreign' being imposed propaganda and false ideologies; 'domestic' being corrosive values subconsciously assimilated.

Thus our nature urges us to protect ourselves against all enemies, foreign and domestic and morally validates our right to keep and bear arms. Freedom imparts that we each seize, respect, enact, and protect it. Fail just one of those persuasions, and we've lost it.

We're all familiar with the golden rule, which states, *'do unto others as you would have them do unto you.'*

Think about that. Very often, the expectations of others determine our actions. Vagrantly left with hopes and desires, our reliance on their moral guidance allows them to prescribe our morality. No quicker shortcut to a subjective morality exists. That moral inversion has been our failing for centuries, yet people still preach it.

Appropriately written, the golden rule should state — *'Do justly unto yourself as you would others do justly unto themselves.'* Acting justly unto ourselves expresses our love for life. So we lead through example, and while that infers others should do likewise, their moral choices are entirely their own. We each are the authors of our morality, based on our lives while respecting the life of all others.

2. Ruled or free societies?

That principle is unquestionably within you. Recall that feelings report whether our actions uphold our life or retard it. Similarly, our actions demonstrate whether we support or deny other people's right to their lives. Creator has modelled the natural law principles of ethics, morality, and natural justice, smack in the core of our conscience and emotional reporting systems, exactly where they belong!

Once grasped that morality or immorality outwardly broadcasts to all others, no difficulty should arise from freely choosing moral actions and bearing all consequences, which is the core principle of natural justice.

Our agreement to allow the state' right' to regulate and control others is our permission for the State to run roughshod over everyone's free will and to trample their unalienable rights into dust. The State knows it well. With your tax dollars, they hire the best in the world to plot your slavery and devise methods to punish you if you do not submit.

> *"The problem is that the people are taught that when violence has been made 'legal' and is committed ' it changes from immoral violence into righteous 'law enforcement.' The fundamental premise upon which all 'government' rests is the idea that what would be morally wrong for the average person to do can be morally right when done by agents of 'authority,' implying that the standards of moral behaviour which apply to human beings do not apply to agents of 'government." —Larken Rose* [3]

In the main, people have not identified that the destruction of any individual's free will choice is the destruction of their own. They do not comprehend that when the State rules against something they disfavour (for which they cheer), the State has confiscated morality in 'principle'; so to govern their actions tomorrow and enforce their decrees with a gun. Few people recognise that children are taught an indulgent indifference to a politic which kills millions. That State or condition is worse than sad; it is criminal, tragic, ruinous, yet entirely preventable.

The day we grant the state permission to regulate others freedom to protect ours is the day we appoint the government to grind our freedom into dust. What you believe is protecting your freedom is murdering it with your approval! Once denied our free will to choose, we become enslaved. Our unalienable rights vanish, and nothing protects us! Today's legislation upholds government; your protection is sufficient only to achieve that goal.

Nothing will change until we divorce the insanity of an animal-like society, whose lawless agents tyrannically rule with a pen in one hand and a gun in the other! Those who declare us irrational animals and forcibly treat us as such, self-confess outlaw intentions. Having forsaken morality, they are the aggressors – the terrorists. Fortunately, they are in the minority. The time has come to declare that your life is precious and inviolable and your so is your right to protect it.

The subject of 'natural law' has roots in Western philosophy, principally in the Pre-Socratic search for principles that govern the cosmos and human beings. The concept is referenced in ancient Greek philosophy by Aristotle and Cicero in ancient Roman philosophy. References found in the Old and New Testaments of the Bible elaborated further in the Middle Ages through Christian philosophers such as Albert the Great and Thomas Aquinas. Modern natural law theories developed in the Age of Enlightenment. They combined inspiration from Roman law with philosophies like the social contract theory and used it to challenge the divine right of kings. These theories often refer also to ethics, politics, civil law, and religious morality.

Important above all is that natural law initially premised on morality became an alternative justification for establishing and upholding the social contract, positive law, and government's legal rights, notably in the form of classical republicanism.

We should not write off periods of olden-day history as tragic altogether – for much of it offered value. For example, Josiah Warren (1798-1874) chose to pursue individualism — credited as the first man to expound and give form to what is now known as Anarchism. John Stuart Mill offered that Warren recognised no authority for society over the individual save to ensure equal freedom for all. The sovereignty of individuals later became an essential focus of Mill and Spencer.

The work of Herbert Spencer (1820-1903), an English sociologist, should not be forgotten. A radical individualist and a moral and political philosopher, he argued absolute ethics in his political and moral theory, specifically that violence and coercion are morally wrong. For some reason, however, he also gave the state autonomy.

Neither should we omit the work of Lysander Spooner (1808-1887). As an American political philosopher, an individualist and anarchist, he offered that—

2. Ruled or free societies?

If justice be not a natural principle, governments (so-called) have no more right or reason to take cognizance of it, or to pretend or profess to take cognizance of it, than they have to take cognizance, or to pretend or profess to take cognizance, of any other nonentity; and all their professions of establishing justice, or of maintaining justice, or of regarding justice, are simply the mere gibberish of fools, or the frauds of imposters. —Lysander Spooner [10]

John Locke (1632-1704, widely regarded as one of the most influential enlightenment thinkers) was the first to postulate that the mind is a blank slate or tabula rasa at birth. In his questioning of the work of others, Locke ostensibly established the method of introspection, that of observing one's emotions and behaviour.

Sir William Blackstone (1723-1780), an English jurist, judge, and Tory politician, also deserves mention. Although noted for his controversial legacy, the main work of which is his Commentaries, likely had they not been written when they were, the United States and other English-speaking countries would not have adopted the common law.

Those rights, then, which God and nature have established, and are therefore called natural rights, such as life and liberty, need not the aid of human laws to be more effectually invested in every man than they are; neither do they receive any additional strength when declared by the municipal laws to be inviolate. On the contrary, no human legislature has power to abridge or destroy them, unless the owner shall himself commit some act that amounts to a forfeiture. — Sir William Blackstone [12]

Frank van Dun (1947-) is a Belgian law philosopher and libertarian natural law theorist who qualifies the above revelations concerning natural law. As a subscriber of the private law society or anarcho-capitalism, he argues that every natural person (individual) has a lawful claim on his life, freedom, and property. Moreover, this claim is absolute, provided it does not prohibit equivalent claims of other natural persons insofar as argumentation is respected. Arguing that the correct interpretation of the non-aggression principle (NAP) is praxeological rather than physical, van Dun's offerings on natural law vs the legal, and Kritarchy, are indispensable to any student of jurisprudence.

The human conscious process informs us that spirituality is value-based communion between our conscious and subconscious minds. Their harmony, cooperation, grace, and reverence for each other and Creator is spiritual self-growth, self-respect, self-mastery, self-esteem, and devotion to a lived life.

Consequently, it is not the role of physical science to interpret our achievements in spiritual terms. Instead, each of us must learn from scientific enquiry and, from that foundation, choose life values and exercise our spiritual essence.

Governing laws within our nature prohibit this sequential process from being reversed. Our physical sciences should not condemn spiritual values, therefore. Science should instead spark spiritual discovery, much as perception sparks our cognitive discovery.

The subconscious mind is devoted to our life succeeding and growing in the spiritual sense, whereby our choice to consciously and consistently pursue the same objective is its perfect accompaniment! Natural laws are simple, easily understood, immutable, and just.

Fortunately, and only very recently, science has recognised that our mind's affinity with spirituality is undeniable, as our two minds are profoundly interactive. Philosophers and spiritual teachers should assist in this enlightenment but seldom do they. They've yet to grasp that spirit interfaces with physicality via our human nature and that our consciousness nurtures value-communion between physicality and the Divine.

Nothing excels for Man, is more direct, or more productive. Nothing but the entire exercise of your faculties pay tribute to you, your spiritual essence, and your Creator more reverently. That best explains us as spiritual beings, living a spiritual life in a physical domain. In so doing, we each can attain self-mastery like nothing ever taught.

Eating nutritious foods, exercising, sleeping, and cleansing is respect for our bodies. Exercising thought and our hearts through relaxation and meditation is respect for our minds. Things of beauty are also respected through travel, visiting galleries or venturing into the great outdoors. Properly preparing and ordering the process of our doing is respect for our being. All these means show respect for natural order, in and of ourselves. Every adult on the planet is conversant with being an orderly self.

It follows 'respect'. is the all-encompassing natural order of one's being. It's the most precious of all virtues. Put the ducks in a row like this. Reason comes first, and it generates rationality. Therefore, there must be a reason to uphold one's life and a rational reason to defend the lives of all others respectfully.

Refusal to think is disrespect. Throughout history, humankind has sought to escape natural law precisely because freedom and authoritarian rule are incompatible. Freedom stands in the way of authoritarians and dictators. Natural law blocked them. Consequently, they deemed it necessary to bypass our lives, so they invented 'legal entities' as substitutes for our living selves. They write statutes (laws) to control us as fictional legal entities, like wooden pawns on a chess board. They hoped success would result and have largely succeeded.

But that insane experiment has failed. Instead, natural justice struck home with a vengeance. The mayhem of today's world, the insanity of its control structures, its tensions, bitterness, family feuds, terror, slave systems, racial tensions, financial frauds and endless wars all testify to nature dealing out natural consequences in exact measure. Remember, when thought denies our being, natural justice strikes penalties identical to the magnitude of our insanities; today's circumstance exactly.

There is no escape clause in the morality of natural law! The more we struggle to preserve our refusal to see and to think, the greater our freely chosen downfall.

Free individuals understand that other people's freedom assures their own, so they do all in their power to uphold it. To be fully autonomous is to be fully responsible, thoughtful and graciously respectful. That is Natural Law.

> *The first test of your own commitment to freedom is to ask yourself, "Am I willing to grant every other individual the right to his or her own life?" And until we understand freedom as individuals, and grant that freedom to our neighbours, all efforts to bring freedom to the world will fail miserably. —David MacGregor* [13]

Respect is total. No political figure on earth can answer yes to MacGregor's first question. His second sentence describes natural law consequences. Nothing will change until the world resoundingly says 'yes' to freedom. Nothing offering any modicum of natural justice can happen until all fictional Legal Entities, falsely believed to be 'lawful', are eliminated! Self, respect, and self-responsibility are inseparable.

Self-respect is first. No one and nothing overrules it. Respectful mastery is understanding self and properly using all of one's faculties.

Self-direction is to choose with respect and accept responsibility for one's actions. Self-confidence is to 'know,' evaluate and choose to act respectfully, all consequences accepted.

Respect for others begins with respectful responsibility for one's thoughts and actions in life-value terms, then acting per those values.

Respect for values and virtues utilises our conscience and mentoring system fully.

A self-made Soul is our goal. Our nature testifies this most emphatically via our feelings and emotions.

Freedom is the only condition in which our consciousness operating system can function as it should. It is the prerequisite of our very existence. Natural governing laws do not pronounce upon themselves; instead, they are the only (already existing) means of functioning. They are innate and immutable. None exists as a limit on our will; instead, they inspire us to be more conscious of how we do things. Such 'invitation' opens the door to 'individuation,' which facilitates 'cooperation.'

Freedom pertains to each (independent) living man, woman and child. It is not subject to approval, constraints or dismissal. Freedom is singularly individual, while liberty is social. Thus when freedom factors into society, resultant liberty results as Creator has determined, not as the state decrees.

It is therefore incumbent on us all as independent beings to preserve individual rights and interests, individual responsibility, and individual 'executive' decision-making ability concerning the conduct of our lives. We must remodel society to protect and preserve our unalienable rights to life; without compromise or surrender.

There is a clear and distinctive fork in the road ahead. First comes the awakened evolution of consciousness and human spirituality. Second, we must implement natural law. These laws are axiomatic. All personal, societal, and business dealings correspond with individual, unalienable rights, rightful freedom, and unobstructed action within our will, drawn about us by the equal rights of all others. Natural law forges unprecedented, aggregate empowerment, capable of overcoming any resistance that might stand in its way.

Life demands our most profound consideration and resolute response. It vitalises a deep understanding of our purpose in being alive at this time in human history and brings us face to face with our destiny.

2. Ruled or free societies?

Once we understand that respect for these natural laws is 'spiritual,' we learn that 'Spirit' is the origin of both nature and humanity. Our lives are spirit in action.

As the consequence of God's free creative act, nature serves as the living theatre in which we each freely act and develop as a moral, spiritual beings. To repeat, we are spiritual beings living a spiritual life within a material realm. What matters is that we each live a virtuous life in which morality is our outward expression of spiritual freedom. All three together are our 'here and now' soul connection to our source Creator, our spiritual reverence.

Our task is to initiate and empower human freedom and thus banish tyranny. Consciousness and natural law afford our most incredible opportunity for intellectual and spiritual advancement and survival as a species. Both forge inspiration to join together in a deeper understanding of the further evolution of humanity. Freedom demands that we act upon our knowledge of natural existential law, with its incumbent responsibilities, exercising our right to self-mastery and protecting the same rights for all others.

"Freedom is the sure possession of those alone who have the courage to defend it." —Pericles.

Accordingly, we must seize, respect, enact, and protect freedom. Life demands our most profound consideration and resolute response. Do you want to live free? The very future of humanity may well depend on how we each respond to this information and act on it.

Freedom is the essential prerequisite of humanity. Responsibility is the crucial prerequisite for freedom.

"Those who expect to reap the blessings of freedom must, like men, undergo the fatigue of supporting it." —Thomas Paine (1737-1809) English intellectual.

Freedom is the power to choose while responsibility is the attitude of accepting liability for one's freely chosen actions. No one but the author of one's actions can be held accountable. It follows that in order to have freedom of action, no limitations apply save for one's own conscience and moral values. Freedom imparts that we accept responsibility for our self-chosen moral regulations, themselves based on the natural laws that govern the consequences of our actions.

American people did not cast off their political bonds to England to live in unrestrained freedom, absolved of all responsibility for fellow Americans or the destiny of their nation. The converse is true. They severed their ties with the wealthiest and most powerful nation on Earth, such that America's different system of governance placed increased responsibility for self-mastery on the people. So it became their task to self-rule, thus nurturing and growing their republic.

America's founders well understood that people who determine freedom determine to work for it. Thus, independence is not merely the separation of one state from another; instead, it is the separation of all people from the state. There is no free ride, no childish belief in me-first irresponsibility without penalty.

"In the long history of the world, only a few generations have been granted the role of defending freedom in its hour of maximum danger. I do not shrink from this responsibility -- I welcome it."— John F. Kennedy (1917-1963) Thirty-fifth President of the USA

Thomas Jefferson nailed freedom when he said—

"That governments is best which governs the least because its people discipline themselves."

Jefferson was no layman. His credentials include American statesman, diplomat, lawyer, architect, philosopher, Founder, 3rd President of the United States 1801-1809 and 2nd Vice President of the United States 1797-1801, author of the Declaration of Independence

"The liberty to do as one wishes without consequence, to make a mess of things and leave them to others to clean up, is the freedom of a child. To act without concern for others, to behave in ways that are destructive or disruptive without facing the consequences of one's actions is not the way an adult behaves. And a society that tolerates or promotes that sort of irresponsible freedom is doomed to failure and collapse." — Thomas Jefferson (1743-1826)

2. Ruled or free societies?

Independence is self-rule. It is to make the right and responsible choices, unreservedly knowing they are correct and accountable. These people master responsibility, thus freedom, thereby exercising their sovereignty. Pretenders do not. They exercise irresponsibility in sacrificing their lives to (ruled) dependency, hence slavery.

The concept of freedom does not belong to any country, race, society, civil or social system. It belongs to every man and woman who claims and practices it. To be human is to have the right to your life and be free to exercise it within the equal rights of all others.

You owe it to yourself to take freedom for yourself. He who fails to assert his rights has none. Moreover, if you must petition for freedom from another, you are not free. The only freedom you have, is the freedom you take unto yourself and insist that others observe and respect.

Freedom cannot be granted by a Constitution, the government, the Bible, God, your parents, a company, or political figure. Freedom is a state of being and actions you create from your natural state. Action is needed to voice, create and defend freedom. We must deal firmly with anyone who trespasses our immutable right to life or who would penalise us when we have harmed no one. It is a crime to trespass the freedom of another.

Those who believe that freedom is granted by God are mistaken. It is true that our Creator gave us the means and power to claim our freedom, but He did not give us freedom itself. Freedom is the success of our actions and achievement; not a parceled gift. Thus we can help others to know that they have the right, means, and power to take freedom for themselves.

Freedom exists in the instant you claim it, and usually vanishes when you fail to defend it.

Freedom manifests in different forms according to what each individual makes of it in his or her own way. Freedom is not what you may do, it is doing what you do with no restraints. Freedom cannot be defined, codified, or legislated. It only exists when is exercised within the reciprocal rights of all others.

Freedom, is achieved through non-violence, which means those who choose violence are not free, by their own choice. Free people must defend against violence or loose what freedom they created unto themselves.

Freedom, in a political context, means freedom from government coercion. It does not mean freedom from the landlord, or freedom from the employer, or freedom from the laws of nature which do not provide men with automatic prosperity. It means freedom from the coercive power of the state—and nothing else.— Ayn Rand

Freedom is not possible in a system of majority rule, or any rule by a central authority. Freedom is only possible when those who choose to live as self-avowed sovereign individuals protect their rights, actions and property unmolested and without impediment provided they commit no harm to others. Even then, their obligation is to the harmed party, not a government.

No collection or wealth management should be allowed to any public entity, agency or officer. No wealth or property must ever be seized or forcibly redirected from the individual whose labour has earned it.

Times have changed, which means the words 'government" and 'legal' have long passed their 'use-by' date. Governments are now universally incorporated, meaning they are not a government. Instead, legality is the instrument through which they administer their fraudulent masquerade as government.

Our task is crystal clear. Suppose humankind took a leaf out of the American 1776 declaration and declared all people free and responsible. Suppose instead of the words 'government" and 'legal' they substituted the words 'protectorate' and 'lawful.' A massive change would occur, as this book describes. Consider this synopsis as its introduction.

For a society to be free, its 'Protectorate' must be strictly controlled and never overrule the people's freedom. Under a proper (free) social system, a private individual is lawfully free to take any action he pleases, so long as he does not violate the rights of others. At the same time, a Protectorate official is law-bound by law in every official act. A private individual may do anything except what is lawfully forbidden; a Protectorate official may do nothing except what is lawfully permitted.

There you have it in a nutshell. A free society is one in which the rights and freedoms of all are protected, without exception. People are free to the extent they exercise responsibility. The Protectorate (government) is strictly bound to protect people's freedom to live responsibly, all else and forbidden. That is the only path to a free society for all individual, sentient living beings. Let's now turn to freedom, respect, and responsibility within the auspices of natural law through the advent of Protectorates as lawful substitutes for governments.

Chapter 3

3. Ethics and Morality

Who mentions ethics and morality today? Has social media swept them under the rug, or are they now an extant relic having little application in a world littered with statutes, executive orders, transgenderism and endless legislations? Bogus doctrines and erroneous philosophies have corrupted spirituality so profoundly that few people understand their inner realm. My book Conscious Ascendance explained that our mental and spiritual capacity is considered second to technology. Chaos and trauma reign, and though cheated, nature is not, always ensuring that we reap what we sow.

Do you see the senselessness of countless pseudo beliefs festering in the cesspit vacancy of conscious ignorance? Spiritual achievement begins with us consciously fueling our subconscious database with life values. Thereby enabled, it interfaces our material world through sensory perception and our soul through spiritual values. Accordingly, consciousness is a life-sustaining spiritual-value transfer process interfacing physicality and our soul.

There you have it all. Life values are crucial and you get to choose what they are. Loosely speaking, values define what's good because they are the things we strive for, desire and seek to protect. Few people would disagree, but there is more to this story, as 'Conscious Ascendance' described. Before we reach those prized goals, we need to consider what values will assist us on that journey. I'm speaking of life values like respect, diligence, honesty and integrity. In simple terms, what makes humans unique is the faculty allowing us to determine how we'll act.

Ethics, therefore, is the process of questioning, discovering and defending particular values and purposes like respect and diligence that help propel us to our target goals like peace, harmony, fulfillment and love. It's about finding out what we are, how to function optimally and efficiently, and how to stay steadfast in facing temptations, challenges and uncertainty. 'Conscious Ascendance' explained that process and how to automate it fully to reduce anxiety and stress to near nil. So let's look at life values to formulate our ethics, thereby building a life and a robust future founded on our spiritual nature.

Ayn Rand described morality as a code of values to guide our choices and actions as they determine our life's purpose and course. Since thoughts precede actions, ethics, as a science, deals with discovering and defining such a code. She posed that the first question to be answered in determining, judging or accepting any specific system of ethics is: *"Why do we need a code of values?"* The first question is not what particular values should we accept but do we need values at all—and why?

'Values' are seldom, if ever, mentioned in discussions concerning ethics and morality. Yet, given that the process of 'full consciousness' is wholly reliant on values, ethics is an objective, metaphysical necessity for our survival. Rand makes clear that our nature presents the choice to be rational and so live, or else suffer. To succeed, we have to hold our life as a value, learn what sustains it, discover life-upholding values and choose to practice them.

Spirit is our connection across all boundaries and barriers. It transcends race, religion, gender, culture, nation and education. Such unity is not a unified or 'collective consciousness' as I described in 'Conscious Ascendance.' Instead, we each have a coalescing spiritual force or spiritual energy that unites all of us in purpose, simply because we are all equal. Some might call this 'spiritual consciousness,' but the phrase 'spiritual unity' is much more appropriate, I consider, in that it speaks of 'unified participation' while preserving the unique spiritual independence of one's conscious process.

In other words, 'ethics' are the code that enables us to conceive objective, life-supporting evaluations and judgements in our cognitive mind, based on our chosen spiritual values. Unethical thinking results from abandoning or rejecting such values. Our ethical study properly embraces praxeology, which is concerned with the nature of value and valuation and the different kinds of valuable things. Thus ethics are a formulated code of values. In short, our lives depend on the values we choose, and that value code is 'ethics.'

Accordingly, to be ethical is to investigate, recommend, systematise and defend concepts of right and wrong conduct, where 'right' concerns life and its maintenance. All contrary is anti-life, meaning 'wrong.' So let's be very clear. Ethics is not rightful conduct versus wrong conduct. It concerns concepts of right and wrong conduct, which is to say, 'ethics' involves our thoughts, not our actions. It is correct thinking regarding ideas, concepts, values and principles. Ethics concerns objective, life-supporting evaluations and judgements in our cognitive mind. Morality comes later. It is the enactment of our ethical principles.

The term ethics derives from the Ancient Greek word *ethikos*, which stems from the word ethos (habit, custom). Later, people replaced the mystical theory of ethics in the Dark and Middle Ages with a social theory of ethics, but sadly, neither view ascribed ethics to individuals.

Dictionaries describe ethics as moral principles that govern a person's behaviour or the conducting of an activity. Does that mean that ethics is simply a bunch of moral tenets? If so, who or what determines morality and who determines the baseline reference for determining morality? Schools of ethics in western philosophy offer three descriptions that might answer those questions.

First, Aristotle posed that virtues such as justice, charity, and generosity dispose that we each act in ways that benefit ourselves and society.

Second, Emanuel Kant posited that ethics is a duty central to morality, wherein we are duty bound as rational beings concerning other rational beings.

Third, the notion of utilitarianism holds that our guiding principle of conduct should be most people's greatest happiness or benefit.

Look closely and see that the Kantian view declares ethics and morality a duty we owe to others. Likewise, utilitarianism ties ethics to collectivism.

But the Aristotelian view stands apart from collectivist notions. It attaches virtues to personal and societal benefits without casting any ideas of an imposed duty and without advocating a collectivised supremacy. Most importantly, the Aristotelian view of ethics is correctly divorced from the subject of (enacted) morality.

Accordingly, ethics is not a bunch of moral principles that society, government, the church or any other administrative body might determine.

Lacking any concrete foundation in 'right thinking,' ethics is presently a collectivist ideal belonging entirely to the philosophers of altruism. They and their disciples developed a universal morality. Its purpose is not to preserve your life and mine but to formulate a code of conduct that gives credence to collectivist rule. To disobey is immoral, if not a crime. History testifies to our acceptance, occasioned because no intellectual alternative was ever offered. Moreover, as later discussed, natural law theorists have played right into their hands.

For those reasons, the word 'ethics' receives scant mention today. When philosophers declare that reason has failed and that ethics is beyond reason's power, such that no rational ethics can ever be defined, what then remains? Faith, instinct, propaganda, revelation, feelings, beliefs, urges, and whims fill the void. When ethics is subjective, 'reason' surrenders to an empty wilderness of non-defined phrases, stolen concepts, and meaningless incomprehensible verbiage. Not surprisingly, bereft age-old philosophies are regurgitated in a modern-day vernacular readily swallowed by millions. Thus deprived, we are left to perish in a nonsensical vacuum today taught and believed to be enlightening.

This intellectual vacancy adds to conscious ignorance, effectively doubling the problem. Thus state and church agree that morality is a necessary component of civil authority, whereby they join forces to determine right and wrong and prescribe both. Never challenged because the intellectual void remains, they hold themselves to morality's (believed) authority. Guess what? That includes the moral right to rule, which is immoral, and the immoral wrong to refuse rule, which is honourably moral.

No more deadly formula exists. Artificial laws authoritatively prescribe morality backed by legal force, which is entirely immoral. We fall for this criminal insanity and pay for it most dearly because morality, as taught, approves of it! Thus we agree on the moral right to rule and the immorality of refusing imposed rule without question. Society suffers yet again.

The Dark and Middle Ages are a testimonial monument to the mystical theory of ethics, later replaced with a social theory of ethics, widely accepted as a *'social theory for the collective,'* as described above.

Whether we refer to this mental debauchery as society, human rights, an ideal for Man's benefit, or goodwill, 'subjectivism' and 'altruism' thrive unchallenged. They flourish on the unstated premise that our ethical duty is to be the selfless, voiceless victim of any need, claim, or demand that others may assert. Subjectivism's compass of reality is fluid, plastic, and indeterminate. A broad consensus is society's final judge, in which Man needs no ethical policies, objective values, personal ethics, and no individual morality. Church, or state, will determine all, or we'll hold a referendum and let the collective have its say. So it is believed that consensus must control the 'social animal.' Society comes first, whereby we individuals are thought not to need lawful policies, objective values, personal ethics, and no individual morality. That is today's tragic story. Humanity agrees sufferance is 'normal' and undoable because no other choice ever presents.

Natural justice has justly replied in the exact measure of this damnable and criminal violation of our right to life. Although meta-ethics and normative ethics died, as later discussed, applied ethics remained, being ethical professional practices written for lawyers, doctors, medical businesses, and even social policies and institutions. Are they for you and me? No; all focus on upholding the (purported moral) stature of their respective (commercial) enterprises. Applied ethics are little more than fanciful 'terms and conditions' pleading universal moral endorsement, as in "we are the good guys." That is not to criticise their ethical value but to emphasise that when personal ethics and responsibility bow to authority or consensus, few people will know they are robbery victims.

Leaving aside ethical practices written for lawyers, doctors, and similar professions, all else falls under the banner of morality, usually government-administered. Perhaps you were taught 'ethics' references codes of conduct in workplaces, medical or legal practices, or principles in religion; in contrast, morals refer to the rights and wrongs of 'society'? Were you also taught that the words' ethics' and 'morals' may legitimately interchange since they both mean the same?

Emanuel Kant held that a concept of duty is central to morality. As such, governments have full reign to prescribe social duty and decree what constitutes morality. Duty bound morality underpins all authoritarian ruling bodies.

To change today's common mindset requires removing ethics and morality from subjective or consensus opinion and church and state meddling.

Were you taught the vital necessity of value choices in life-sustaining terms? Few thinkers agree moral questions are answerable. Either right and wrong are considered the province of taste or opinion, or such matters are for governments to assess and enforce, whereby all debate cancels before it begins. Any idea that objective facts might help us scientifically determine how best to live our lives cancels, as 'natural law theory' testifies. Discovery subsides since if there are no moral truths to discover, nothing further can be learned. Not surprisingly, many of today's ethical thinkers are reluctant to pursue anything beyond banalities exhausted centuries back. Two matters arise.

First, humanity has relentlessly pursued technology at the expense of consciousness and spirituality.

Second, although blessed with complex light-speed faculties that almost defy description, we still have not bothered to understand their contribution to a fulfilling, ethical, and moral life.

Do you see the senseless tragedy? Blessed with an ability to unite humanity as never before imagined, we have not recognised its source, its simplicity, or spiritually empowering nature. We have never discovered the importance of spiritual purpose, choosing instead to sacrifice it to a currency of materialism, technology, greed and plunder, paying a hefty price for so doing. Two so-called 'ideals' are primarily responsible.

Philosophic materialism is the view that non-physical things do not exist. Spirituality is senseless; all talk of 'spirit' or 'spirituality' is sheer mysticism. People are nothing more than matter in motion, whereby physical nature is King. This theory is a scam that denies every mental faculty used to describe it.

Philosophic idealism holds that everything is an idea, energy, or consciousness; there is no such thing as matter, physical objects, or bodies. Physicality is a hologram, an illusion because everything is energy or frequency. This theory also defeats itself. Physicality must exist to express the view; moreover, ears, eyes, and brains must exist before others can hear or read such claims.

Ayn Rand eloquently summed up the absurdity of both when she said–

"A body without a soul is a corpse, a soul without a body is a ghost."

Others argue that the ultimate goal of spirituality is to transcend the self. Self is an illusion. Wherever you look, people say, inwardly or outwardly, the 'self,' the 'I,' or the 'ego' cannot be found. Forget your body and brain. Consciousness is not yourself. It just emanates from your body and brain. Neither is there a thinker; thoughts simply emanate from your consciousness. This argument is another scam because it denies the very 'self' to whom spirituality matters.

Ethics recognise and comprises three major areas of study today, vis—

Meta-ethics deals with moral propositions' theoretical meaning and reference, including how truth values (if any) are determined.

Normative ethics deals with the means of determining a moral course of action.

Applied Ethics concerns ethical practices written for lawyers, doctors, and similar professions.

Do you see a problem? Ignore life values, and meta-ethics and normative ethics are left foundering with no metaphysical foundation. Reject the importance of life, and theories and beliefs are all that remain. Conjecture rules our lives.

'Applied ethics' remain as codes of professional practice or for social policies and institutions. We, as individuals, are excluded. In truth, 'applied ethics' are little more than 'terms and conditions' in fanciful moralistic terms. That is not to criticise their value but to emphasise that when personal ethics and responsibility cancel, personal guidance concerning ethics is virtually non-existent.

If meta-ethics concerns the values of moral propositions, and normative ethics determines the morality of actions, then ethics concerns thoughts and not actions. Indeed, full consciousness shows emphatically 'ethics' pertains solely to thinking and our deliberations before choosing any action. 'Morality' entirely belongs to subsequent action(s), not thoughts that precede it.

The fundamental principle of Meta-ethics is vital and very simple, specifically–*Life demands that one always act to support and sustain it, never sacrificing its supreme value to anything lesser.*

That statement embraces every ethical consideration, every desire, goal, and purpose. Free will is vital. Meta-ethics is properly the deductive science of correctly appraising life values and choosing accordingly.

We can decide to be ethical or unethical, to think ethically or unethically— evaluate, choose, reconsider and choose anew. No one is affected or harmed but ourselves. Meta-ethics then becomes a science concerning particular values required to sustain our lives.

Whoa! Hold up. Isn't 'normative ethics' 'the means of determining a moral course of action'? If so, normative ethics swallows every subject of Meta-ethics. Only one science remains, called 'ethics.'

Nothing could be more simple. As the author of our actions, we originate our morality or we do not. Necessarily, we are fully accountable for that doing or not doing. Do you see? Spiritual values are life determined, and we choose among them according to purposeful goals. That rolls 'meta-ethics' and 'normative ethics' into one. In other words, we 'ethically' determine a 'moral' course of action. Do you see? Our desires and values are transferred from our conscious mind to the subconscious mind for moral enactment. Unethical thought upholds immoral actions.

Now meta-ethics is redundant. Our course of action is supportive of life or it is depleting or destructive. Either way, our values, ethics and intentions are fully exposed. So now 'ethics' can be taught as an objective science deriving from our biological and psychological human nature. Moreover, the relationship between 'private' ethics and 'public' morality is now clear.

Ethically: Life demands our deliberate choice to support and sustain it, never sacrificing its supreme value for anything less.

Morally: Life impels that we never act to deprive another of their life or the means to support and sustain it.

Those two premises can be described as ethical and moral intelligence. So two sciences suggest – ethics and morality.

A science or code of ethics. This concerns thoughts and values that uphold our private lives, as consciousness advises via its natural laws.

A science or code of morality. This code derives from ethics but solely concerns what behaviours and actions uphold the lives of all others.

Ethics should properly teach Creator's personal invitation to live the fullest, most beautiful, and bountiful life possible. It should also impress that natural laws are for our guidance, fulfilment, advantage and protection, knowledge, understanding, and holy joy.

Creator encrypted these laws within our being so no one could erase them. Nothing could be more natural or scientific than the exact nature of what we are. Therefore, ethics may be summed logically as objective, life-supporting evaluations and judgements. Its results should properly formulate the morality of our actions, for which we, as authors, are fully accountable.

This spiritually based, objective Science of Ethics embraces four straightforward principles.

Life: Nothing is more pertinent to every man, woman, or child on earth than life itself. Life is the base reference for all that concerns it, including the natural laws of identity, causality, independence, respect, equality, integrity, individual rights, free will and commitment.

Virtues: Virtues are attitudes, values, or developed character traits that enable us to act in life-supporting ways that foster and master our potential. These uphold our spiritual essence, which the above-mentioned natural laws embrace.

Respect: Respect is the voluntary endorsement of the vital need to support our life through the lawful exercise of our faculties. Respect also applies to other people since their well-being reflects our own. Individual Rights are crucial, for without, the right to life is ripe for plunder. Respect embraces all the above-mentioned natural laws.

Justness: Justness is the sum of just actions, a testament to our morality. Justness relies on the Natural Law of Just Consequence, which culminates as Natural Justice, uniting every natural law.

Thus we have internalised ethical principles founding judgments of right and wrong. Ethics, as now defined, pertains to each of us as individuals, independent one from another, respective of our desires, goals, ambitions, productivity, and life-sustenance.

The natural law of ethics states that choosing life-supporting thoughts, values, and determinations serves oneself, and those, when acted upon, outwardly express one's morality.

Nature has determined that we adapt material reality to our purposes. Thus life-sustaining thinking and reasoning must underscore our actions to be fully effective. The (value-based) code of life-sustaining principles that guide and ultimately determine the moral correctness of our behaviour and actions is 'ethics.' It relies on our wholesome integrity and the objective engagement of our every physical, mental, emotional and spiritual faculty. Unethical thinking and reasoning occasions no harm to anyone but ourselves.

The relationship between self-contained ethics and publicly expressed morality is now abundantly clear. Previously, morality has been considered a social necessity bound to imposed statutes (laws) intended to provide security, comforts, and protections. That error says that moral standards are a social ethic to be made uniform, legal, and rightly enforceable. People would presumably run amok were morality left to each individual, resulting in imposed laws and moral dictates being accepted without question. Rules and commandments endure, seemingly because no alternative exists.

Can you overturn that absurdity in your mind? Of course, you should, because a collective morality forced on us and backed by gunpowder rules is immoral, if not criminal. It is time to forget collective morality as an ideal. Why? Because when singular men and women are accorded their true nature as independent living beings, morality is instantly snatched from the social arena and restored to our separate domain where it rightfully belongs. Every man, woman, and child is the author of their morality or immorality and accountable for it, precisely because actions are of their free choice.

> *Morality is your conscious will to live according to your nature, never depriving others of the same opportunity. —Kenneth Bartle*

But, many will scream indignantly, *'how can uniform moral uprightness be achieved if each chooses their own?'* The answer is simple. There is no moral 'collective' since society is an aggregate of individual beings. Violence and aggression are personality disorders, not social disorders. Moral problems are singular, not plural.

Of course, groups or collections of individuals and governments can commit violence. Nevertheless, only one person signs a statute into law. No living being who fills a puppet role or position granted by positive law or government is excused or forgiven. (Witness decisions given at the Nuremberg Trials.) No one is exempt, whether a government official or not.

Aggression is of vital concern without question, but until our individual, unalienable right to life holds precedence, the principle of non-aggression lacks definitive reference. Conversely, once we focus on our right to life, its protection follows necessarily.

Our life and nature, and its governing laws, determine the foundations of ethics, morality, and justice. After that, our personally committed actions manifestly confess our agreed (moral) responsibility for them.

Of course, many people will question this idea. *"Morality must have consensus approval, surely?" "How could one man or woman ever uphold morality, given others may hold different opinions?"* Are they good questions? No, they are tragic misunderstandings dating from childhood. Parents and grandparents teach universal morality while religious persuasion and governments reinforce the notion. Legal authority enforces it, dissenters contemptuously charged with advocating immorality.

The question begs. Whenever and however I act, who commissioned my so-doing? Who enacted my morality or immorality, exactly? Was it me, or was it some self-appointed 'moralist?' God forbids I ask such questions because "everyone knows" we must legislate and enforce morality for everyone's benefit.

That tragic error illustrates precisely how the mindset of authority takes root. If these self-acclaimed 'moralists' truly understood morality as they profess, they would know with absolute certainty that to command another's mind is immoral, if not criminal. The governing laws of our nature forbid overrule of our choices. You are the living proof of this natural law.

Do you see today's problem? Once 'duty' is made central to morality, governments have full reign to prescribe social duty, thereby decreeing what constitutes morality. Authoritarian rule is thereby instituted and reputedly validated, which is today's (insane) social contract.

To change the common mindset and reverse that immoral standing, consider the often repeated saying, 'service to others comes before service to self.' Does it? The truth is that your freely chosen value-based ethics purposefully service yourself. After that, your just and moral actions are indeed services to others. You've shown what is possible and upheld their choice to emulate your achievements. Of course, we may choose to assist others, but that is not our moral duty. Think further. As described in 'Conscious Ascendance,' Life-values' are your ethics. They can be uploaded to the subconscious mind and put on autopilot. Do that, and your morality goes on autopilot.

'Moral relativism' and 'moral realism' are opposing ideologies. 'Moral relativism' holds that no absolute rules determine whether something is right or wrong. Governments depend on opinion, consensus, social context, culture or several other factors. Consequently, right or wrong are not absolutes. Morals and ethics can vary from one situation, person, or circumstance to the next. Moral relativism seems to grant autonomy, therefore. It seemingly permits us to act in our interest. The government collects a bonus because it can change the rules and thus deny freedom.

Conversely, 'moral realism' holds that there are objective moral truths. Where are they to be found? You know the answer already. Since we each are the author of our actions, we author our morality, or its lack, and are fully accountable for the consequences.

Moral relativism thrives because conscious ignorance has concealed the objective absolutes of moral realism. Natural law theorists flounder similarly, believing that some innate morality prescribes natural law. Yet, had these theorists researched and learned how consciousness works, they would have discovered that *natural law theory* is back to front.

Because natural law upholds life's supremacy, its prescriptions are objectively moral. That sequence is irreversible, whereby morality cannot ever prescribe natural law. 'Moral realism' is not a theory, therefore. Natural law upholds morality, as the study of 'full consciousness' indubitably shows. People can choose to act morally or immorally, but never can they escape natural law consequences. Are you beginning to see how morality has been butchered? Our guaranteed free will to enact morality is what governs it. It permits pinnacles of material and spiritual excellence because your mind is free to roam the cosmos, while you are fully accountable for your expressed morality.

To better understand your nature and the role of ethics, please study this table closely. It shows the divisions of Objectivist Philosophy, each differently defining the branches of philosophy, including the rationality and methods of each, respectively. Please read down each column, then across each row.

Philosophy	Rationale	Method
Metaphsics		
Existence	What is there?	Reality, identity, causality
Epistemology		
Knowledge	How do I know?	Senses, reason, logic, discerment
Ethics		
Thought/Values	How should I think and live?	Rational self interst
Morality		
Action/Respect	How should I act/treat others?	Respect, integrity, cooperation
Law		
Force/Justice	Legitimate force/natural law	Restraint, justness, natural justice
Aesthetics		
Art	Happiness	Romantic inspiration, sprituality

3, Branches of Philosophy

Metaphysics is the branch of philosophy that deals with the first principles of things, including abstract concepts such as being, knowing, identity, time, and space. As Ayn Rand described it—

"Metaphysics identifies the nature of the universe as a whole. It tells us what kind of world we live in, and whether there is a supernatural dimension beyond it. It tells us whether we live in a world of solid entities, natural laws, absolute facts, or in a world of illusory fragments, unpredictable miracles, and ceaseless flux. It tells us whether the things we perceive by our senses form a comprehensible reality, with which we can deal, or some kind of unreal appearance, which leaves us staring and helpless.

Perhaps you're now thinking that your values fuel your ethics, that your individuality spells independence, and that natural laws oversee the whole process. If so, you're a winner!

- **Epistemology** is the theory of knowledge, especially concerning its methods, validity, scope, and the distinction between justified knowledge, beliefs and opinions.
- **Psycho-epistemology** studies our cognitive processes as concerns (value) communication and interaction between our conscious mind and the automatic functions of the subconscious. That exchange is precisely what the Value Transfer Wave reveals, as described in my book Conscious Ascendance.
- **Ethics is personal**. How should I think and live? What is in my rational self-interest, always remembering that my advancement ultimately benefits others?
- **Law is order;** thus, natural law is natural orderliness. Initiated force violates the 'natural law of no trespass.' Consequently, corrective force legitimately restores the natural order. Its measure is justness and natural justice.
- **Morality** is our ethics projected into the social realm through our actions. How do I respect and treat others with integrity for life, and how can I cooperate with others for mutual benefit?
- **Aesthetics** is the last branch of philosophy, the study of art based on metaphysics.

We're all familiar with the 'golden rule' that says, "do unto others as you would have them do unto you." Everyone preaches it. Although the idea is noble, no faster shortcut to a subjective morality exists. It is up for grabs to all comers. It gives governments carte blanche approval to dictate duty and morality and enforce both.

3. Ethics and Morality

Suppose the golden rule was paraphrased and re-written like this. *"Do morally unto yourself as you would others do justly unto themselves."* Instantly, life emerges as the benchmark for determining your ethical intentions. Your moral actions correctly follow, and they tell of your life-upholding choices. They reveal your moral stature and speak of your love of life. You lead through example, and while that may infer others should follow, their moral choice is entirely their own, including all consequences.

This principle already exists within you, as mentoring reports (emotions) advising of life-upholding outcomes or their lack shows beautifully. Morality and natural justice are the very nature of your being.

Once grasped that ethics concerns our desires in life-value terms and that morality or immorality is outwardly broadcast to all others, choosing a just path having beneficial consequences should be second nature.

Necessarily, such a code of morality would be independent of human opinion, rule and strict enforcement. Howls of protest would undoubtedly follow.*"How on earth will immoral behaviour be arrested if we each are our moral governor?"*

The answer lies in the Natural Law of Just Consequence. Every instigator of an immoral action publicly confesses guilt through their action(s). So the question is answered. Once guilt is established, the particular trespass or violation of another's life is confirmed.

Morality is not a social mandate. It is not 'collective.' Each of us is accountable for our morality or lack thereof. Free will, ethics, morality and justice, are all-encompassing. Our right to live is exclusively independent and immutable. Our life is what we are. Our singularity, beautiful uniqueness, and the natural order of our life, ordains boundaries separating us from others. Our rights, words, deeds, works, and property are separate from another's and other things. Nothing could be simpler or more in tune with nature herself.

- **Morality** is the enactment of self-mastery that honours and ensures freedom for others.
- **Ethics** are our personal benchmark.
- **Justness and morality** are our social benchmark, the sum of just actions and testament to our morality.

So now we have an answer to the question — *'how can uniform moral uprightness be achieved if each chooses their own?'* As a collective, we cannot, as history has long proven, but as individuals, we can.

The relationship between 'private' ethics and 'public' morality is now evident. These objectively based founding precepts offer a universal code of morality.

- **Morality** is the outward manifestation of ethically based principles underpinning life-sustaining actions. Conversely, immorality manifests lack, or refusal of ethical considerations, lack of moral discipline, or lack of justness.
- **Protection** is our unalienable right to our life and the inalienable right to our property. (Later discussed.) Such protection arbitrates just restoration when needed.
- **Convivial Society** results from moral actions in aggregate. Independence, one from another, engages with respect for each other. Co-operation amongst equals, or one's likes, results in mutual benefit. (Later discussed.)
- **Living Justice:** Those who prize ethics and morality as spiritual progenitors of life relish these steering virtues because others learn to respect and employ justness from joint dealings. Moral actions invoke reciprocity. (Later discussed.)

A new definition of morality is now evident.

Morality is the conscious will to live according to one's nature, never depriving others of the same opportunity.

Grasp its vital importance, for here lies the source of justness, inwardly to ourselves, and later broadcast to the world as our morality. Briefly, 'actions, and behaviour, publicly testify our pre-conceived moral stature and self-confessed moral accountability.'

To live according to our nature is to practice the life values that our nature requires. In mental terms, such values and virtues amount to 'rational moral principles.' The principle (or integrity) of rationality means using reason and logic as our means of knowledge, through which we can adjudicate values as our ethical guide to actions.

Let's consider some of these virtues or vital principles.

- **Morality** derives from employing the virtues of rationality.
- **Honesty** means rejecting irrationality: not faking reality in pursuit of life values.
- **Productiveness** means a rational, not arbitrary, approach to creating material values.
- **Independence** means thinking for and supporting oneself through one's efforts.

- **Integrity** means adhering to rational principles when tempted to compromise them.
- **Pride**, or self-esteem if you prefer, means continually striving to act as morality requires, to do one's best and achieve one's goals.

Were you taught those principles in school or university? Scan the first words of those bullet points, and you will see the framework of morality that schools should teach at all levels.

Life differentiates ethical thinking and intentions from the morality of subsequent actions and behaviours. Because ethics and morality both derive from our very nature, in that order, both should properly be treated as a science, entirely removed from subjective or consensus opinion and state meddling. Now two codes or sciences unfold in sequence.

1. A science or code of ethics devoted to how men, and women, should think of life values and life itself, singularly and collectively. Ethics is choosing to master oneself through honouring Creator in our thoughts, desires and ambitions.

2. A science or code of morality, describing how men, and women, should act, based on the science or principles of ethics, respective of self and the lives of all others.

Ethics and morality are properly reunited because their functioning sequence is now correctly reversed. Natural law theory is also reversed. People previously assumed natural law proceeded from a (believed) innate morality. Accordingly, self-proclaimed moralists set forth what they determined natural law to be.

Once grasped that ethics transition to morality through actions, that sequence cannot be reversed. The fact that ethics is the progenitor or morality is Creator's recipe for (morally based) individual freedom, from which is the means to implement free organic societies.

Science has recently concluded that our brain has evolved to understand that exclusion, aggression, violence, and isolation are no benefit to us. Also, that morality is (almost always) a natural response in human beings. Our nature explains why that should be. Ascribing ethics to the thought process and morality to behaviour allows massive benefits to emerge. Consider this list.

- All of today's beliefs concerning ethics and morality overturn.
- All 'collectivised' jurisdictional claims over ethics and morality are invalidated.
- Ethics and morality are separated from each other as sciences but

united in purpose, much as our two minds are separate in function while serving like purpose.

- Both ethics and morality are removed from the (collective) social arena (public/political domain) and placed squarely in the individual (private domain) of sovereign individuals to which they rightfully belong.
- Unalienable and Inalienable rights now reign, as later discussed.
- Justness and justice only concern moral actions, not prior ethical intentions that only affect ourselves.
- Present-day natural law theories that hold morality determines natural law are inverted, thus emerges a truthful vitality that no one ever suspected.
- Common law, or constitutional law, now has teeth that no one can deny or erase!
- Authoritarian government switches to self-governance under natural law.

We each have an inherent and immutable right to life's continuance as Creator intended. Then, as free societies begin to form in ways you've never imagined, a profound spiritual swelling will arise in your heart that words fail to describe.

From the preparatory school onwards, ethical and moral education can be formulated, written, and taught across all curricula. You have a revolutionary forward path in that life is yours to live, full consciousness and natural governing laws are the means, and Creator has your back all the way!

Once ethics are discovered and understood, ethical and moral education follows. What better could we ask?

Gone are rules enforced with fines, prisons and guns. Instead, natural laws encrypted within our nature show that our free will determination of value and purpose is spiritual. Each interface with the other. Thus we are spiritual beings living a spiritual life, albeit in a physical vessel and environment.

Today's much supported moral theory of jurisprudence maintains that (blanket applied) law defines morality, while ethics is held rightful. Similarly, self-proclaimed moralists presume the right to determine what natural law is. These versions of morality then cancel, deny or overrule what is independently natural. Having put the cart before the horse, today's theory of jurisprudence shows as immoral in substance and principle.

3. Ethics and Morality

This chapter has shown the proper order. Morality does not determine what natural law is. As described in *Conscious Ascendance,* our entire conscious process is the progenitor of ethics and morality subsequently. The sequence in which an orderly process invokes ethical thinking, later expressed as a moral action, is irreversible. Every ethic needed to support personal life lies within every man and woman, on tap for our societal dealings with others. What better could we ask?

Ethics is the instigator of morality, and your free will conducts its orchestra, as this chapter has described. So hold tight; it gets even better.

Chapter 4

4. Justness & Natural Justice

The last chapter expressed our ethics and morality regarding their voluntary origin. Now the justness or unjustness of our actions needs revision in terms of lawful justice, not a legal agreement. So let's begin with separating justness from justice. Very briefly, 'justness' evidences moral actions, while 'justice' serves to remedy unjust actions.

Self-evident truth holds we all are created equal by nature yet unique in expression, endowed with certain rights among which life, liberty, and the pursuit of happiness, are immutable and unalienable. Natural law within all men and women is beyond self-evident. It is axiomatic, whereby all personal, societal, and business dealings are properly correspondent with unalienable individual rights, rightful freedom, and unobstructed action within our will, drawn around us by the equal rights of all others. Tragically, humanity has rejected or ignored those truths for millennia and still does, and that demands our most profound consideration and resolute response.

Just as the principle of justness encrypted in our nature demands our attention, it works the same way for society. Unless we justly and morally deliver to others, we violate our own lives, which we professedly uphold. If we hold our own life in contempt, as valueless, we confess the need for correction.

That brief overview answers many questions. Still, greater understanding is needed because not only can this information change lives, it vitalises a deep inner knowledge of our purpose in being alive at this time in human history. It brings us face to face with our destiny. This interpretation may confront some people, but the very future of humanity may well depend on how we each respond to this information and act on it.

Question. If 'moral justness' is so simple, could it be preemptively taught in classrooms of seven-year-olds? Yes, of course, and it should. The need for natural justice courts would greatly diminish as a result. This truth offers great hope in the face of rampant domination and control often enforced with violence, utterly destructive of our nature and the natural laws that govern it. There is nothing to fear, no doom or gloom. Our task is to initiate and empower human freedom. That will catalyse personal and societal responses to promptly cancel continuance of much injustice.

While physiology and psychology identify problems that impede our ability to respond to today's crisis, our human sciences still do not recognise the solution within our nature. We think of ourselves as only a tiny part of a vast and incredible universe. This closed perspective and self-limiting isolation forbid a greater understanding of ourselves, our conscious and spiritual abilities, and our place in the physical and newly emerging spiritual universe.

Fortunately, we can free ourselves from that deprivation. Consciousness and natural law afford our most fantastic opportunity for intellectual and spiritual advancement and survival as a species, offering inspiration to join together in a deeper understanding of what will serve the further evolution of humanity.

Do you prefer to live as a servant or enslaved person to authoritarians with whom we share equal natural status, yet who coerce or force us into a system of Corporate Feudalism that makes Colonialism look tame in comparison? Many people recognise that predicament, but unless we act to implement the fulness of freedom and the right to self-govern and act upon that right with full responsibility, we have neither rights nor freedom.

Nature invokes us to take the next necessary steps and accept full responsibility that goes with the right to self-govern. But we need to wake up! Wake up to 'justness' because that is absent today. Our identity is stolen, lives taken over, and our unalienable rights denied, yet we stand about as willing victims, never considering any alternative could exist. Do you want your freedom? Nature gifted it and encrypted the natural laws of your governance. You can put freedom aside as a noble idea and agree to your stolen birthright, or you can accept nature's gifts and stand up for them, use them and protect them. Freedom means you must act, seize, use, and protect it. Omit one of those four initiatives, and freedom cancels.

Our body is our vessel, and so we refuse what poisons it. Likewise, consciousness is our driving force, so we should not let anything in our mind violate or disfigure it. Declare yourself to be a child of nature blessed with the full ability to attain and preserve self-mastery. Stand up for yourself as nature intends you should. Understand and utilise your power. Send intruders and interlopers packing. Standing up for justness is the first step.

When millions vote for benefits, comforts, and security to be legally extracted from others, as though such theft ensures a just and moral society, they have voted for immoral rule. Once agreed to be herded, branded, and corralled as social animals, injustice, immorality, and crime result, as one's vote approves.

Humanity is at a critical junction where one road leads to a bleak future, and the other offers an unprecedented spiritual age. Its attainment requires independent minds with sufficient confidence to dispel all social pressures to conform. Therefore, we each are obligated to begin knowing and stop believing. Stop blindly accepting what governments and so-called "experts" want us to believe. That is where justness begins.

We must stop giving away our power, free our mind, grasp hold of its incredible abilities, and learn to master our consciousness. If our desire is a free, symbiotic moral society, we must first enact it, then protect it, and that leads to the subject of justice.

Today's socialised ethics beg we all act morally from duty or obligation to achieve social ends determined and administered through government. That's all back to front. All body and mental processes must 'justly' deliver from one to the other, or they violate the life they professedly uphold. The principle of justice embedded in our nature means that other people should not determine what we should morally defend. Instead, our spiritual nature should highlight values we ought to choose, thence to morally and spiritually enact as individuals.

- **Justness** manifests one's moral choice of action. Each man and woman serves justness by not interfering with or forbidding any other person their ability to live and sustain their life.
- **Justice** serves to remediate unjust or immoral actions — served each offender as a correction, remediation, repatriation or restoration in the measure of their offense.

The tool of justice is the correction or restoration of the natural order, not punishment. Its task is to steer offenders back to an ethic-based morality, moral congruence, and acceptance of others' right to life. Is recompense involved? Yes, in many cases, although mitigating circumstances may prevail. No victimless crime can exist; thus, no penalty, remedy or restitution can be levied against such inventions. Every violation of life is a perpetrator's confession to forego their right to freedom.

Although democracy may substantially reduce the chances of an all-encompassing dictatorship, it nonetheless opens the door to every political opportunist who will scramble to occupy every political position and then do whatever a majority of voters, even a slim majority, supposedly approve. Their misguided vision of good is the chance to write morality and justice as they wish it to be. Yet, no matter how much they believe the cause of liberty has advanced, freedom is not guaranteed through democracy, even for one person. Individual freedom cannot exist in a democracy.

Accordingly, government feeds on itself. Its differentiated social positions of power carry privileges, immunities, perks, and rewards. These attractions inevitably lead to the expansion of public control in satisfaction of an insatiable urge to satisfy ambitions, career opportunities, rivalries and rank. The blank cheque of society's majority approves its 'justice system' with no challenge possible. The nature of this beast prohibits checks and balances because 'subjects', 'servants' or 'citizens' are firmly locked into the same social structure. They, too, are enslaved to the same perverted morality that purportedly upholds justice. Damnable ambiguity, inconsistency, and incompatibility arise from this insatiable monster. That drives the (assumed) need to strengthen the legal system, and so perverse injustice has no perceivable end. Social justice is a contradiction in terms.

The answer to my question is yes. Moral justness can be preemptively taught in the classrooms of seven-year-olds. Ethics and morality instilled in the minds and hearts of everyone from an early age would unquestionably stall the practice of justice. So what is the hold-up?

The simple truth is that many powerful and influential people and ardent ideologues would feel deprived, denied or mistreated if natural justice held sway, which they would interpret as a gross injustice. Truthful (natural) justice will curtail or forbid specific unjust actions that today's actors consider fully legal and therefore moral. That is another example of how immorality sustains and builds on itself. Should it surprise that new legislations are passed weekly if not daily?

Natural justice expressed in its most elementary ('Justice for Dummies') form is the quality of being fair and reasonable. *"Everyone knows that"*, people will say, instantly dismissing any thought of studying the subject more closely. So it is that people also dismiss natural law at lightning speed, as though if it's natural, then nature will take care.

Some people regard natural law as old-fashioned, a stone age relic, entirely useless with nothing to offer in the computer age. Others consider it a broad reference framework to mitigate public criticism of legal decisions. Today's overpowering thrust of legalities supports that for many intellectuals, 'natural law' is little more than prescientific metaphysical speculation. Others, if not so misled, will likely conclude that human advancement in economic analysis and efficient policy includes safeguards of order in the human world; thus, the science of law and any quest for justice are fundamentally irrelevant.

These dismissive attitudes or excuses are ignorant, if not arrogant. Dismissal of what is 'natural and just' without investigation is nothing but an arrogant assertion of one's ability to command nature or dismiss it.

Natural justice exists to correct immoral, unjust actions like those described. It is the practice of remediating unjustness, just as our human nature works. Whereas one's actions serve justness or unjustness, natural justice serves remedy as needed. Unethical thoughts lead to immoral acts, which invoke restoration of moral order and possible remediation.

That is the role of natural justice. It determines if someone violated another's rights and whether to institute a remedy according to the victim's harm. Our actions may or may not serve justness upon others. The difference between justness and justice is now plainly evident. Justness indicates one's morality. Unjustness is immorality.

These truths seem to have eluded us for millennia. Injustice and immorality stare us in the face because while ever it is ruled wrong to rape, pillage and plunder, today we legally enforce rules that pillage and plunder as morally correct. Present practice begs us to act morally from duty or obligation to achieve the social ends governments desire, yet those ends are often immoral and unjust.

The alternative is to preemptively act morally and with justness, not because it's the dutiable or social thing to do, but because it is in our vital interests. Actions that justly and morally spill into our societies endorse that natural justice exists. The principle is straightforward when founded on life values and spirituality.

Physical needs should not determine what we each ought morally to do; instead, our spiritual nature should evaluate what and how we should morally and spiritually enact our needs and desires.

Once firmly grasped that spiritually founded natural laws advance our material life, all falls perfectly into place. Proper reasoning, rational thinking, evaluation, integrity, purpose, and value selection based on life emerge as a (spiritually based) Science of Ethics, its core tenets graciously encrypted within us all.

Do you see? Every man and woman has the free choice to embrace the will to live and employ its necessities. Accordingly, 'justness' serves oneself and all others. Now we can add 'Justness' and 'justice' to the code of ethics and morality.

- Each man and woman serves justness by not interfering with or denying any other person their ability to live and sustain their life.
- Only innocent individuals (persons) are free. One found guilty of injustice, or unjustness, cannot justly be considered to be a free individual, independent of the victim. Accordingly…
- Justice is served to offenders, as a correction, remediation, or restoration, in the measure of their offense. The tool of justice is 'correction,' not punishment. Justice concerns the remediation of trespass, respectful of its causal action(s).
- Natural justice steers offenders back to an ethic-based morality, moral congruence, and acceptance of others' right to life.

Whereas' justice' in today's courts fundamentally preserves its underlying legal systems, natural justice does the opposite. It serves the people through reliance on natural law encrypted within every man, woman and child. Hence the term 'natural justice' substituted for the word 'justice.'

The general principle of (natural) justice is that only innocent individuals (persons) are free. Those who choose to step outside natural law are outlaws. Those people found guilty of injustice or unjustness cannot justly be considered free individuals independent of the victim. To quote Frank van Dun, the philosophy of law holds "Justice is for mature adults who are supposed to know the difference between the real world and the games people play."

Victims of crime acquire natural justice from the criminal's unjust action(s). Stated differently, whosoever victimises another voluntarily gives up their' rights.' These now belong to their victim(s) for the sole purpose of correction, remediation, and or recompense. This right remains until that particular action or aggression is restoratively closed.

In other words, the victim acquires natural justice from the perpetrator's unjust action(s). They have the right to remedial measures and compensation in restoring the natural order that (correctly) should have existed in place of the crime. That is the general principle of Natural Justice according to natural law.

"One's actions, in violation of the individual rights of another, constitutes their unspoken consent for natural justice to be administered in (full) measure of their trespass." —Max Emmons Taylor Jr.

How simple is that?

"The primary practical objective of the juristic study of Natural Law is to propose rules or practical principles that, if followed by human beings, are likely to maintain, strengthen and restore respect for the natural order of the human world. They are the principles and rules of justice. — Frank van Dun

Moral justness invokes the personal need to be accountable for one's actions, including acceptance of justice measures. Van Dun continues...

That does not mean the requirements of justice are contradictory. A person who inadvertently or in a temporary fit violates the Natural Law can always volunteer to undo his transgression or to submit to a procedure of arbitration to determine the kind and amount of restitution he owes to another. No violent action against such a tortfeasor is necessary." —Frank van Dun [8]

Those principles are the converse of today's collectivised justice, positive law, legal justice, or any variant thereof. So-called justice that serves the state, or any form of 'collective,' is morally bereft from its conception, capable of nothing but injustice in theory and practice.

Creator has modelled the principle of natural justice right in the core of our conscience and emotional reporting systems, exactly where it belongs. Nothing could be more productive or more in tune with nature itself.

The moral principle is straightforward. No man or woman can violate another's life while claiming to preserve their right to life. Transgressors forego their right to freedom voluntarily. Every violation of another's life self-confesses an act of natural law trespass.

You will now understand that all body and mental processes must justly deliver from one to the other, or they violate the life they professedly uphold. The principle of justice exists in our nature.

No one decides justice - It just is.

These descriptions show the vital relationship of consciousness to natural justice. Our conscience and emotions inform us of what is upholding our life or hindering it. We are alerted to correct behaviour and to that which needs remedy. We're gifted with the means to determine the natural justness of our thoughts and actions. The principle of natural justice is encrypted deep within the core of our conscience and emotional reporting systems, exactly where it belongs. Accordingly— we do justness or fail that responsibility.

Readers of *'Conscious Ascendance'* will see how our conscious process and natural law relate to natural justice. Once they understand the spiritual mechanics of consciousness, they will have already grasped the moral principle that no man or woman cannot violate another's life while professing to uphold their own. They will recognise in social terms that every action violating another's life is one's confession of guilt. So they will have grasped the essence of criminal law, and that crime is one's (self) confessed violation of natural law. Observably, therefore, justice follows from understanding natural law. Once grasped that no such thing as a victimless crime can exist, Natural Justice—

- allows that all charges be transparently public for all to see;
- allows all evidence to be made public;
- allows the accuser and accused to testify openly and in public such that much healing can take place from the telling of one's story while jurors and others listen with objective, reflective, and compassionate intent;
- allows the accused an opportunity to confess, repent, or express regret, offer restitution, and receive forgiveness if agreed. It will enable the accuser (victim) to provide forgiveness;
- requires that where court procedures and jury deliberations continue, they do so openly and publicly;
- Rehabilitation for the offender is allowed if required. If charged, the accused has a formal opportunity to confess, repent, offer remediation,

and seek public forgiveness. Where an offender refuses all offers of restoration or repeats the offense, detainment or imprisonment logically follows from the offender's choice not to repent.

Free symbiotic societies will defend that one's life choices can never corrupt the necessary (right to life) processes of another. Your life is truthful proof of this natural law concept. Most of our twenty natural laws concern personal ethics. As the authors of our actions, we bear the total weight of natural justice. In sum—

- Aggressors wilfully confess responsibility for remedy or restoration of the natural order.
- No judge rules against them because they have already ruled against themselves.
- Natural justice steers offenders back to an ethic-based morality.
- Natural justice is the correction or restoration of the natural order, not punishment.
- Recompense may be occasioned, despite mitigating circumstances may prevail.

That list explains the importance of 'independence.' Morality shifts from being a social convention to its proper place as the conveyor of justness, originating from its fully accountable place within each (individual) living being. 'Natural justice' upholds that fact of life.

Will the unjustness of state rule ever be reversed? Will natural justice ever emerge? Not while the state writes legal and moral rule books and enforces both with gunpowder statutes and armies! Neither will state rule vanish while human sciences ignore the natural laws of our being as though non-existent. Tyranny and slavery will continue while political authorities violate our right to life.

It remains that when millions vote for benefits, comforts, and security to be legally stolen from others as though a just and moral society, they have voted for immorality and injustice. Any surprise they are herded, branded, and corralled as social animals?

So we are obligated to begin knowing and stop believing, primarily understanding free, symbiotic moral societies exist within ourselves.

Incomprehensibly, thousands if not millions of people daily fight in courts, attempting to reconcile the natural laws of their life with the positive law of artificial beings, as though some conciliation or meeting ground is humanly possible. It is not. It is impossible!

Today's justice systems are perceived to uphold our rights as living beings. The truth is very different. Every positive law court and legal procedure is bound to keep state rule. Since rule and freedom are incompatible, Positive Law Courts must banish natural law because it is outside their jurisdiction. Although we may present natural law evidence in these courts, the court deems we are an artificial legal entity within a legal jurisdiction. Natural law evidence is wholly inadmissible, therefore. No reconciliation or compromise is possible, between natural and artificial, now or ever! Every presenter must know that fake order (law) will preside in such courts, whereby their natural law case is lost before it begins.

I promised to show how the justness or unjustness of our actions needs revision in terms of lawful justice, not a legal agreement. Independence is paramount. Nothing of this kind will ever happen while 'authoritarian society' rules that justice is fodder for herd-like consumption. Paramount to this success is our 'individual right' to life, as described in the next chapter.

Chapter 5

5. Independence & Individual Rights

Individualism, independence and 'rights' are inseparable. Individualism is the habit or principle of being independent and self-reliant. Self-reliance depends on one's right to act in support of their life. When 'collectivism' substitutes for 'individualism,' rights become government permissions which today is considered 'normal.' Free societies are impossible thereby. People suffer but are unaware of their sufferance because it's normal. So let's undo both.

Given there is no such thing as a collective brain or any thought, we are each individual beings of creation. We can divide a meal but cannot digest it in a collective stomach. We cannot use our lungs for breathing for another man or woman. We can impart our thoughts to others, but we cannot think through their brains. Every function of our body and spirit is private. We can learn much about society through studying the nature of who and what we are. But we can know nothing about our singular selves through social study because the interrelationships of many people's free will choices are indeterminate.

There you have individualism in a nutshell. We can share or transfer the 'products' of our body and spirit, but never can we share their private' functions.' That reiterates that we can change the content of our consciousness, but we cannot change its process. Our conscious and subconscious minds are individual, although both work for the same cause. Individualism is the principle of being independent and self-reliant.

That fact highlights what individualism is, whereby as human beings, we each are separate, one from another. Independence refers to self-centred thoughts, actions, self-reliance, egoism, and self-mastery. Do not let 'egotism' confuse you; it is the word most people refer to when they use the word 'ego.' Egotism is excessive self-conceit, usually at the expense of others — the polar opposite of 'egoism,' which is self-esteem earned legitimately.

Independence means that our actions are free from collective or state control. We each have the right to support and uphold our life and to pursue happiness within the equal rights of all others. Free people have no ambition, urge, or necessity to become absorbed in a greater mass. Nothing persuades casting themselves to the wolves in the surrender of self. Because these free individuals imagine and create on a scale that surpasses collective demands, their work naturally spills over to the benefit of others. Free people know that the greatest good comes from liberating all individuals to pursue their highest aspirations, their creative and productive abilities. Independence is the door to freedom and human progress, the secret to free societies. Therefore, it is prudent, if not vital, that we withdraw from the 'collective' mindset; it is the principal reason every government in earth's history has failed or will fail.

No monarch, dictator or government has fully upheld the *'Individual Rights of Man'*. None can without relinquishing their authoritarian rule over the populace. Were you taught that in grade school? No, because the state wants conformists and so it controls education. Neither were you taught human consciousness. Thus the core principles of individualism and independence have lain dormant for centuries. Disastrous consequences have resulted.

Collectivists have long hammered the notion of family, group, community and social support. That is good. It is vital to our self-interest to uphold and support those around us. The problem is that collectivists will do all possible to foster group identity at the expense of being independent. They fear independence like they fear hell itself. Why? Because they know their survival depends upon mass obedience. There cannot be one individual — there can only be one mob — hence we are compelled to adapt to a legally contrived environment like animals, all escape routes blocked.

Today's economic lockdowns and virulent (health) crimes against humanity are no accident. From centuries of ignorance and abuse of individual rights, they are another inescapable reminder that natural laws govern behavioural consequences.

Collectivists and authoritarians firmly intend that you remain passively inert, utterly ignorant of your power, because, like a malignant, infectious disease, your entrapment helps their cause immensely. Passivity spreads and multiplies in populations. Strong people become weak, and weak people develop dementia. Sport and entertainment offer relief. Millions of people adore heroes and heroines in all walks of life, including artists, musicians, political 'leaders,' and most notably, Hollywood movie stars.

The irony is that to escape our fear of independence, we naturally gravitate to those who fiercely project the qualities of liberty and independence. If that truth became known, people would soon see that the more independent they become, the more they would appreciate independence in others. Then, heroes and heroines are no longer diversions or relief from fear or stress; instead, they are like-minded celebrants of our intellectual and spiritual advancement.

People would also grasp that ideologies, beliefs and doctrines do not shape free individuals. Instead, free thought and our desire to advance enhance the freedom of others. Strong will exists to discover life through imagination and creative power, for without, freedom withers and dies. As the free individual imagines and creates on a scale far surpassing societal regulation, others benefit. Free individuals know that the greatest good comes from liberating all individuals to pursue their highest aspirations, divorcing them from the collective mindset. It becomes evident that group or unity consciousness will not substitute for what we each are.

> *'The boughs of no two trees ever have the same arrangement. Nature always produces individuals; she never produces classes.' ~ Lydia Maria Child*

A new life-supporting perspective emerges, where life is the only goal and purpose. Wrong and evil do not disappear; they merely present as uncivil or criminal deviations from the cause and purpose of life. They are not equal in life or equitable competitors; instead, they are gutless, nuisance-like diseases, manifesting as abusive aberrations. Nonetheless, they require correction and remediation.

This understanding of the Creator's intention and endowment is contrary to almost all taught. It is inverted today, upheld through rules that sustain its inversion or perversion. It is time to re-appraise psychology, psychiatry, philosophy, religion, politics, trade, society, competition and cooperation. Many commonly held beliefs, bogus ideologies, politics, subjectivism, and authoritarian government deserve scrapping. Even libertarian persuaders should re-appraise their goals. It also begs that we redefine justice. Almost every precept ever taught is called into question! By those means, independence may be steered back on course; not one state from another like the 1776 'Declaration of Independence,' instead, freedom from any state that violates our right to life.

We must attest that we live. Life is our immutable hallmark. The difference is that all who claim an opposing (legal) jurisdiction have voluntarily divorced from 'life.' They have wilfully joined the club of ineffectual, dead, legal entities. Their choice to abdicate life frees you and me from their 'forced rule' and widespread tyranny. They walked out on life. You didn't!

Consequently, the phrase consent of the governed needs questioning. Why? Because governments that (forcibly) rule according to (statute) permissions, (forcibly) rule our consent. Mind-controlled brainwashing is rampant. Governments mould whatever 'consent' they desire to achieve their goals. Francis Bacon offered the alternative to this insanity centuries ago—

"Nature to be commanded must be obeyed."

Here lies the most beautiful thing. Since the natural laws of our nature govern the consequences of our actions and behaviour, as consented by our Creator, no further consent is required. Think what that jaw-dropping revelation means. It means that when free societies are correctly founded on the 'nature of those governed,' as universally consented, we must ensure that free will is always protected.' Consent' cannot ever be denied because it is the very nature of what we are. And, because we have free choice to override it, we must indubitably ensure no one else does.

'Natural law' may now acquire absolute power as our Creator granted. Although never witnessed in all history, it strictly provides that 'unalienable rights,' freedoms and 'natural justice' are upheld and forever protected. Therefore, no better precedent exists than to self-govern according to what we are. Consider how that would impact the health industry, just for starters.

5. Independence & Individual Rights

Although never realised before, a revolutionary about-face of this magnitude is ours for the knowledge and willpower to achieve! Full consciousness and its natural laws are our passports to humanity's glorious future. Nothing less will suffice! Grasping the truth of our nature is now the battle for humankind. Nothing has precedence, is more relevant, nor is more urgent.

Some people argue that free organic societies can only work in low-population, primitive cultures. Moreover, in today's high-speed, hi-tech, highly regulated society, such orderliness is wishful thinking and impractical. In reply to this criticism, what drives people's constant appetite for regulation? To argue that we can only function when one rules or regulates another is to say that society can only flourish when one Man can punish another. The ruling, conformist societies have never worked in our history, and never will they. Free production, and free, uncoerced exchange, are anathema to regulation. The truth is that the denser and more high-tech the environment, the greater a free (non-ruled) society is enabled to serve it.

To believe that we can only function with a publicly appointed boss, president, or dictator, aided by armies of administrators who write rules for citizens to obey while robbing them, is insane. Nevertheless, all social and essential services can continue through those presently employed or contracted. Return the employer's role to the people and send the government packing. To that end, no public purse will excuse their ineffectiveness, inefficiency, or lack. Witness how free trade succeeds when allowed free rein.

Josiah Warren reported concerning the Time Store in Cincinnati, which opened in May 1827. The Store applies symbiotic principles to the management and the interchange of labour, including merchants, lawyers, physicians, and teachers. The individual's autonomy was always strictly preserved and was invariably respected. No legislation of any description assumed control over people at any time or in any case. What resulted?

> *Such was the complete individuality of action that hundreds dealt at the Time Store without understanding much of its principles or its objects; but they perceived that it was their interest to do so, thus demonstrating that the business of the community can be brought into this condition by a natural and irresistible process; without combination, without organisation, without laws, without*

government, without the surrender of any "portion" of the natural liberty of the individual; demonstrating also that reformation need not wait till the world becomes learned: but the practical operation constitutes a process of re-education which no one can estimate without experience, and which the learned are most backward in acquiring. —Josiah Warren [14]

No one has any need to wait for deliverance. All that's needed is protection from rule, aggression, and violence. Freedom is your birthright. Respect for others is your responsibility and yours alone. Your life is what you are, and your joy in this world is to live it!

Protection of individual rights is for a Commission of Justice or equal, a 'protectorate body' in place of government. Such should properly be constrained to moral justice serving our lives, and rehabilitating transgressors, never wavering from or forsaking that specific commission or charter; or it is guilty of trespass. No such body can be permitted to infringe your right to life through authoritarian rule, legal or otherwise since that commits an injustice. A 'Protectorate's role must be severely delimited, as later discussed.

We each stand on the cusp of personal and societal change, having no precedent in human history. Unprecedented opportunity exists to entirely divorce from societal domination and control that has damnably beleaguered planet Earth. The choice to be free is one we each must make. Importantly, we must know what that choice is, how to exercise it, and how to protect it. Independence means being singularly alive in body, mind, and spirit. From that understanding, we can reach out to others whenever and however we choose. Independence demands we will stop clutching a group-laden life raft rotting from mental bankruptcy. Jon Rappoport put it succinctly–

"Your deepest power is alive. It's personal. It's stunningly energetic and dynamic. It connects with your deepest understanding of what is true and good and right. But it never sacrifices itself on the altar of what others insist is good and true and right. It never deserts you for an abstract ideology someone else has devised. That ideology was formulated, in fact, to separate you from your power."

We are blessed indeed

- Creator's model shows how we can function independently while contributing to society.
- Our contribution to life guarantees self-protection.
- No better model of 'independence' exists, nor can it.

Choose to exercise your creative power to fulfil what you most desire, and that process will positively affect others. You testify to the success of your method and your means. Your 'win' will lift them and remind them of their inherent power if only they choose it.

A society's communal power arises out of that independence. Your creative power is yours, individually and independently. The more you develop it, the less fear you will experience. The more you develop independence, the more you expose and reduce oppression. Using your knowledge of consciousness is the key to individualism and complete autonomy.

Who today has lived without government authority? We know nothing different because we've never challenged statism or its legal and purportedly moral superiority. We've little understood who and what we are and never grasped that all social intercourse is properly individual before it is communal. The government has known from its inception that its criminal conduct could only succeed while citizens remain ignorant of its counterfeit methods; additionally, men and women remain convinced that collective society must dictate daily existence. Fully practised yet mistaken ideologies have allowed governments to conceal evil, denying or refuting everything that might reveal it.

The alternative is to allow and encourage a symbiotic society. That means abandoning societal rule and instituting (protected) self-rule, a centuries overdue mission. So make this declaration yours today.

Personal declaration of independence

Self-evident truth holds all Men created equal in nature while unique in expression, endowed by their Creator with certain rights, among which life, liberty, and the pursuit of happiness, are immutable and unalienable. Natural law within all men and women is beyond self-evident, axiomatic in nature; all personal, societal, and business dealings correspondent with unalienable, individual rights, rightful freedom, and unobstructed action within our will, all within the equal rights of all others.

Notwithstanding, false and misleading theologies, ideologies, and philosophies have hidden, perverted, misconstrued, and overruled nature's laws and Man's right to life as though non-existent. Blinded, deluded, and deceived, Man is branded a social animal, enslaved to political society with no disclosure. Forbidden redress through legal yet immoral rules, deceit, corruption, and criminality in defiance of a free people, and denied the right to life, Man is insanely forced to uphold bloody-minded tyranny as the only liberty possible!

When legislations constrain men, and women, contrary to their nature, through any fictional or covert invention, and when criminal abuse and violation of Man's right to life reduce existence to animal-like status under absolute despotism, the cessation of criminal evil demands. When injuries, violence, and usurpations, consistently repeat for the direct object of tyranny over Man, so undeniable criminality summed as moral right to rule and immoral wrong to refuse rule is historical fact—open to all seekers of truth—no need to re-state it.

Accepting equality and individual station as the laws of nature entitle and Creator consents, it is men and women's unalienable right and duty as living beings to abolish all legislation to divorce from criminal and unjust legal authority entirely. Each, and all of the One People of Earth, impelled to determine complete separation and independence from all enforced (state) power and rule, now chose to institute and secure new and lasting protections deriving just powers from those whom the laws of nature and nature's God has endowed.

In complete absolution of centuries-old criminal violation of Man's right to life, let the (natural) laws of nature and Creator submit to a candid world for the lawful upholding of human life, contrary to every abomination and violation. To that effect—

1. Natural law (Law) is the natural order of human beings, capable of rational, purposive action, speech and thought, the natural order of the human world, expressing method, system, process, order, equality, uniqueness, all inviting free choice, within free and cooperative rightful action.

2. As a species, Homo sapiens sapiens possess like faculty (governed thought processes), in union with independent free will thoughts, undeniably testifying all men and women are equal, independently free—humankind their aggregation—not collection.

3. Independent faculties are guaranteed inclusive of individual responsibility, liability, and accountability; actioned consequences are inescapable. Respect for the lives of others reciprocally ensures

one's own, never sacrificing life's supreme value to anything lesser.

4. Individual right to life is the unalienable right to the action of living, faculties of movement, feeling, thought, and speech, drawn within the equal rights of all others.

5. Where the rights of all others are respected, no one can offend through any application of his own.

6. The right to act in support of life is unalienable; the right to the product of one's efforts is inalienable.

7. Individual rights preside over all other life forms and preclude collective rights.

8. To secure the certain individual right to life, unless all men created equal, unequivocally protect their right to life and their unalienable right to do so, against all violation, cancellation or usurpation, they will have neither the right to life nor its protection.

9. No authority is granted to any individual to command another — all commandments refused — no man or woman a human agent; no legal or other instrument presiding contrary.

10. All thoughts and intentions are self-contained, unable to violate another's right to life or property.

11. Subsequent actions and behaviour that violate another's right to life—when proven—publicly confess immorality, immoral action(s) and trespass of natural law. Fraud, blackmail, rape, theft and murder do not occur accidentally.

12. Actioned trespass of natural law, admits to its lawful cessation, agreement to remediate harm and endure restoration, respectful of that transgression.

13. Criminal action forfeits freedom; rightful justice is remedially

acquired by the victim, without which no rights and liberties can exist.

14. Natural justice binds. Because free society and natural law are co-dependent, each must guarantee non-violation of the other, or both vanish.

Natural laws of perfected self-governing are the 'separate and equal station to which the laws of nature and nature's God entitle each man and woman.' Therefore, as perfectly modelled for transfer into Man's societies, so decent respect for natural law declares separation from all contrary, all men and women from the state, Creator's natural laws of proven and perfected societal governing commissioned forthwith.

Thus endowed, I do, with complete rectitude, solemnly publish and declare that all men and women in their nature and life are unequivocally and eternally free from all artificial order; free from authority, and state, no dispute save to 'nature and nature's God.'

With firm and unwavering reliance on steadfast integrity and protection of Source, I now pledge my sacred honour to my fellow men and women; within my immutable right to life and its protections, I humbly make this my solemn, private, Declaration of Independence.

Autograph______________________________ this ____ day of __________ _____

Witness _________________________ this ____ day of _________ _____

The Universal Declaration of Human Rights (UDHR), to which Australia is a signatory, was adopted by the United Nations General Assembly in December 1948 at the Palais de Chaillot, Paris. People believe this document enunciates the rights to which all individual human beings are inherently entitled, which guarantees their liberty. Does it indeed?

Article 1 states—*"All human beings are born free and equal in dignity and rights." As though that clause did not exist, Article 29 (3) states—"These rights and freedoms may in no case be exercised contrary to the purposes and principles of the United Nations."*

Even simpletons should scream indignation at that insanity! Article 29 completely smashes Article 1. Freedom, rights, equality and dignity, are politically and categorically overruled without exceptions! Your born (living) nature and your right to life are subject to United Nations permission—all counterclaims denied. You are a chattel, enslaved to UN authority! You have no rights, period!

Just as it is immoral to take the freedom or rights of another, it is not possible for one to give freedom or rights to another. We each must conceive and secure our own freedoms and we must oppose those who deter us from doing that.

No individual may rightfully be obligated by his silence or by presumption or implication of any law, policy or custom. Tragically and without excuse, today's courts uphold policies that obligate individuals without full disclosure and without their consent.

Charity is done by people, while 'redistribution' is done by theft. Institutions who steal wealth have no moral capacity to distribute it justly, honourably or equitably. Not surprisingly, governments themselves consume most of the wealth they take.

So-called Human Rights are not rights at all. Under maritime law, we each are just a person, a legal persona, a mask. Legally, we are dead. Our flesh and blood living being is refused by today's legal systems. Given that dead legal entities have no ability to action anything, how can they possibly have rights?

As mentioned at the head of this chapter, independence announces one's right to act as an independent living being (ILB). But what are rights? Good question; better yet, 'what are 'individual rights,' specifically'? Various descriptions can be found; for example—

- Individual rights are the rights each individual needs to pursue their lives and goals without interference from other individuals or the government. Individual rights are those considered so essential that they warrant specific statutory protection from interference.
- An individual right is a person's freedom to act in a social environment, also defined as any action or behaviour individuals can freely undertake.
- Individual rights provide moral protection for individuals against unchosen and characteristically harmful incursions other individuals or groups might choose to inflict. An individual's rights specify the domain over which he rightfully exercises control; if others intrude on that domain, they trespass on him. As John Locke put it in Two Treatises

of Government, rights allow individuals *"to order their actions, and dispose of their possessions and persons, as they think fit without asking leave, or depending upon the will of any other man."*

Of those three descriptions, the first and last are most pertinent since both speak of protection for individuals. So please hold that thought until I return to it later.

Ayn Rand defined the core issue explicitly

"A right is a moral principle defining and sanctioning a man's freedom of action in a social context."

A natural right is the right to act, specifically (self) control over our faculties, without violating another's rights. There is no rightful claim to a thing or some outcome, for example, to receive an education or health care. We each have the right to seek such results but we've no right to demand that someone provides them. Observe what that means in practice –

Our rights are guaranteed when our actions preserve other people's right to life.

Conversely, activities that violate others' rights forfeit our own.

Frank Van Dun, describes natural rights as individual

"A natural right in the strict sense is that which is naturally under a person's control, his body with its faculties of movement, feeling, thought, and speech. By extension a natural right is what a person brings under his control without violating any other person's natural rights."—Frank Van Dun.

His explanation highlights two of the most fundamental facts of human existence concerning natural law that today are least understood.

One's right to life and freedom is assured, provided that you uphold every other individual's right to their life. Exercise of one's rights to uphold the rights of others preserves and protects those rights from ever being repealed or denied.

Transgressors whose immoral and unjust action(s) voluntarily forfeit their freedom admit that restorative natural justice is theirs to bear, according to the measure of their voluntary transgression.

In other words, actions that preserve others' rights guarantee one's own. Conversely, activities that violate others rights forfeit one's own and invoke natural justice in like measure.

Without, there can be no rights and no freedoms! You are the instigator of your rights; no government or United Nations can be.

Individuals may associate, cooperate, and collaborate, but no associative dealing can negate our right to life. By preserving individual rights, everyone's right to life is protected. Accordingly, just as there is no collective lung, heart, or digestive system to be sustained, no group rights are possible, yet everyone is protected.

Because Natural law seeks integrity, morality and justice, and not compliance, it cannot be an alternative system to that of Positive Law (statutes). Free will can be abused, plundered, violated, usurped or negated. Many people do. They portend that free will is the right to do what they prefer, when so chosen, to whomever, regardless of all consequences. Some claim this right is God-given, hence the Divine Right of Kings. This abomination has secularly translated into every government that has existed, premised on the (self-claimed) right of a few to rule all others. (Refer to Chapter 11 also.)

Rand's description and Van Dun's descriptions of rights tell of two truths. First, rights apply to the actions of individual living beings, as they concern the upholding of life and its sustenance, and second, both are properties of our individual, independent self. No act, decree or legislation of Man can alter that fact.

The source of Individual Rights is not divine or congressional law, therefore, but the Natural Law of Identity. Nature urges us to sustain our lives through our effort. We perish otherwise unless another person steps in to fulfil that function, aged care, for example. Consequently, our right to life is not the right to a product, service, result or outcome, but only to the actions of living. Without that right, life is curtailed, decreased, deprived, violated, invalidated, or legally annulled. Thus Individual Rights are conditions of existence every man, woman and child requires for their sustenance and survival.

Since no 'unified' life exists, no collective 'human rights can exist. Individuals may associate, cooperate and collaborate, but no associative dealing can negate our free right to life. Therefore, every political purpose and society should endorse the applicability of individual rights, as here summarised.

- One cannot rightfully live without the individual right to act, so to live.

- Whosoever preaches or decrees otherwise holds death as their premise.
- No claim of right may negate or usurp the unalienable rights of any other living human being.
- Our human body, thoughts, emotions and actions are indeed our life; therefore, our responsibility is reciprocally valid for all others equally.
- No collective rights are possible without usurping each individual's right to their life.
- Natural individual rights impose no obligations on one's neighbours except to abstain from violating their rights.
- Individual rights guarantee one's freedom to think and act.
- Our right to act and live cannot exist or be just without fully accepting the reciprocal right of all others equally.
- Whereas animals must adapt themselves to nature, and Man must adapt nature to himself, the individual rights of Man to live necessarily preside over all other life forms.
- We each have the inalienable and immutable right to live as rational beings, and nature obliges that we do. Nonetheless, our free will allows us to think and act outside ourselves and others and reap just consequences in like measure. (See the Natural Law of Just Consequence.)

Many people consider 'Unalienable Rights ' and 'Inalienable Rights' mean the same thing. This confusion seemingly arises from the words Latin and French roots, in which the prefix 'in,' is a Latin negative prefix, and 'un,' is the English prefix. Others consider it mere spelling difference. Utter nonsense!

Precisely because the words Unalienable, and Inalienable have never been properly defined, I have chosen to make that distinction and define their crucial differences for the advent of free societies.

The key word is alien, that comes from the word lien, the etymological root of which is the Anglo-French 'lien', meaning a loyen, bond or restraint, from Latin ligamen, arising from ligare, to bind.

Thus if lien means to bond or bind, then its opposite connotation means to undo that bond; to alienate one aspect or element from its other(s). Where a part cannot possibly be split, divorced, separated or alienated, then the bond is undoable, obviously. It is unable to be broken, or severed, unable to be alienated. Hence I have used the word, 'unalienable' to indicate that the bond is unable to be undone using any means whatsoever.

5. Independence & Individual Rights

Do not let corrupted vocabulary mislead. It is likely that unalienable and inalienable are deliberately made ambiguous so that few people will ever learn what each word really means. As a deliberate ploy, that ambiguity permits people to believe that government is attendant upon their natural rights, when in fact, government only addresses the (so called) rights (permissions) of (legal) citizens.

It is therefore imperative to get to the truth of the matter. In the United States 'Declaration of Independence,' Thomas Jefferson, carefully chose the distributive plural (of) the word laws, to include both the law of nature, and the law of God who presides over nature. Jefferson declared that all men are equally endowed with 'unalienable' rights. Thus "the laws of nature, and of nature's God" are the foundation of our 'unalienable' right to life. Being that our rights are of nature, so they are inherent, intrinsic, and immutable.

The natural rights of life and liberty are unalienable —Bouvier's Law Dictionary, 1856 Edition.

Alfred Adask nailed it...

"It is impossible for any individual to sell, transfer or otherwise dispose of an 'unalienable Right.' It is impossible for you to take one of my 'unalienable rights.' It is likewise impossible for me to even voluntarily surrender, sell or transfer one of my 'unalienable rights.' Once I have something 'unalienable,' it's impossible for me to get rid of it. It would be easier to give up the color of my eyes or my heart than to give up that which is 'unalienable.' —Alfred Adask [6]

Accordingly, Unalienable Rights are immutable, impossible to erase, respectful of and within the equal rights of all others. They express our right to action, our immutable right to live and sustain our life, all contrary directives or proclamations null and void.

Our inherent and inseparable right to life is not separately granted or bestowed. It is of our nature. It is the right to think, and act, the right to use and exercise our faculties in support of life. It is the right to live free from molestation, and to protect that right. Every abrogation, or refusal of these facts, represents death in some form. Neither is the right to life 'self-ownership,' as many will claim. One's life is not one's property. Life cannot be a (personal) constituent property of what you are, since it is what you are. You are your life.

> *"Natural rights are therefore not to be confused with the so-called 'human rights' of the United Nations' Universal Declaration of Human Rights of 1948. On the basis of that Declaration I can say that I have rights to life, liberty and property, but not to my life, liberty or property." —Frank van Dun*

One cannot (separately) own what they already are. Notwithstanding, every man, woman and child has the unalienable right to life and thus to sustain it. As van Dun makes clear, the difference between *'self-ownership'* of one's life and one's *'unalienable right'* to life is profound. The first is one's claim. The second is one's inherent self. Accordingly, Unalienable right means our immutable right to live and sustain the life we are, drawn about us by the equal rights of all others. All aggression, trespass, or violation of our 'unalienable' right to life is outlawed.

How can we uphold our life if we do not also have a 'right' to the fruits of our labours? Do we have a right to the product of our actions? Yes, indeed, but please comprehend the difference. There can be no guarantee we will earn any property but that we will own it if and when we earn it.

Our right to life is the source of all rights. Property rights are our only means because no other rights are possible without them. With no means to sustain our lives through our effort, we each are dependents, but on what or whom? People who produce while others dispose of their products are enslaved. In sum, therefore...

- We each have the right to act in support of our life.
- We each have the right to the product of our efforts.

The difference now is crystal clear. Our 'unalienable' right to life is our right to be, not to own. Our 'inalienable' right is to own, not our lives, but that which upholds and sustains what our nature decrees we are.

John Locke (1632-1704), an English philosopher and political theorist, offered a very valid distinction concerning 'property.' In his Classic Labour Theory of Private Property, he asserted that *"the Labour of Mans Body, and the Work of his Hands, we may say, are properly his."*

Further, *"that whatsoever he removes out of the State that Nature hath provided, and left it in, he hath mixed his labour with, and joined to it something that is his own, and thereby makes it his property."*

Sir William Blackstone agreed. He held that, *"bodily labour, bestowed upon any subject which before lay in common to all men, is universally allowed to give the fairest and most reasonable title to an exclusive property."*

The American Declaration of Independence endorsed that philosophical history unmistakably. America's founders correctly showed that the unalienable right to act in support of our life is immutable; unable to be removed by any means.

That means we have a right to the product of our efforts: to the fruits of our labours. This right is not inherent in our human nature; instead, it is ingrained within our efforts to produce products and services.

Our cultivated or manufactured products comprise raw materials and our labour efforts and cannot be separated. The effort remains a part of that product even when ownership entitlement is transferred, for example, when the product is sold, gifted, or bequeathed.

John Locke grasped the principle fully. In effect, he said that land is a raw material to which the 'property of labour' can be added, for example, to improve a parcel of land. According to the unalienable right to action, *"the land and his labour are joined such that the improved land, by the property of his effort, becomes his property."*

In other words, our 'right to property arises from adding labour to improve land that, before our effort, (to use Locke's words) is *"the state that Nature hath provided, and left it in."*

Locke's idea conflicted with the Divine Right of Kings, wherein the king is the universal lord and original proprietor of all the lands in his kingdom. That is what America's 'founding fathers' sought to escape. Their tool was to expressly include action to improve land and one's life by entering the phrase 'pursuit of happiness.' In effect, the 'Declaration of Independence' encapsulated the significance of Locke's work and, in one term, embraced and co-joined the natural laws concerning Man's life, his freedom to live it, and his right to enjoy the fruits of his labours.

The word property has three very different meanings.

1. First, it refers to possessions like goods, effects, stuff, chattels, assets, valuables, etcetera.

2. Second, it means holdings to which one has a title—for example, a house, land, estates, acreage, real property, or realty.

3. Thirdly, property means a constituent or attribute— a quality, characteristic, feature, trait, mark or hallmark. For example, length is a (dimensional) property of a piece of string, and wet is a (constituent) property of a raindrop.

Meanings #1 and #2 infer or permit ownership. Definition #3 does not. Our beating heart cannot be a separable property of life, or vice versa, since neither can exist without the other. Our right to life is wholly inseparable from life. Our 'right' to own property is non-separable from our right to life because it provisions life's sustenance.

The principle is clear-cut. To sustain and uphold our lives, we must be able to keep and own the proceeds of our efforts — the fruits of our labour. Any refusal violates our life-sustaining efforts and our right to live. I have defined this right to property as our 'inalienable right,' our right of entitlement (or belonging) to that which our efforts have produced. 'Inalienable rights' are thereby conferred, without which the product(s) would not have materialised. Those labours cannot be subtracted or deleted.

The difference between 'unalienable' and 'inalienable' is now clear-cut.

- The right to act in support of our life is unalienable. (Unalienable means unable to be removed.)
- The right to the product of our efforts is inalienable. (Inalienable means within the product.)

Now consider the implications.

- The unalienable right to our lives prevents service corporations, governments, or anyone else from violating our life. Theft, including tax, is outlawed.
- Inalienable rights deny anyone or any group from confiscating our (lawful) property. The subject of one's property, an item, or product, can be aliened, but no one can take, confiscate, usurp, plunder, defile, or steal any individual's inalienable right to their property. Theft and eminent domain are outlawed thereby.

Neither of these rights apply to any group, race, culture, society or collective, nor can they. Both belong to flesh and blood living beings; thus, both are 'individual rights,' divorced from today's legal jurisdiction.

Ownership of one's efforts may transfer to another, whereby the (in-built) inalienable right to that product exchanges for value, whether gifted, bequeathed or sold. The right of ownership or right of entitlement transfers; thus, the new owner's inalienable right to own that particular property is acquired. (This has far-reaching implications for contractual matters.) Products can be sold, gifted, or bequeathed—the producer's inalienable right to their effort's product transfers by voluntary choice to the new owner.

I consider those descriptions the most proper and lawful description of unalienable and inalienable rights ever offered. They cannot apply to inert fictional legal entities because dead entities cannot action anything. Thus, our individual rights are categorically denied authoritative misappropriation by anyone, any group, or government for any purpose. Group rights cannot exist and need not exist. No one is disadvantaged since everyone has individual rights without exception.

Inalienable rights and unalienable rights are co-dependent since both reference life itself. You cannot have one without the other! A producer who does not own the result of his effort, whose production is usurped or stolen, does not have the right to live. State denial of property rights effectively turns men and women into state-owned property.

Does this explain 'human rights' rule under the auspices of the United Nations, in contravention of its (Article 1) statement that *'all human beings are born free and equal in dignity and rights'?* Do you now see why states rule 'equitable title,' be separable from 'legal title'? Do you see the deadly trap of claiming that we each own our lives, thereby permitting government to usurp our ownership?

Does all that help to explain, why the Thomas Jefferson Memorial in Washington DC has the word INALIENABLE engraved in twelve-inch high letters, despite that Jefferson used the word 'Unalienable'?

No one, no association, cooperation, collaboration, or dealing can negate our free and unalienable right to life. We must protect individual rights if humanity is to be free. Consider the implications.

- Whereas animals must adapt themselves to nature, and we must adapt nature to our purpose, we have the respectful and responsible right to do so.
- Our nature is such that we each have the immutable, unalienable right to live as a rational being.
- No one can rightfully live without the individual right to act, so to live.

Whosoever preaches or decrees otherwise holds death as their premise.

- No claim of right may negate, or usurp, the unalienable rights of any other living human being.
- No trespass of any other living being's right to life is permissible under natural law.
- Our right to act, so to live, fully accepts the reciprocal right of all others, equally so to do.
- When our actions preserve other people's right to life, our own rights are guaranteed.
- When our actions violate others' rights, we forfeit our own. Trespassing another's rights self-cancels our (individual) rights, respective of that particular action.
- Our body, thoughts, emotions, and actions, are our life and responsibility, reciprocally valid for all others equally.
- No collective rights are possible without trespassing one or more individuals' rights to their life.
- Individual rights guarantee one's freedom to think and act. They impose no obligations on one's neighbours except to abstain from violating their rights.

To stand for freedom at the expense of one's own life buys freedom for millions of others. To trade freedom for comfort or convenience costs freedom for all others in society.

Substitution of a 'protectorate body' in place of government would reduce command to nil and boost societal abundance far beyond our current imaginations.

The concepts of 'safety', 'security' 'order' and 'necessity' are the most commonly used excuses to deny freedom. The result is the abolition of freedom matched by increased institutional control and exploitation of private individuals having no particular benefit to society. Government empowers itself as the "solution" to the "problem" of fear thus generated.

Freedom must be seen and protected for its life-sustaining value. Failure to protect your own freedom is to weaken or destroy the freedom of others. Differently said, our protecting the freedom of others, assures our own.

Those who assault our freedoms point to the compliant as normal and the non-compliant as deviant. It is just the opposite. As asserted in *Conscious Ascendance*, conscious power is individual, the highest condition of which is ethical and moral self-mastery. That self-realised state is the source of one's freedom. Deny that learning and its practice, and freedom vanishes.

The plunder of rights, and goods across centuries, is now laid bare. So you can see why 'unalienable' and 'inalienable' construe to mean the same thing. Why group rights leading to gang warfare are ignorantly upheld, and why individual rights are condemned as selfish.

> *Whoever claims the "right" to "redistribute" the wealth produced by others is claiming the "right" to treat human beings as chattel. — Ayn Rand* [15]

This chapter began by stating that individualism, independence and 'rights' are inseparable. The uniting key is your life. When your autonomy and rights are sacrificed to state rule, so is your life. It is necessary, therefore, to accord your independence and individual rights their proper place, fully and unconditionally protected. Natural law is the means, but before dealing with each of the twenty natural laws, there must be a platform on which they can rest securely, as the next chapter describes.

Chapter 6

6. Blueprints for natural law

Independence, ethics, morality, rights and justice introduce the blueprints of natural law, of which there are twenty. They are presently unknown, utterly dissimilar from that currently perceived as law. This chapter is crucially essential, therefore. Its express intent is to prepare a foundation on which the twenty laws stand so that you will have no doubts concerning their validity and authenticity. Please study this chapter with your mind open to considering new concepts.

From my study and many years of practice of Ayn Rand's Objectivist philosophy, I had long known that governments do not exist, but instead 'corporations' masquerading as government. So commencing in 2012, I sought to learn how the Australian government might be re-purposed. Knowing that statutes offered no merit, I turned to 'Common Law.' Little satisfied me, save learning 'Natural law' underpins it. So I changed course and promptly hit another brick wall. Natural law rests in moral theory predominantly, hence the term *'natural law theory.'*

Objectively, I postured that our human body consists of an enormous diversity of cells, tissues, organs and systems, plus mental processes and that none, in good health, could disagree with another in the service of one's life. I argued that although all are different, each serves to sustain life and nothing more. Equally tasked, every cell organ and faculty are individually unique. Further, if this common purpose is to have full effect, human consciousness must play a significant role. So I put 'natural law theory' aside and turned my full attention to researching human consciousness. Unfortunately, that hit another roadblock.

As late as 1989, Stuart Sutherland (1989), a British psychologist, wrote in the International Dictionary of Psychology:

> *"Consciousness is a fascinating but elusive phenomenon. It is impossible to specify what it is, what it does, or why it evolved. Nothing worth reading has been written on it". —(p. 95).*

Science regards consciousness as subjective due to free will, whence it cannot be a science. David Chalmers put forward the idea that consciousness will likely never be known, thereby coining the term, 'hard problem of consciousness.' Thus with nothing left to inquire about and nowhere to turn, neuroscientists invented 'panpsychism', which states that every atom has an element of consciousness.

I was shocked. To know nothing of consciousness and thereby have no means of correcting conscious ignorance or preventing its recurrence is almost beyond belief! That mental vacancy, I concluded, permits so-called governments to wreak wide-scale havoc and untold suffering on a global scale. Moreover, it leaves us vulnerable to deliberate mind control, forcing our submission into a totalitarian dictatorship. Perhaps our ignorance of consciousness is deliberately plotted for that purpose, but I digress.

I pressed on — *"no theories, just give me facts!"* I sensed that if we humans, ordinarily in good health, are governed through natural processes that uphold life while permitting free will thought, then they are indeed common to all, despite free choices. So my mind questioned whether Creator had offered us a law blueprint within our nature. Moreover, if that works for each of us personally, could that blueprint apply to our societies? Would we need to write societal laws additionally? Could a community exist that would enable our will to run free yet prevent each of us from violating someone's desire to live as they might choose? Wishful thinking or facts never discovered?

It became apparent that no examination of this kind would stand scrutiny unless factually grounded in our human nature. I questioned whether we are all equal by nature despite being different in form, talents and expression. So I was determined to discover regularity and consistency that keeps our lives on track while allowing our will to run free.

6. Blueprints for natural law

What, then, is consciousness? For our will to be free, indeed Creator must have provided boundaries that would ensure it? The answer emerged over several years of concerted research, described in my (2017) book, *'Law from Within,'* now updated and superseded by my book *'Conscious Ascendance.'* Not only did I discover what consciousness is, how it works and why, twenty natural laws emerged from our human nature, all coexisting with free will. These laws are immutable and unable to be altered. Our 'will' is 'free' to roam the cosmos, yet the consequences of our actions are governed. Better still, these laws may translate into society without alteration or addition.

I got it! I got it in full! Instead of laws prescribing or commanding our actions and punishing non-compliance, inherent laws honour our choices while governing the consequences of our efforts. Our activities are judged summarily, not prescriptively censured in advance. With that reversed understanding of the *'law,'* the whole subject inverted. My vision for Australia's future skyrocketed, applicable to all human societies on this planet and beyond. Three separate quotations tell the story.

Thomas Jefferson's words explain the vital role that full consciousness plays—

> *"If a nation expects to be ignorant and free in a state of civilisation, it expects what never was and never will be."*

Albert Einstein confirmed Jefferson's words concerning ignorance...

> *"No problem can be solved from the same level of consciousness that created it."*

Buckminster Fuller explained the task ahead...

> *You never change things fighting the existing reality. To change something, build a new model that makes the existing model obsolete.*

The remainder of this book describes that new model. My mission succeeded. All of the roadblocks collapsed, unveiling a vision for free, organic societies worldwide, unlike anything ever witnessed or dreamt.

Our body is a physical housing for our life on earth, home for our organs, systems, brain, mind, emotions and soul. Our skeletal system of bones and joints connects to many systems, including nervous, circulatory, lymphatic, respiratory, endocrine, digestive, urinary, and reproductive systems. Nature organises our physiological systems and processes for our thriving and maintenance in an orderly manner.

'Order' is often considered to mean command and compliance. But in the sense of life and its processes, it means to form, structure and maintain in an orderly fashion. It means a state of 'orderliness' in arrangement and functionality. Such organisation implies arranging our separate systems into one indivisible body, where the function of one system induces the process of one or more others. Orderly patterns of interconnectedness and interoperability exist. Observe also that the word 'systems' is effectively another way of saying 'orderliness.'

Neuroscience achieves wonders, but unless this orderly harmony and correspondence are considered a science, no laws governing their function are discoverable. The natural order of human nature remains undiscovered. Sadly, we live in ignorance of the incredible powers of consciousness. We may suffer as a result and not know that we suffer. Differently said, we may never know what joy is humanly possible. However, once mental orderliness and conscious process are correctly understood, it becomes clear that all our faculties interconnect in the most orderly fashion possible. We are functionally complete, lacking nothing, provided we have the will to learn.

Frank van Dun, explains that from etymology, the word 'law' means order or orderliness. It follows that biological parameters ensuring physiological orderliness are natural laws. They are inherent in our created nature, regardless of how you define your creation; innate and immutable. None are theorised or written for us by other humans.

Given this (systematic) orderliness within ourselves, it would seem logical that our outward expressions toward others would 'naturally' follow suit. If 'natural law' is our guidance exactly, shouldn't this automated life-preserving protocol require that we harmoniously interface and collaborate with others for the same purpose? Yes, it should, but we have the free will to say no.

Consequently, natural law cannot rule. It can only advise. It is as though 'life' taps us on the shoulder, saying, "look, I know you've got to deal with others, and that can prove difficult at times, but can we do it my way, please?" You respect' natural law' when you agree to act in harmony with self-preservation as the first principle and respectfully accord others the same right to their lives.

Just as Positive law has overwritten Natural law for centuries, we are accustomed to looking for solutions outside of ourselves, in society, church, legal dealings, government, trade unions, family, and so on. Not surprisingly, it is quite a monumental task to grasp that natural law is not the solution to problems; instead, it exists to keep the human machine running smoothly, both for ourselves and our dealings with others. This gift of efficiency and efficacy is its beauty and simplicity. Once grasped that nine-tenths of today's problems manifest from pre-scripted rules, the opportunity to avoid that imposed vexation becomes extremely attractive.

Our physical bodies organise across six levels in a structural hierarchy, from elementary to very complex. Orderliness begins right there. Take speech, for example. The lips, tongue, throat, jaw, larynx, and diaphragm must all work together in near-perfect synchrony. This symphony requires our brain to become a master conductor, even to utter simple phrases. Look further. Our endocrine system is a chemical messenger system consisting of hormones. The hypothalamus in the brain is the neural control centre. A group of glands secrete hormones directly into the circulatory system to regulate the function of distant target organs. After that, feedback loops modulate hormone release to maintain homeostasis.

This process is no accident. Natural laws govern our biology, yet nothing prescribes or demands what we eat, drink or inhale. Cells, tissues, and organs in our bodies are all unique and independent, yet all cooperate to support and uphold our life. We each are living testament to natural laws encrypted in our physiology. Subjectivity and theorising have no place.

Pieces of the puzzle came together. Patterns of order (orderliness) are consistent and equal in all humans, while free will is correspondingly unique and independent. Thus natural Law emphatically upholds equality, jointly upholding our uniqueness as individuals. Therefore, it makes perfect sense that if the 'content' of our free thought is separate from our mental 'process,' unbridled freedom within a governed (natural law) process is eminently feasible! There is no conflict, nor can there be! It is perfect! We are all equal in freedom, each having a governed mental process, not to inhibit our free will choices, but to ensure that free will predominates!

That understanding caught me off guard, but its truth is pure beauty. Unlike anything history has shown, personal, political, and societal implications explode. Another revelation struck home. Creators' laws and Man-made laws are incompatible. I did not need to study common Law, maritime Law, positive Law or any other legalities. No law library sufficed. I needed instead to explore the wholesome beauty of our human nature and grasp how its different functions uniquely contribute to the wholesomeness of life, personally and socially.

As separate human beings, we are each capable of purposive thought, speech, and action, mainly directed at material things and resources. Our ability to act is not only necessary; it is our exclusive, naturally ordained 'right to life.' Free will and our 'right' to action are our 'lawful' means of living and sustaining our life. To that end, our body and all its parts exist and function in concert. None can be separated, divided or deconstructed, save through death. In short, our means of action is a (faculty) 'property' of our being, while actions are our 'right'.

Therefore, given that natural laws govern the consequences of our actions, why should they not also apply to morality, respecting 'just' social and business dealings? Results from that question far exceeded my expectations!

How could nature offer us the best life unless its purposeful functions respected the laws governing themselves without reservation? How can we give ourselves the best life possible if we are not consistently honest with the governing laws of our nature? Now step into the social realm. How are we to thrive in a free society that affords the best life possible without fully respecting the governing laws of our nature?

Is that understanding so problematic? No, it is the most simple and direct invocation of all! If natural Law is the Creator's blessing on our lives, then we do not need to demolish every artificial Law in history. We need only learn, express and employ what's been there all along! There is no need to unravel or overturn the spiritual, the new age, enlightenment, or unity consciousness.

All fraudulent inventions can be dismissed, especially concerning legal entities, straw men, birth certificates, statute laws, and all legal agencies and deficiencies in the 'Constitution.'

Governing laws exist and work to preserve our lives. Learning natural Law is thereby reduced to only three core matters—

- Understanding our true nature and rights as individuals.

- How natural Law is inherent within our body, mind and soul, wholly insistent on our wellbeing.
- How we can most efficiently and profitably function in nature and put that morality and justness into societal practice.

In short, identify what exists and use it. Falsity will fall of its own accord, which is how natural Law works! It notifies errors and allows us to confess them, remediate them, and graciously move on as lessons learned. We advance through moral will, thought and achievement, which should be recognised and taught across all curricula. Most transgressors of Natural Law are merely slow learners, not outlaws. People legally forced to submit to manufactured laws are victims, not lawbreakers.

> *"Justice in the general sense is the art or skill of acting in conformity with law, with due regard for the rights of other persons. In the particular 'technical' sense it is the art or skill of discovering rules, methods and procedures that effectively and efficiently provide for the ... and, if need be, fortification and restoration of the law of the human world. The discovery, refinement and systematisation of such rules, methods and procedures are the proper province of jurisprudence as a rational discipline." —Frank van Dun* [9]

Natural Law offers 'compassion' as one of its superior qualities, natural justice in like measure. Jurisprudence should be the foremost concern, but sadly it is virtually non-existent today. Law is not what someone said or wrote, whereby all must obey. Statutes are not law. Law, so-called, is statutory rules. Suppose we are to overcome the prevailing mindset that ranks 'collective' subservience higher than independent morality. In that case, it becomes ever more necessary to learn and practice the object of natural law, its ethics, morality, and justice. Frank van Dun reasons the rejection of natural law.

"The practice of Natural Law also has been eliminated completely by the legal profession. Very often, the study and the practice of Natural Law are scorned if not ridiculed.The reasons for this desultory attitude towards Natural Law are many. However, the most important reason for the negative attitude is that the legal profession has discovered that there is much more money to be made from focusing on highly politicised

complex, constantly changing systems of social regulation than it ever could hope to make from the study and practice of Natural Law." —Frank van Dun

Do you see massive simplification, intelligible education texts, massively reduced costs, and crime reduction? Nothing is more important for intelligent living beings than to study the Creator's laws governing the consequences of their actions.

As a side-note, through all of van Dun's extensive writings concerning Natural Law, 'natural persons' are distinctly differentiated from 'artificial persons,' those being (fictional) 'legal entities' concocted within legal systems under the banner of 'positive law.' He assertively reasons that "natural persons are always living human beings born of nature," despite all legislation decreeing otherwise, as in Australia.

In his treatise, *'The Lawful and the Legal,'* Frank van Dun writes—

> *The word 'law' means order, hence Natural Law is simply the natural order. In the sense in which Natural Law is relevant to jurists, it is the natural order of persons, specifically, the order of natural persons: human beings that are capable of rational, purposive action, speech and thought. In short, Natural Law is the natural order of the human world. Laws are patterns of order. Hence, Natural Laws are patterns of natural order–and, in the juristically relevant sense, patterns of order among natural persons. —Frank van Dun* [8]

He also explains the two (conflicting) deviations of the word 'Law.'

- **LEX:** 'Law' was first derived from the Latin word Lex, representing the mobilisation of armies, and the organising of military campaigns. Thus Lex was a 'command,' which came to mean any general directive, rule, or law issued from the highest political authorities.
- **IUS:** The word 'law,' was also translated from the Latin word 'Ius', which refers to a bond or obligation that arises out of a personal commitment made in solemn speech.

Eventually, the Latin word lex changed to 'Lex Naturalis,' purportedly to give moral legitimacy to statute laws and commandments. Unfortunately, 'lex' remains attached to authoritarian commands that we call statute law.

How can the directive content of any natural law be determined? It cannot. No directive exists. 'Lex' has the power to oblige, coerce, or force without consent, but natural law has no such power. To use the term 'lex naturalis' in the sense of 'natural law' is to bind or oblige people without their consent, which abrogates free will choice from the outset. Thus 'naturalis' attached to 'lex' is a contradiction in terms that reeks of political domination and control.

Conversely, the word law was also more appropriately used to translate the Latin word 'ius,' because ius has nothing to do with exercising political authority.

> *"Ius denotes a bond or obligation arising out of a personal commitment made in solemn speech ('iurare', to swear) and in a more general sense the order of human affairs that arises out of such mutual commitments. In other words, 'ius' presupposes a condition in which people meet as free and equal persons and arrange their affairs by mutual agreements, contracts or covenants." — Frank van Dun*

As explained here, and more particularly in *'Conscious Ascendance,'* Creator has used internal order, unity, interdependence, interoperability, harmony, systematisation, and sequence patterns. This orderliness corresponds with the Latin word Ius, as a solemn oath bond, which allies with the proper meaning of the word 'law.'

'Lex', which presupposes that one man can unilaterally oblige or rule another, is the exact opposite. It follows that the order or law of our human world ordains and maintains the condition in which people may enter into rational discussion and negotiation. Each takes the other seriously, thus carrying out any commitments they jointly agree to undertake. This collaborative bond is precisely what the word ius conveys. Mutual obligation to respect one another is inescapable, as long as the commitment is reciprocal. Moral adherence is mutual respect. That is a form of natural law collaboration.

Today, most people believe there is no such thing as 'natural law,' if they have ever heard the term. Instead, many hold 'natural law' is little more than a set of ill-defined background principles intended to deflect (moral) outrage among the public away from legislators' and judges' decisions.

Initially, freedom and property were relatively safe from private and public aggression within natural law constraints that society respected. However, in time, people understood that desire for wealth and personal betterment led them to material progress. Subsequently, as the nineteenth century closed, the idea that (progressive) material progress is the 'natural law' of the human world replaced that understanding. Do you see the disastrous switch? Wealth and welfare as the proper natural rights of men meant that 'justice' was then morally if not criminally) re-interpreted to represent the efficient production and 'fair' distribution of wealth. In other words, 'justice' was removed from the personal realm and implanted into the public domain exercised by governments.

Natural law is today more commonly referred to as *'Natural Law Theory.'* That splits into two factions,' *Natural Law Theory of Morality'* and the *'Natural Law Theory of Positive Law.'* The 'morality theory' holds that humans possess intrinsic (in-bred) values or morals that strongly influence our reasoning and behaviour. We are fundamentally good people, and this acceptance arises from our inbuilt propensity to always do the right thing. Accordingly, morality is inherent in all people, witnessed by close observation of values intrinsic to human nature. Thus a system of natural law can be deduced through reason and applied independently of the enacted (positive or legal positivism) rules of a state or society.

That description sounds superficially plausible and desirable, but a serious question arises. If rules of right and wrong are inherent in people, then they are undoubtedly facts of nature, not theories. Further, if values are intrinsic within our human nature, they cannot be theoretical either. So the question is; are natural laws a fact of human nature, or not? If that is so, then natural law is not a theory.

What, then, is true? Do we have an inbuilt tendency towards good or a natural propensity to act morally? Do we have inbuilt character traits and virtues, and do they define what natural law is? Does this innate 'inbred morality' prescribe what natural law is? Yes, answers today's adherents of the *'Natural Law Moral Theory.'* That is precisely how it works.

But does it? If we have an inherent morality or predisposition to do good, our mind is regulatory biased from day one. Therefore, free will cannot exist. Where choice and determination, known as free will, are foreordained, all reasoning is nonsensical.

What if the opposite was true? Suppose natural law was factually inherent in our human nature, our being, and no inbuilt morality existed? Suppose those natural laws defined ethics and morality but left acceptance or rejection as our choice. In that case, natural law factually exists within our nature, and no natural law theory exists. These natural laws would advocate, commend, and advise ethics, fueling our (unbiased) free choices. Moral or immoral actions would follow subsequently.

Do you see? Once (innate) natural law is shown to uphold morality absolutely but never impose it, the 'natural law theory of morality' is no longer a theory. Instead, it exists as the baseline guide for ethics and morality, fully supportive of free choice. Do you sense a moral revolution never spoken of before?

If indeed we each author our morality in the manner described, what justice or protection society might have if any? Laws are needed most surely, to preempt our security? To answer, let's examine the 'natural law theory of positive law' concerning what's legal and illegal.

To ensure protection, natural law theorists invented a 'natural law theory of positive law.' Its purpose was to establish what is legal versus illegal while ostensibly upholding or endorsing the 'moral theory of natural law.'

The result was 'Lex naturalis,' or the 'natural law theory of positive law.' Its moral underpinnings differ from 'Legal positivism,' which has no moral foundation. Consequently, there are rival views about what 'law' is and what unites morality with justice. Thomas Aquinas, globally known as the guru of natural law theory, held that any 'positive law' which conflicts with or is inconsistent with either natural law or divine law is not law at all. Therefore, there is no moral obligation to obey it or legal obligation to obey. Augustine and Martin Luther King supported this view. Others argue it is impossible to have a legal system without fidelity to the rule of law and formal justice.

Enough already because the matter is now crystal clear. The evidence is incontrovertible. 'Patterns of natural order' existing in our biology and mental processes, and orderly governing of their functioning, constitute a 'bond or obligation that arises out of their mutual commitment' to uphold life. And that is the exact definition of 'ius naturale.' Accordingly, 'natural law' is a fact of life.

Evidence is indisputable. If we ingest toxins or poisons, we pay the price, however high that might be. Likewise, anxiety, stress, and trauma are unavoidable if we hold toxic thoughts, propaganda or bogus ideologies in our minds. It becomes apparent that just as our heart protects our lungs and vice versa, so patterns of natural order protect our two minds. Better yet, free will falls wholly within that protection because Creator sandwiched its functioning sequentially inside the automated subconscious process. Can you think of anything more beneficial, committed, or protective?

Grasp that natural law is not primarily concerned with societal regulation or arresting criminals; instead, it involves the beauty and fullness of spiritual life on a material plane. In those two milliseconds of conscious comprehension, you will have advanced more than humanity has in two centuries!

It gets better! The fact 'existential natural law' is inherent within us, it authenticates, validates and protects itself and us equally. No legislator, authoritarian dictator, or even satan can erase it! No commandment, rule, or statute can overrule its natural bonds or natural law. That means all forms of 'lex,' including lex naturalis,' with the potential to violate the natural order, are entirely excluded. All are outlawed since 'commands' violate free will and your freedom, which is immoral and unjust.

Free will is protected from all interference save what we permit. A new future for humanity dawns once grasped 'natural laws protect our free will choices while governing the consequences of our actions and behaviour.'

The conclusion is unmistakable. 'Existential natural law' is incompatible with 'natural law theory.' The implications are profound because natural law suffers no loss, no diminishment; on the contrary, rescued from anonymity. It gains a new irrefutable foothold that no one knew existed, thus amplifying its potency considerably. Belief that an innate morality points to natural law no longer exists. Instead, factual natural law advises our character and our free choice to exercise it. Self-governance assumes prominence and responsibility, whereby all imposed rule cancels. No protest is admissible without the claimant refuting their nature, which action instantly nullifies all claims.

The (believed) morality of 'what we in nature do best' was and still is promoted as a societal platform to uphold (moral) freedom. Tragically, that allowed natural law to be excised from the 'private domain' where it rightfully belongs, then placed square in the 'public domain' under the authoritarian rule of 'positive law,' all reinstatement denied. Whatever moral progress may have resulted from the work of natural law theorists is now factually rescued from arrest and given new life of inestimable proportions.

Two matters remain for correction. First, until the misuse of the word 'law' is corrected, 'natural law' cannot be explained, taught, or implemented. Second, we must show and confirm that natural law exists within the nature of every man, woman and child; theory no more. When these two matters synergistically reinforce each other, 'existential natural law' will undoubtedly change the course of human history.

As described in the following chapter, the twenty natural laws encrypted in our physiology and conscious processes exist to serve our lives, personally and socially. But unfortunately, these laws remain hidden so long as human and sociological sciences refuse to study human consciousness. Worse, the benefits of natural law are never shown, much less explained.

Natural laws do not command — no prescription exists nor can it, else we've no free will. Natural law governs the consequences of our actions and nothing more.

Your whole being works for self-preservation as its baseline reference. 'Life' has a 'natural order' to its intrinsic process geared to your thriving as you choose. Think of it as complete harmony, intrinsically orchestrated to ensure that its 'self' continues, meaning that you 'live' in pursuit of happiness. Thriving is the goal, the art of self-preservation being the bottom line.

Let me quote briefly from the first chapter in *'Conscious Ascendance.'* Animal life is perceptual. Man's life is conceptual. Animals depend upon the environment which already exists, sufficient for their sustenance. They adapt themselves to nature. We do the opposite. We adapt nature to ourselves. We build bridges, roads, tools, contracts, orchestras, airplanes, computer software, restaurants and more. All testify excellence of thought and physical ability. Our most outstanding efficiency in all this activity comes not from conforming to legal demands but from forethought, kindness, grace, morality, ethics, gratitude, diligence, good judgement and much more, all of which spell 'Natural Law.'

It is a tragedy that many people are brainwashed to believe that without a ruler, there can be no order. It is doubly sad that so many cannot grasp their natural order and embrace it to the point where no ruler is needed but their morality, which nature upholds every minute of every day. How can so few relate to the law as orderliness, having no directive content, one so brilliantly conceived it comes with its own fail-safe protection system?

The answer has escaped everyone. Natural law obliges everyone without the need for consent. Our orderliness arises from the inbuilt necessity for one faculty to uphold the next, and so on. Natural law practice is one's consent to live. Dissidence is the opposite. The most vital elements of natural law are not yet taught. Many are oblique, hiding, out of sight, mainly because of prejudice and past indoctrination. They must be revealed and made known if we are to grasp our fullness of being, precisely because the only law that permits that approval is natural.

The first principle is that law is not a command, a system of directions, or control, even for the (so-called) 'common good.' Natural law is nature's invitation to live your own life, with the profound blessing that you do so, all rolled into one! Its invocation is to be welcomed with open arms, prized, praised, practised as virtue and placed high on one's value list. Then people will inspire to preserve their lives and values through their conduct and thoughts, voluntarily committing to its finite protection for their family in perpetuity. We cannot choose natural law. We can only choose to respect it — or disrespect it.

It is imperative, therefore, to rid common belief that in 'natural law', the word 'law' stands for commands, rules, directives, or decrees. The opposite is true. Expressly, a (natural) 'law' proclaims something should be done or not done. In turn, doing or not doing is left to the discretion of those to whom the law addresses. As stated, natural law is an invitation or invocation, nothing less or more. Specifically, it is an objective condition that many people may in fact, value and even admire. As discussed in 'Conscious Ascendance,' its spiritual 'life-value' component inspires people to formulate rules of respectful, ethical and responsible conduct, and imparts that they restore it, should it be impaired.

From a historical perspective, some people may define 'natural law' as 'rules of law.' Importantly, we should never forget that natural law primarily exists as the means to an end, expressly our invocation to thrive and prosper. Natural law secondarily exists for any restoration of the natural order (ius) to satisfy that end. Most importantly, once natural law is understood in its primary creative context, only resorting to its remedial and restorative powers on demand, then 'natural law' stands for 'justice' on both counts. Accordingly, natural law may be referred to as rules of justice because the literal meaning of 'justice' (Latin: justicia) is entirely conducive to 'ius'. Justice is respect for law in the sense of 'ius' as a social bond.

'Natural law' is no longer a mystifying concept, or irrelevant. Frank van Dun explains how it stands for the natural order of a peaceable and thriving human world.

6. Blueprints for natural law

"Order in the human world certainly implies that there is no confusion among persons. This is the case when words, works and actions can be traced to their true authors and when their consequences — to the extent that these objectively or materially affect others — are either borne by the authors themselves or else by willing or consenting others. When human affairs are in order, no person need fear that others realise their projects, or take credit for his words, actions or works at his expense but without his agreement. No one can successfully hide his own responsibility for what he said, did or brought about. There is then no confusion as to who is innocent or guilty of a crime, who owes a debt to whom, who was and who was not a participant in some particular undertaking or practice, who participated voluntarily and who was forced or tricked to participate, which exchanges were concluded by mutual consent and which were not, and so on.

Order or law in the human world is that condition in which each person is free from the threat of injurious actions from others, able to live his life and to enjoy his property in an environment of peaceful, friendly relations. 'To each his own' is therefore the defining characteristic of law. To maintain that order requires respect for it, i.e. justice, as the guiding principle of human action. That respect includes the constant will to leave or if necessary to return to each his own — that is to say the will to avoid causing physical damage to the person, work or property of any other, to honour lawful contracts and to provide full restitution or compensation to those to whom one has nevertheless caused unlawful harm, as well as the will not to hinder those who seek lawful remedies for unlawful wrongs done to themselves or others." — Frank van Dun[8]

Readers of 'Conscious Ascendance' will recognise how those words connect natural law in personal terms to natural law in societal terms. They reinforce how ethical thoughts manifest as moral actions. Because morality is of our own making, we become architects of the natural societal order, the natural law of the human world. Let's explore further.

'Conscious Ascendance' expressed equality and our uniqueness as independent living beings. It stressed that we are alike in freedom, blessed with an inherent capacity for independent action, speech and thought, and for rationally communicating our thoughts, intentions, and expectations to one another. Moreover, as free agents, we get to determine a value hierarchy that magnifies our ethical prowess, which then manifests as value-charged morality. We, each, are the authors of our morality, respecting the lives of all others.

Accordingly, objectively accurate answers exist to questions about the authorship of anything we say or do, also as concerns our lawful property. Our individual rights must never invade or infringe upon others' unalienable right to life and their inalienable right to property, thereby causing unlawful harm.

It follows that natural law applies to our 'equality' in nature, not to our differences in nature. Equality results from our universal nature with our innate or genetically given freedom of action, speech, thought and rational communication. In that crucial respect, the very heart of our complete conscious process determines we are all alike. Age, gender, body weight, the colour of skin or hair, proficiency in language or math, and all other constituents of nature are not determinants of natural law. Thus nine-tenths of perceived disorder vanishes instantly. Natural orderliness founded on equality renders all those distractions irrelevant.

Although freedom is our reality, it may be temporarily destroyed, as in a traffic accident. Such may well be the consequences of one's actions, thus proof of natural law in the personal domain. But when infractions caused by others arise, only then does the question of lawful or unlawful destruction of a person's fundamental freedom arise. In other words, natural law is the order of ourselves in the first instance; differently constituted by interactions of many individually separate human beings.

Here is where authoritarian commands and dictates often cause mayhem, distress and loss in many forms. As the authors of our actions, our respect for natural law requires us to estimate advantages and disadvantages, personally and societally, based on ascertainable or established facts.

No absolute obligation can emerge from such deliberations; else, free will is rejected. Alternatively, parasitic outsiders prescribe our commitments and thus trespass free will. Frank van Dun offers that natural law—

> *"does not forbid every vice which a man of virtue would not commit, but only the more serious vices which even the multitude can avoid. These are the vices that do harm to others, the vices that*

would destroy human society if they were not prohibited: murder, theft, and other vices of this kind, which the human law prohibits."

Astute readers will recognise a profound ideological shift from dictatorial rule at all cost to the free exercise of moral virtue for our gain. Self-governance, in other words, is directed to thriving and flourishing within the providence of natural law. To that end, in the societal sense, justice is the art or skill of acting in conformity with natural existential law, having due regard for other people's rights. In the particular 'judicial' sense, it is the art or skill of discovering rules, methods and procedures that effectively and efficiently provide for the defence and, if need be, fortification and restoration of the natural law of the human world. Properly, it is for 'jurisprudence' as a rational discipline to discover, refine, and systematise such rules, methods and procedures and disseminate them across educational curricula at all levels.

Concerning prior discussion concerning individual rights, Van Dun offers that people can use the word 'right' in two different but related senses. One captures the static aspect of a right, the other the active part.

"In the static sense a person's natural right is the place or space he occupies lawfully in the natural order of the human world — it is his property. That space is first of all determined by his physical being as a person, and is therefore immediately filled by his real freedom. It is therefore only by his lawful activity, that is insofar as he respects the rights of others, that a person can add to his natural right. In the dynamic sense a right denotes any personal action or pattern of behaviour that is in accordance with natural law." —Frank van Dun

Accordingly, natural law and natural rights are two sides of the same coin. That must be so since both apply to individual living beings, not societal groups, societies, states or nations. Accordingly, one's natural right denotes the space of real and organic freedom coincidental with his being and his work. Moreover, because natural law is an existential fact of nature, natural law practice is an objective goal, fully correspondent with natural rights as the means to reach such goals.

Natural law may now be defined, first in personal terms, second in social terms, nevertheless as one statement–

Natural law is the set of universal, eternal and immutable conditions governing behavioural consequences of volitionally conscious beings. Absent compliance with these maxims inherent in the nature and state of Man, the peace and happiness of society can never be preserved.

As already said, natural law does not rule or command. It governs behavioural consequences only, whereby it unceasingly upholds free will. Those who transgress natural law are outlaws, their actions testifying wilful admission of the fact.

The power of natural law is manifestly inimitable on the personal level. Yet ignorance of its existence is beyond question. Doubt is found only in the minds of those who refuse it. Revolt against these laws is not forbidden or prohibited. These laws cannot be disobeyed; we can only disrespect them. Whether we know of them or not, as described in the next chapter, still they govern the fundamental conditions of our lives. They envelop us, penetrate our biology and psychology, drive our processes, regulate our bodies and movements, and preserve our thoughts and values. Any pretence or belief that we can reject them only demonstrates their omnipotence. Common sense is the nearest approximation to adopting unrecognised natural law, the most immediate form of self-governance.

Jefferson did not explicitly reference Natural Law fundamentals in the (1776) Declaration of Independence, but his embrace of it is unmistakable. The document preamble stated—

> *We hold these truths to be self-evident, that all men are created equal, that they are endowed by their Creator with certain unalienable Rights, that among these are Life, Liberty and the pursuit of happiness.*

What Jefferson immortalised in his words is probably the most profound and succinct description of natural law one could write. Jefferson grasped that truth is immutable, and so is the natural law of humankind. He caught that life is its own 'self-preservation order', and its 'truths' are self-evident in every manifestation of your nature.

There is a law that makes your heart beat and your lungs efficiently function when walking, and this law is eminently self-evident. No one consciously orders their functions, heartbeat following heartbeat, or lung expansion following contraction. The self-evident truths of these immutable, unalienable laws confirm that we humans are all equal and respectful of all necessary for the (self) preservation of life, liberty and happiness for the whole family of Man.

Jefferson's understanding of life is those self-evident truths that apply to life and forbid all attempts to quash them. Humankind should be greatly indebted to him and the Declaration of Independence, for not only did he disenfranchise America from the tyranny of England, but he also opened the door for every man and woman to escape tyranny wherever they live.

The American Declaration of Independence is renowned for its unmistakable contribution to freedom, proven benefits, and Man's advancement, attested in literature worldwide. Jefferson opened the door to America's release, but broader in principle, to the emancipation of humankind and the cessation of global tyranny.

It should now be clear 'existential natural law' exceeds anything past generations have ever known or practised over millennia. With spirituality as its core principle, its fruitful exercise is the greatest tribute one can ever offer their Creator. Natural law is not a product of the human mind. It is Creator's gift. It is our invitation to prosper and thrive materially, emotionally, and spiritually, as never taught before.

It remains that we will have neither rights nor freedom until we awaken to the fullness of freedom and the right to self-govern and responsibly act upon that right. Humanities' future and societal freedom depend on the inherent principles of natural law, our respect and incumbent responsibilities, the actioned exercise of our right to sovereign self-mastery within the individual rights and protection for all others. For that, Creator has our back, all the way!

Do you now see how natural law upholds morality without ruling our free will? Do you think it is likely that profound changes will occur when today's accepted notions of ethics and morality are cancelled? Consider these outcomes to glimpse the future in which you can play a significant part.

- Present theories holding that morality determines natural law are inverted.
- Creator has modelled the (natural law) principles of ethics, morality, and natural justice, smack in the core of our conscience and emotional reporting systems, exactly where they belong!
- All of today's beliefs concerning ethics and morality overturn.
- Morality is no longer a social or legal convention; instead, individually accountable according to the natural laws governing our nature.

- All 'collectivised' jurisdictional claims over ethics and morality are thereby invalidated.
- Independence removes the whole subject of morality from the (collective) government-ruled domain and puts it into the private domain, where it rightfully belongs.
- Not only is the right to bear arms and defend against all foreign and domestic enemies encrypted in our nature, but urged! In consequence, therefore—
- Self-governance replaces authoritarian government within the auspices of natural law.
- Statute law that wilfully renounces life through imbecilic inventions surrenders itself indisputably.
- Natural law, applicable in common, attains immutable power and dominance that no practitioner of jurisprudence ever suspected it possessed.

Thus 'existential natural law' stands in its jurisdiction, contrary to all positive law. Nothing obligates that we prove it. It is axiomatic, meaning we cannot exist without it. Those who refuse it already use it. Judges need not rule against transgressors since they have voluntarily ruled against themselves.

The name 'Natural law' is now validated and authenticated axiomatically; one must use it to refute it. Indeed, its substantive authenticity may add valid legitimacy to 'constitutional law' as never in history, provided that it never contradicts itself, as ignorantly attempted through 'lex naturalis.'

No living, flesh and blood beings need legally extract themselves from maritime law and its statutes because its juristic practitioners and adherents have already effected their separation voluntarily. They chose to violate natural law by inventing fictional entities and enforcing our compliance, that trespass of natural law their confessed guilt. They chose outlaw behaviour of their own free will. Refusing human flesh and blood disavows or renounces one's nature; thus all who do must explain the crime of forcing others to do the same.

Our task is to attest that we live. Life is our immutable hallmark, and that is our separation from all who claim any opposing jurisdiction.

Thomas Hobbes, who lived from1588 to 1679, was also a paradigmatic natural law theorist. *He held that the laws of nature are divine and that all humans are thus bound, making it easy to know at least the moral basics*. Moreover, he postured that *the fundamental good is self-preservation and that the laws of nature direct the way to this good.*

Hobbes's distinction is astoundingly accurate! Reread the last sentence and contrast it with the views of Thomas Aquinas, who held 'morality' defines natural law. Hobbes saw the opposite: natural law allows us to discover morality. This turnaround is monumental but ignored. No author in my research has mentioned how natural law theory is displaced or replaced with natural law as fact, save for Frank van Dun.

This about-turn is crucially important because all forms of positive law hell-bent on tyranny show as criminal. Nature disallows excuses; thus, positive law inventions and all its frauds that trespass life are stopped dead in their tracks. No maneuvering space remains, zilch, zero, nada.

I promised to prepare a foundation on which the twenty laws stand and to certify their validity and authenticity. You will now recognise how and why they are unknown and vastly different from all perceived as 'law.' This subject is so refreshingly new, so please do not fear contrary viewpoints or arguments. This knowledge will undoubtedly shake some people to the core. Still, once they recognise Creator's bountiful gifts to us all, they will understand exactly which side of the dividing fence is defective. The next chapter will leave no doubts.

Chapter 7

The process of full consciousness and human physiology reveal twenty governing laws of our human nature. Here, I describe each, based on the platform built in the last chapter, to show how (personal) natural law may be applied verbatim to the social or societal realm.

Initially described in my book *'Law From Within' (2017)*, I repeated these laws in my 2022) book *'Conscious Ascendance.'* The source of each was described but not referenced. I suggested that readers follow the given clues, find the page numbers of those topics, and pencil them next to the relevant law in the appendix. That cross-referenced study should have boosted the reader's knowledge, abilities and confidence and eased almost all of their fears.

This book comprehensively unites with *Conscience Ascendance* as one complete, indivisible work by dealing with natural law in societal terms. Because natural law applies to oneself and society, those twenty laws had logically to repeat here. However, instead of re-describing the source in our biology and conscious process, each law is authenticated and validated, additional to jointly referencing this information with *'Conscious Ascendance.'* Significantly, consciousness cannot be separated from natural law since it regulates the conscious process.

Let's begin with a brief synopsis of *'Conscious Ascendance.'* [Please skip ahead three paragraphs if you have already that book.] Multiple patterns of physical and mental order exist, and that particular 'orderliness' constitutes the natural laws of our being, serving to uphold and sustain our lives. 'Order,' in this sense, means to structure in an orderly fashion.

Like two individuals, our heart (hydraulic) and lungs (pneumatic) work cooperatively without pause for our entire life. A similar relationship exists between our kidneys and liver. Our body has levels of organisation that constructively build on each other, such as different cell types and tissue types that make up organs to form different organ systems. Our hearts and lungs differ, yet both work for the same purpose. So too, our conscious and subconscious minds. Values are communicated between them, much as blood conveys nutrients to our cells and organs. Human consciousness is a value transfer system that interfaces physicality and spirituality.

All the separate systems are interconnected; thus, the function of one system induces all others to join in as one indivisible entity. Cells in every tissue, organ and system, plus various mental and emotional faculties, are all independent, yet each is a cooperative part of the whole. There is an orderliness of interconnectedness and interoperability, which is what the word 'systems' conveys. So we can be confident that what is good for us is what is complete or perfecting for each of us, according to our nature.

Such orderliness or 'law' governs our functioning, the cooperation of our systems and faculties and the independence of each. Without it, we could not function at all. We could not live. 'Life-supremacy' is the bottom line. This mutual commitment' to uphold life is the very 'bond or obligation' that defines 'ius naturale,' known as natural law.

Diagram 4 shows how the twenty natural laws fall into four groups clockwise from law number 1. Each one connects to all others, which reinforces their wholesome unity. Furthermore, each law has a counterpart or supporting law found diametrically opposite—for example, 3 points to 13 and 6 points to 16.

Ten Fundamentals of Natural Law

Comprehension of these laws requires they be studied with their diagonal counterpart to thereby grasp their relationships, and their source in our nature. The following ten fundamentals apply to all twenty natural laws, following after that. These fundamentals polish the foundation given in the last chapter.

7. Twenty natural laws

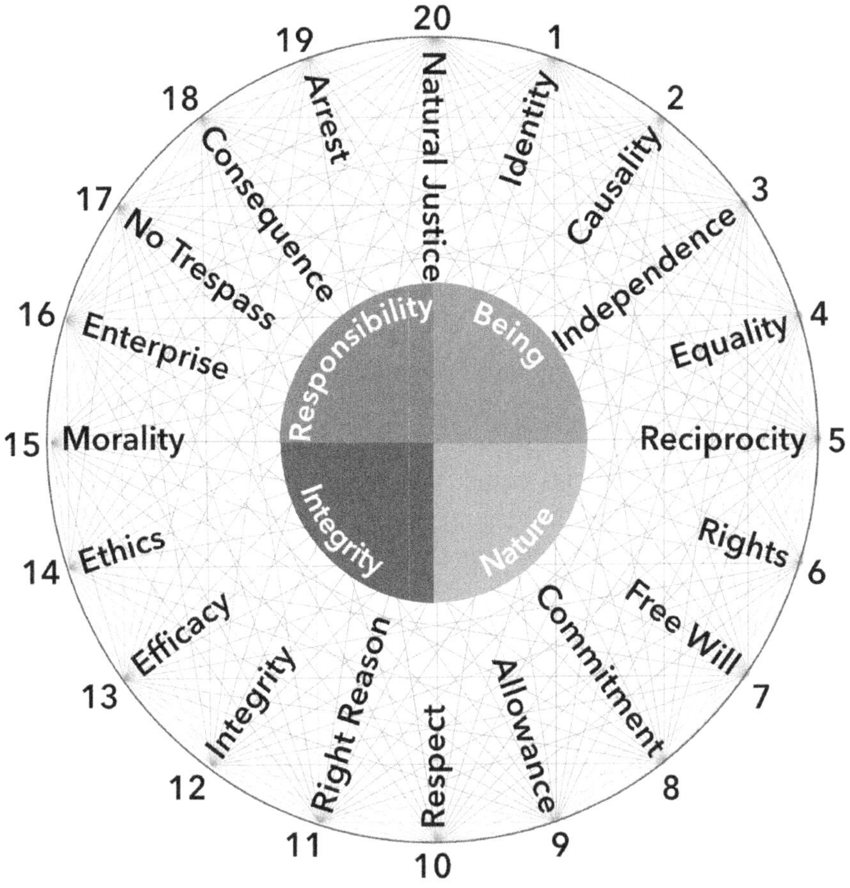

4 Natural law (flower) diagram

1 Natural Law is to be respected; not obeyed

Natural law cannot be obeyed or disobeyed. It has only to be respected. Every living man, woman and child has free will to respect natural law, treat it with hostility or contempt, or even refuse it. All consequences are one's own, whether for good or evil.

2 Natural law is of Man; not for Man

Natural law is inherent in our human nature, unable to be subtracted from or added to; thus, any contravening law trespasses from the outset, which denies its authenticity. Completeness leaves no gaps; therefore, we ignore natural law at our peril. Natural law does not rule in the usual law-book fashion; rather, it exists within our nature as life-sustaining moral guidance, always accessible.

3 Natural law is objective, not subjective

Natural law does not refuse subjective opinion, but such is irrelevant if it offers no spiritual or life-sustaining purpose. Actions that respect natural law are objectively lawful in that they uphold life and serve justice. Activities that do not are unlawful and unjust, mitigating circumstances admitted.

4 Natural law is immutable

Natural law is inviolate. No one or any construct can overrule without such action confessing unlawful power or force.

5 Natural law upholds independent human life

We are not 'all one,' as multitudes today proclaim; we are each one, and society is many. Free societies are the aggregation of independent living beings, all species-equal yet unique in expression and thus independent. No (common) lung, organ, brain, stomach, mind, or consciousness exists. The individuality of human life cannot fuse into one unified entity; therefore, without we each sacrifice our unalienable right to life to a (mass)' collective,' that has no life and no consciousness.

6 Natural law grants no authority

Natural law permits no jurisdiction for one individual to command another, as witnessed by neither of our two minds overruling the other. The principle of integrity, and one's unalienable right to life, are evident. Natural law grants no permission or authority for one to trespass upon another's life.

7 Natural law refuses all authority

Free will is the overseer of acceptance and refusal. Therefore, in the order it is protected, natural law denies all orders and all authority save its own, whether from a partner, neighbour, pulpit, parliament, congress or any other.

8 Natural law admits no trespass

Whosoever knowingly initiates the use of physical or coercive force, or fraud against others, negates and paralyses the victim's means of survival. Those who forbid people's right to life automatically relinquish their right to so choose. Such 'outlaws' are not free. It follows that the right to exercise force to arrest such assaults is morally justifiable. Murder and self-defence are opposites.

9 Natural law seeks integrity

Natural Law, and Positive Law (statutes), apply to different things, so they cannot be alternative systems of rules applicable to the same thing.

7. Twenty natural laws

The natural orderliness that governs our being is complete and without lack, entirely given to maintaining our life with immutable, undivided, wholesome integrity. Natural law obliges that we act in spiritual accordance with the same integrity of purpose that upholds our bodily life. Spiritual integrity is vital to sustaining and enhancing inestimable joys that result from living a life of moral integrity! Consciousness facilitates that goal.

10 Natural law supports our life respectful of all others

Integrity, lawfulness, and justice are the foundation and culmination of natural law, the full expression and manifestation of body, mind and soul. Therefore, when our (consciously initiated) actions outwardly manifest honesty and integrity found within, without which our mental and bodily life could not exist, the orderliness and morality of societal structures are obliged to correspond.

All that remains is to arrest violence and trespass. Nothing less will suffice. Nothing more is needed. Tragically, so long as human and sociological sciences refuse to study human consciousness in the manner here described, these laws will remain hidden.

Remember that the primary purpose of these laws is a thriving life within the equal rights of all others. Each law relates to all the others, implying that the brief descriptions below are purely a (note form) introduction. Jurisprudence and natural law students should study these laws, their source, and their interdependence in more detail. Your understanding of full authentication is best served by reading both my books as though one volume.

The first two laws are crucial; both rely on "existence exists." That phrase is axiomatic, meaning any attempt to refute it admits it; it states that there is something, as opposed to nothing. Existence is present in everything, every circumstance, and event, directly or indirectly available for us to understand. Therefore, nothing that exists can deny or refute itself.

Except for (chosen) actions, there are no facts of random occurrence that could have been different, as against facts that must be. An entity's very nature determines what it can do and dictates what it will do in any given circumstances. Can a non-material essence exist? Yes, indeed, theories are one example. But if you cannot identify a non-material core from one or more characteristics, it has no identity, whence conscious identification is impossible. Consequently, it is bereft of any life value—nothing of worth offers.

That discussion shows the absolute necessity that each of the twenty natural laws is validated and authenticated through the nature of what we are, not who we are. This qualification leads to the first natural law

1 Natural Law of Identity

A thing is what it is and that as the thing is, it acts; conversely as the thing acts, it is.

Authenticity and validity: Except for (chosen) actions, there are no facts of random occurrence, such that could have been different, as against facts that must be. An entity's nature determines what it can do and dictates what it will do in any given circumstances. An objective ethical morality wholly relies on identity and identification. Whatsoever has no identity cannot be consciously identified, thus has no valid ethical or moral import. Devoid of any life value, nothing of worth offers. This law derives from existence, from every constituent of physical matter, their separateness and existent interrelationships, from every man, woman, and child, every tissue, cell, organ, system, and faculty of our physical, mental, and spiritual being.

Application: Because life is a process of self-sustaining action, we are prompted to identify the fundamental nature of ourselves, the true identity of what life is, and thenceforth determine what life ought to enact. Our nature requires that we recognise our true self and what life is to reason how to act and live. This law is universal. It applies to our every thought, consideration, and personal interaction with others, every politic, and society.

2 Natural Law of Causality

All action is caused and determined via the nature of the entities that act; no real entity (thing) can occur through chance, or without cause; a thing cannot act contrary to its nature.

Authenticity and validity: The Law of Causality is the inevitable consequence of the Law of Identity. Existence and identity must exist before our consciousness has cause to identify that which exists. Efficacy of our mind depends entirely on existent reality and our discovery and use of both laws. Nothing can causally act contrary to its nature. Accordingly, committed actions certify our moral nature as the cause. Because thoughts and intentions do not, causal responsibility lies with the actor. This natural law exhibits within every man, woman, and child, physically, mentally, and spiritually.

Application: The laws of identity and causality apply to personal ethics, which later manifest as just or unjust actions. Not only do these two laws have a significant bearing on individual outcomes, but they also authenticate our efforts and thus determine the causal path of natural Justice.

3 Natural Law of Independence

All men and women are unique and independent, according to their nature of equally being Man, qua Man.

Authenticity and validity: Independence is undeniable, the immutable separateness of every individual man and woman's being. Our life, our every breath and heartbeat, are testament to our (individual) being, without which we cannot exist. The natural order of our nature governs every independent faculty and body function. The separateness of every breath and heartbeat testifies to their independence, without which we cannot exist. Likewise, our free will (cognitive mind) (8%) must be independent of the automated subconscious mind (92%) to ensure authentically productive psycho-epistemological functioning. All body and spirit functions are private; thus, they are individual and always independent. Although shared as experiences of life and value exchange, their source belongs to each alone.

Application: Our separateness as human beings is the natural law of the world. We each are not only capable of doing, thinking, and saying things independently of what others are choosing to do simultaneously, but that separateness is crucial to a free, thriving society. Our separateness as human beings is the natural law of the world. This law is fundamental to our biology, psychology, and praxeology (the study of human action and conduct); to our lives, thoughts, feelings, and activities. Independence and our unalienable right to life are inseparable.

Accordingly, our independence must be upheld and protected unequivocally. Independence marks each one of us separated from each other.

Our rights and autonomy must unite as one accord to separate and protect us from all domination and control. Independence cannot be refuted but can be refused. Our future depends on which of those we choose.

4 Natural Law of Equality

All living beings of the Homo sapiens species, are alike in nature and faculties, equally endowed.

Authenticity and validity: Appearances and traits materially differ, but the property which defines uniqueness is conceptually equal to all. Individual identity serves not to diminish equality but to emphasise its broad compass, including the individuated faculty of our free mind. This union of individual faculty with unique free expression testifies that all living beings are equal in kind but are unique in expression and form.

Every cell, organ, system and faculty of our physical, mental and spiritual being is equal in purposeful function. None are hierarchically superior, dominating, or authoritative. All support life equally. Appearances and traits differ, but their independent uniqueness serves equality of purpose, namely life.

Application: Absent equality and independence, our right to life and property, freedom, and convivial society are impossible. Conversely, it is imperative that our mental process, which testifies to universal equality, be united with free expression. That attests to universal independence, whereafter our (declared) individual rights must prevail. They should adequately protect our freedom and form the core of our business and societal structures, thence included in all educational curricula from infancy.

5 Natural Law of Integrity

The state of being whole, undivided, integrated, ethically intentioned, and committed to one's life, fully accords with the natural laws of one's nature.

Authenticity and validity: Integrity embraces the truthful, honest, holistic cohesiveness of our physical, mental, emotional, and spiritual faculties. It underpins every value, desire, and spiritual goal supporting the totality of life. The undoable, irremovable bond (Ius naturalis) unites the entirety of our physical, conscious, subconscious, emotional and spiritual being.

Application: Integrity invokes the state of being whole, undivided, integrated, ethically intentioned and committed to live. Its lack almost inevitably results in diminished quality of life in some form or to some degree. To live is to commit to living and accept what our actions deliver. We cannot escape the moral accountability that our efforts express. Courage falls within the law of integrity.

At the societal level, integrity manifests most profoundly as respect for the lives of others. Our resounding success from using integrity fully endorses that we use the same ethic in all personal and societal intentions, actions, and goals. Its lack results in diminished quality of life to some degree. (Refer also to the law of Just Consequence.)

This law applies to all personal thoughts and actions, truth, honesty and respect. Consequently, it falls squarely within all personal, social and business dealings, contracts, societal order, and the jurisdiction of natural justice, whereby it should rank as fundamental across all teaching curricula.

6 Natural Law of Individual Rights

Every man, woman, and child is an independent living being, having individual, immutable, and unalienable right to his or her life, free and independent from any trespass, usurpation, or violation whatsoever.

Authenticity and validity: The separate contributory functioning of every biological and psychological constituent that upholds our lives relies wholly on its right to do. Absent our right to act; no life would exist. Our right to life is unalienable, immutable, and inviolate. No one can live without performing the self-sustaining actions of living or without the right to act in support of their life.

Application: Our unalienable right is our right to act, live and sustain our life within the rights of all others. Our inalienable right applies to the product of our action(s), our entitlement to that which our efforts produce. Right to the fruits of our labour is inalienable and inviolate.

Because individual rights are moral principles that restrain society members from interfering with another's actions, they must be implemented and protected absolutely. Individual rights impose no obligations on one's neighbours except to abstain from violating their rights. When all people are protected, no collective rights need to exist, nor can they.

This law pertains to every unique living (human) being, every politic and society, and all personal, business, and societal dealings with others. Therefore, individual rights should be instituted as inclusive in a country's "constitution' and taught from an early age. (Refer also to the natural laws of No Trespass, Allowance, Just Consequence, Respect, Reciprocity, Commitment and Natural Justice.)

7 Natural Law of Free Will

Free choice of thought and actions of any and all Living Being's, are guaranteed inclusive of the responsibility, liability and accountability, naturally and inherently flowing therefrom.

Authenticity and validity: Volitional consciousness is axiomatically inherent in every man, woman, and child; thus, it distinguishes Homo Sapiens from all other life forms. It is fully supported, preserved and protected through automated subconscious functioning. Specific material and spiritual values, initially of your choice, uphold that subconscious process. Human life is impossible without free will; it cannot be removed or erased. More than a yes/no switch, it establishes the value database that fuels our subconscious mind and thereby authors our feelings, conscience, and emotions.

Application: Free will thought imparts full responsibility for our actions, which confirms our right to act and bear the consequences. No exceptions, escape routes, let-outs, excuses, or pardons exist for refusing to exercise free will, whereby no artificial law may reject, deny or overrule it. Individual rights uphold free will, which directs respect, responsibility, and accountability, thereby upholding morality, justness and natural justice. None are separable, whereby they must be maintained and protected. No Man-made construct overruling our free will enacted responsibility is permissible. (Witness decisions given in the Nuremberg Trials.)

Free will imparts and embraces the essence and vitality of every natural law herein described. Those who claim free license to overrule free will, regardless of asserted authority, mastery, or divinity, are imposters, renegades, pirates, or psychopaths. Their claims are false, without merit, value, or substance!

Free will is unimpeachable and indestructible. Nothing can override free consent, thus confirming that torture or traumas that violently and criminally force submission are neither free agreement nor consent! Because some people may obtain permission surreptitiously without the victim knowing, e.g. through propaganda or misguided ideology, mental vigilance is essential, per the natural laws of identity and causality. Refer also to the natural laws of Identity, Allowance, Causality, Commitment, Independence, and Equality.

8 Natural Law of Commitment

To live is to commit to action(s) and bear the consequences.

Authenticity and validity: Our entire biological, psychological and spiritual nature authenticates the law of commitment since it enacts what we choose to commit. This authentication includes 'life' itself, material, mental, emotional, and spiritual maintenance, preservation and accomplishments, satisfaction, joy and happiness. The subconscious mind is committed to fulfilling our chosen desires. The same commitment drives our conscience, emotions, self-preserving instinctual responses, and intuition. Commitment is the willed intention to achieve a particular outcome or result from a chosen action and bear responsibility for that action. Commitment is the 'will' part of our 'free will.' Our commitment to that which we choose determines our actions, moral responsibility and accountability, regardless of what thought or evaluation prompted them (mitigating circumstances accepted). Without commitment, nothing happens; thus, nature offers no alternative, as automated for other life forms, but to 'commit.'

Application: Human nature necessitates using our mind, always remembering that not choosing is to choose and bear the consequences. As authors of our actions and behaviour, we cannot escape moral responsibility and accountability expressed through our actions.

This law imparts responsibility and accountability to all personal, social and business dealings and natural justice. Our free choice to act is our commitment to accept the outcome and its consequences, for better or worse. (Refer also to the Natural Law of Just Consequence.)

9. Natural Law of Allowance

Every man, woman, and child (including infants and those mentally handicapped) are endowed to venture forth and progress at their choice and pace, in service of their life, but are not absolved from refusing so to do.

Authenticity and validity: Subconscious mind relies on values that our cognitive mind prior determines through free choice. Infants have not yet acquired this ability, yet they must be enabled to function, thus gaining an ability to develop their choice of values. This law is their means. It derives from their ability to learn rudimentary actions and tasks without having any cognitive ability or means to express or direct them. Thus infants, young children, and those who suffer from a mental handicap are enabled to choose their actions and experience the emotions of success or failure. At the same time, they progressively grow in cognitive stature, understanding, and spirituality. Our subconscious mind may fully function, including for emotions, although the mental mind is unable but not unwilling to perform at its fullest potential.

Application: This law universally applies to every man, woman and child. Ethically, morally, and spiritually, this law invokes that we each recognise and accept others' rights and ability to progress at their pace, according to their choices and skills. It facilitates ever-increasing mental efficiency over time, making clear that mental and emotional development is necessary for a complete and prosperous life. It encourages learning and spiritual maturity to become habituated throughout adult life. Through this window, habituation of the learning process enables consistently higher percentiles of truth to amass in our intuit database, fostering increasing reliability and certainty with the least effort.

While this law encourages learning at our own pace, it does not excuse the consequences of refusing. It must be that way since maturity evolves from our increasing mental ability to supplant the Law of Allowance, thus progressively accepting full adult responsibility through exercising value-based choices. Adolescence is that platform of maturity.

This law allows for lessons of support and correction and for those teachings to be freely woven into the tapestry of our conscious and subconscious minds, thereby facilitating and stimulating mental growth and development. This law speaks of graciousness, politeness, integrity, gratitude, and respect. It enables the development of mental competence consistent with choice and without penalty.

No (purported) Law we've invented can match what this natural law allows. Man's laws can only trespass it. It offers a foundation for all education, cooperation, collaboration, relationships, marriage, and parenthood. With particular relevance to schooling at all levels, including adult education, devotees and students of Steiner, and Montessori education, will recognise its potency in a flash! (See the Natural Law of Efficacy)

Abuse of the Law of Allowance

Wilful ignorance, apathy, indifference, or lazy refusal to exercise one's mental faculties are not excused.

Authenticity and validity: [This is not one of the natural laws in the strict sense, instead the flip side of '9, the Natural Law of Allowance.'] Whilst that law alleviates or overcomes (temporary or prolonged) innate cognitive disability, wilful adult reliance on our (subconscious) automated processes is akin to existing in a state of animality. But that is impossible because we are not so equipped. Every attempt is fraught with failure to some degree. The Law of Allowance cannot be abused with impunity. We reap what we sow. Most anxiety, stress, and mental trauma result from attempting to escape the 'natural law of just consequence.' But we cannot escape natural law. Our success or distress, physically, mentally and emotionally, confirms our purposeful need to direct these outcomes and not attempt to escape that responsibility. Consequences result in all cases, and we determine them fundamentally.

Application: This Law alleviates or overcomes legitimate impairment of some kind but offers no excuses for refusing to work toward our benefit. Those who rely on (nature's) bridging pathway provided for children, thus pretending they can thrive in adulthood, will suffer. Wishful thinking, mysticism, and subjectivism are good examples of blissfully attempting to bypass conscious understanding.

Abuse of this law does not result from an impaired or debilitated mental faculty; instead, one's abstention, apathy, indifference, or lazy refusal to exercise cognitive abilities. It is a coma-like belief that one's advancement will automatically happen from one's daily activities; hence no purposefully initiated betterment is ordinarily necessitated. It remains, however, that no excuse is permitted, and no allowance exists for choosing to be mentally vacant, deprived, or retarded. Harmful consequences that inevitably result are our free choice, as justly deserved. It follows that the Law of Allowance does not and cannot compel self-initiated development, for that would trespass free will. Instead, it justly allows the full consequences of one's choices for better or worse, whence the (parallel) 'Natural Law of Just Consequence' adjudicates all outcomes. Therefore, abuse of this law falls within the jurisdiction of Natural Justice.

10 Natural Law of Respect

No man, woman, or child can uphold their unalienable right to life without correspondingly respecting the equal right to life of all other sentient living beings.

Authenticity and validity: Every organ and organ system in our body thrives because each respects the right of every other organ and organ system to live and function independently, thereby contributing to life as the supreme value. Our life entirely depends on self-respect for virtues, spiritual life values, health, hygiene, emotional satisfaction and spiritual accomplishment; natural order, our welfare and its governing laws. Respect is inherent in the natural order, absent which disorder is certain.

Application: To uphold natural law is to show respect. Self-respect, and respect for others, should be one's core principle in life, physiologically, psychologically, emotionally and spiritually. Personally, every constituent, organ, system, process, and faculty of our being serves the individual success of all other supportive entities, regardless of uniqueness, difference, or diversity, else its function and life are compromised or snuffed out.

Societally, respect manifests through moral or immoral actions as the primary factor in all matters concerning natural justice. Whosoever disagrees with this fundamental fact of life should take their petition to Mans Creator, not to an (irrelevant) court of legal jurisdiction.

Respect necessitates that Individual Rights be instituted, thence protected from all trespass and violation. Those who uphold the natural law respect it. Those who disrespect it trespass it. The relationship of respect to natural justice should be the core ethic taught in all curricula, from infancy onwards.

11 Natural Law of Reciprocity

Respect for one's individual life, and reciprocally for the right of all others to live, ensures one's freedom, so too the right of all others of the human species.

Authenticity and validity: Every functional element of our body serves its interest by collaboratively assisting all others. Reciprocally, that assistance bears on and binds the two parties, such orderly bond being the exact nature of 'ius naturale,' being natural law. Value exchange between the cognitive and subconscious mind is reciprocal, absent which neither could function. The aggregate success of every constituent and faculty of our being guarantees continuance and maintenance of the (societal) environment in which each singularly prospers. Reciprocity is inherent and immutable, biologically and psychologically.

Application: Creator has ruled that our lives are independently conditional upon maintaining a societal environment guaranteeing that each life may prosper. However, such protection cannot ensure that each will thrive, for flourishing is the prerogative of free will. We must translate this law into a free convivial society, thereby upholding reciprocal individual rights to life, property, and freedom. Moral discipline asserts that where the rights of all other individuals are respected, no one can offend another through any application of their own. Freedom to live according to one's nature and personal choices applies to everyone; all contrary claims are anti-life. Any quarrel is with Creator and none other.

This law applies to every unique living being, every politic and society. The institution of this law cancels every Man-made statute or directive that violates Creator's invitation to live. (Refer also to the Law of No Trespass.)

12 Natural Law of Right Reason

Reasoning discovers truths that are not self-evident, thus to adapt material existence to life-sustaining purposes.

Authenticity and validity: Every constituent of our physical, mental, emotional, and spiritual being has a purposeful reason for its existence and assignment. That reason is immutably inherent in our very being. Its source lies in different constituent biological purposes, functions, interactions and interoperability; also in our volitional consciousness. Communication and value transfer between our two minds is psycho-epistemology.

Application: Reasoning is the intellectual ability to logically think through connected steps in search of truths that are not self-evident. Rational beings understand themselves through reason. They consider cause and effect, truth and falsehood, ethics and morality. All discovery and learning, logic, enquiry, contemplation, investigation, determination, evaluation, and commitment properly reside in reason. Right reason facilitates our ability to change attitudes, traditions, and institutions, and to convert beliefs into knowledge within the realm of ethics, free will, self-determination and actioned morality. The word 'right' implies that life is the benchmark, that it is right to be moral and wrong to harm others. This Law correctly applies to every unique living being, every politic, and society.

13 Natural Law of Efficacy

Related conscious faculties, permit efficacious functioning, correspondent with valid, truthful, value-based mental content.

Authenticity and validity: In good health ordinarily, the exact nature of what we are, authenticates and validates the efficiency and efficacy of our being. Every physical, material, mental, emotional, and spiritual quality is the glowing quintessence of efficiency and effectiveness, none less, save through illness, injury or death. Thus established, we should employ every means to maintain it.

This law derives from the ability of our subconscious mind to automatically active and monitor our desires and actions at blistering speed, thus freeing our cognitive mind to investigate, deliberate, and choose life-sustaining values. This law, found in perception, conscience, emotions and feelings, imagination, and intuition, facilitates subconscious mind programming for desirous auto-functioning.

Application: This law allows anyone who places a high value on their life to speed past all others who must mentally wrestle every issue and do so with a high degree of truthful certainty. Mental efficacy depends on existent reality and that we know it. Our success depends on whether our values enhance our life or hinder it, which means we each hold the key to mental ability, efficiency, and emotional stability. When data is misleading, corruptive or false, efficient cognitive functioning is severely handicapped, if not denied. We are the guardians of our abilities according to our choices.

This law teaches that we each are responsible for our efficiencies, efficacy and success. Also, all erroneous beliefs, fictional laws, mysticisms, and perverted meanings, including misconstrued language and stolen concepts, will deprive or mislead cognitive understanding to hinder or cripple cognitive comprehension. This law applies to every material, mental, emotional, and spiritual aspect of self, every goal and ambition. It also applies to every element of education, politics, society, and every personal, business and societal dealing with others. (Refer also to the laws of allowance, commitment, respect, free will, integrity and reason.)

14 Natural Law of Ethics

Ethics constitute the science of choosing life-supporting thoughts, values, and determinations, that when acted upon, outwardly express one's morality.

Authenticity and validity: Ethics is inherent in the moral fibre of life itself. Truthful, honest, wholesome cohesiveness of all our biological faculties and our intellectual, emotional and value-based spiritual nature all testify to ethics. Our nature obliges that we adapt material reality to our purposes and that our actions rely on prior ethical, life-sustaining thinking and reasoning.

Application: Ethics is the chosen code of principles residing in our mind that govern the moral correctness of our behaviour and actions. Ethics constitute rightful, life-sustaining thoughts, not actions, our honest guide to thinking and reasoning in a manner supportive of life. Because unethical thinking and reasoning occasions no harm to anyone but ourselves, we've no choice but to be ethical or fail. To pursue physical, mental, emotional and spiritual accomplishment and success is to choose ethically. Thus ethics is our chosen codebook of values for determining what will later become life-upholding moral actions.

Teachers should include the science of ethics and morality (from its source perspective) within all education curricula. (Refer also to the Natural Law of No Trespass, the Natural Law of Just Consequence., and the Law of Natural Justice.)

15 Natural Law of Morality

Actions and behaviour publicly testify one's pre-conceived moral stature, and agreed moral accountability.

Authenticity and validity: Every cell, tissue, organ, system and function of our body and mental faculties necessarily and justly upholds every constituent of life. Each is responsible and accountable for supporting the whole. That task, when extrapolated into societal terms, is morality.' Morality and immorality are not biologically innate; but their principle is psychologically intrinsic. We are responsible and accountable for our actions and behaviours affecting ourselves and others.

Application: One's actions let the ethical cat out of the bag, such that morality expresses through our actions; moral, amoral, or immoral. Immoral actions may harm ourselves and others, for which we are wholly accountable and responsible. Morality is not a social mandate. It is our lawful responsibility concerning how we choose to behave. Our ethics manifest as our morality by which we are fully accountable, mitigating circumstances admitted. Immoral action does not break the natural law but instead reinforces and amplifies its necessity, thus cogently pointing to necessary correction or remediation. Proven trespass of natural law, proven guilt, is the perpetrator's confessed agreement to bear natural justice as a self-intentioned outlaw. Outlaws are not free. Their immoral or unlawful behaviour confirms they have consciously chosen to surrender their freedom.

16 Natural Law of Cooperative Enterprise

Cooperative effort with others, will return more benefit than most individual's can achieve alone.

Authenticity and validity: Indisputably, all our body functions and constituents work collaboratively with all others for synergistic benefit, likewise our mental processes. Cooperative Enterprise exhibits through every individual biological and psychological component and faculty collaboratively working with fifty-trillion cells, two hundred cell types, seventy-eight organs and thirteen organ systems. Add two minds possessing nine higher faculties, all collaboratively supporting and maintaining life, all orchestrally free will conducted, including conscience and emotions, plus intuition and imagination graciously assisting. No dispute or conflict exists save through disease.

Application: Collaborative enterprise satisfies the natural law of no trespass in all respects while upholding the laws of equality, independence, right reason, efficacy, and morality. Any cooperative enterprise requires that individual rights prevail over any instituted societal or business structure. Group rights are thereby ousted, eminent domain likewise. Business and contractual dealings depend on independence, voluntary cooperation, and one's unalienable right to life.

17 Natural Law of No Trespass

No independent living being has the right to trespass, or to violate another's life, or property.

Authenticity and validity: This law is self-evident in the nature and function of every biological organ and system, and our conscious process. Any trespass, such as a pulmonary embolism, is cruel, if not fatal. Our heart and lungs are proactively separated. No attribute, constituent or faculty within our nature may trespass any other.

The conscious mind cannot change the subconscious process because it is fully automated. Correspondingly the subconscious process cannot overrule free will, or there is no free will. Because no part of the mental process can trespass on free will, which is the intentional driving force of life, nothing and no one has the right to trespass or violate another's life or property.

Application: This law informs no trespass of any other (volitionally conscious) sentient living being's right to life. Notice that respect for all others, and no violation of the rights of others, are effectively identical, per the law of reciprocity.

Two persons cannot be free and equal when one of them is controlling, managing, threatening, harming, blackmailing, or extorting the other. This law does not say that one cannot trespass or violate another's life because that would infringe on one's free will. It says instead that no one has the 'right' to do it. Our right to act and live fully accepts the reciprocal right of all others equally.

Trespassing another's rights self-cancels one's rights respective of any relevant action. No claim of right may negate, usurp, or overrule the unalienable rights of other living human beings.

Independent rights of Man preside over all other life forms.

No form of eminent domain may hereafter exist. (Eminent domain' means resumption/compulsory acquisition or expropriation; e.g. the power of a state or a national government to take private property for public use.) That is trespass, respective of our right to life and the fruits of our labours.

18. Natural law of just consequence

Nature serves just consequence, whether respected or not.

Authenticity and validity: The outcomes that our biological functions and conscious process deliver, all result from the nutrient or spiritual value of what we choose to be physical or conscious fuel. Aside from natural causes, commonly referred to as Acts of God, all actions result from choices we each make. We each are the author and practitioner of our efforts, just recipients of their consequences thereby.

Application: This law mimics Francis Bacon's statement, 'Nature to be commanded must be obeyed.' (Given free will, the word 'respect' is more accurate than the word 'obey.') Additional to this law applying to every unique living (human) being, every politic, and society, is a core tenet of the science of ethics and the foundation of the Natural Law of Justice. Our moral obligation is to learn of this law and learn from it. It is the core of our conscience and emotions, not forgetting bodily dis-ease.

Whereas the Law of Allowance applies to alleviate or overcome legitimate impairment of some kind, the Law of Just Consequence precludes its abuse. We each are the author and practitioner of our actions and just recipients of their consequences for better or worse. All outcomes justly and exactly belong to whoever caused them. Although this law does not prescribe that a result will be the exact measure of one's moral or immoral action, it will more often than not. Other people's efforts or mitigating circumstances may apply. 'Just consequence' means it justly belongs exactly to whoever caused it. That endorses natural justice. This law is the essence of natural justice. It permits what one chooses, whether for good or evil and makes no mistakes.

19 Natural law of Forceful Arrest

Creator's approved arrest of all initiated force protects Man's unalienable right to life and inalienable right to the fruits of one's labours.

Authenticity and validity: Our bodily endocrine system exists to maintain homeostasis, meaning physical order, or ius naturale. Our emotions serve the same purpose as concerns our chosen values. They offer free will the means of arresting harmful energies, ideologies and philosophies. As our nature testifies, including our instinct, body, immune system, conscience, feelings and emotions, we must arrest all initiated coercive or physical force and all acts of aggression that violate our free will and right to life. Force, and mind, are opposites.

Application: Initiated force demanding we act against our judgment negates and paralyses our means of survival. Those who initiate coercive or physical force, for whatever purpose and to whatever extent, intend to harm or destroy our capacity to live, regardless of all claims to the contrary!

Without protection or self-defence, we are at the mercy of all who initiate force, including governments, fraudsters, blackmailers, tyrants, rapists, psychopaths, terrorists, thugs, warmongers and murderers. The precondition of a civilised society is the barring of physical force from social relationships. Nature has established that if men and women wish to deal with one another, they may do so through reasoned discussion, persuasion, and voluntary, un-coerced agreement. Therefore, the security of each person, and their property against predatory attack, emerges as a most necessary condition of society.

Those who invent legal statutes to herd and rule men and women cannot claim the sanction of reason, just as no advocate of contradictions can claim it. Freedom demands self-control. Self-control requires the security of each person and their property. Therefore, protection of Individual Rights is the only proper function of a 'Protectorate,' that being a lawful substitute for government, including a Commission of Justice. (Refer also to the Natural Laws of Cooperative Enterprise, Allowance, Morality, No Trespass, Just Consequence, and Natural Justice.)

20 Natural Law of Justice

Innocent, natural individuals are free. Proven trespassers of natural law are outlaws, perpetrators of deliberately enacted transgressions; voluntary bearers of natural justice.

7. Twenty natural laws

Authenticity and validity: Natural justice is why conscience and emotional reporting faculties exist within every man, woman and child. Their (reported) approvals, or censures alternatively, respectively point to justly maintaining one's values and respecting oneself and others. Our nature is given to upholding, maintaining, and protecting life's sanctity, which defines the baseline reference of natural justice.

Application: As the author of our thought-based ethics, our subsequent actions translate into moral justness or immoral unjustness served upon others. Free persons do not commit crimes — those who have (prior) chosen to relinquish their freedom do. Those who walk over people's rights to grind their lives into dust reject morality and justness. Their actions outwardly broadcast the need for restorative justice, to return to a state of natural order and its laws. Those who violate the natural law are not innocent of their actions. They elect to be outlaws.

It follows that natural justice must bear upon those who violate natural law since corrective force is all that anyone has the right to choose. Those who act within natural law are innocent and free—they offer justness, whereby no legal instrument may preside contrary. Therefore, lawful remediation is the path of natural justice.

Our task is to grasp the full conscious process showing the raw source of these twenty laws, their ramifications and personal and societal applications. From that study, authoritarian compulsion and force will emerge as the tyrant it truly is. Remember that—

> *"No problem can be solved from the same level of consciousness that created it", Albert Einstein.*

'Existential natural law' exceeds any other form of law known to Man. It is not a product of the human mind. On the contrary, our Creator's gift enables our mind to function. That is our personal invitation to prosper and thrive materially, emotionally and spiritually. Spirituality's core principle and fruitful exercise are the greatest tribute one can ever offer their Creator. No invention is necessary. Our discovery and practice are.

Until we awaken to the fullness of consciousness, its freedom and the right to self-govern and responsibly act upon all three, we deny ourselves and suffer the penalty.

As promised, I've described how these twenty natural laws translate from the personal realm described in *'Conscious Ascendance'* into the social or societal realm of 'Freedom.' It now remains to show how that advance is for the betterment of humanity, never tempted to revert to past failures. Please enjoy this glimpse of the future as it unfolds.

Chapter 8

8. Organic societies

If asked some carefully worded questions, there seems little doubt that most people would agree most of the twenty natural laws are plain common sense. Yet, tragically, people realise that society is not serving their lives as it should, and they have no answer. This chapter bridges the gap between what does not work and what will. It considers society from a radically different perspective, one that assists you and your efforts to voluntarily contribute to society. That is not to say, 'no pay,' instead that your pay is both material and spiritual, resulting from you volunteering to engage that double benefit.

Some consider awakening as expanding their consciousness or raising their vibrations. Others believe we need to return to the (US) Constitution. Others foresee a spiritual transformation, while some hold out for a global currency reset, a return to the gold standard, a disclosure of extraterrestrial beings, a critical mass for worldwide ascension, etcetera. Others want a political or legal re-ordering, e.g., a return to common law. What, we might ask, do all these awakenings have in common? What is triggering these people's motivation for change? Is it mere dissatisfaction, or is there something more significant? Some say there are energies at play. Others talk of unity consciousness that supposedly we can rise to or embrace.

There may be elements of truth in all the above, but the real reason, I submit, is one that human society has never experienced previously. I refer to the 'information explosion' made available through the internet. Truth, along with every bogus philosophy and ideology invented, is open to far greater numbers than ever before. In less than two decades, dialogue has exploded through email, SMS, video, social media, podcasts, e-books, and blog sites. This outpouring of information allows people more opportunities to employ it in their lives, to test hypotheses, compare results with others, concur, experiment, evaluate, and learn.

But what exactly are these people learning? What truth? How much remains as beliefs, false ideologies, or restated mystical revelations? How many so-called energy vibrations premise on the collective and not individuals? These are all vital questions because if people accept and absorb nothing but a (modern-day) rehash of ideologies that never worked and can never serve their needs, then dissatisfaction is greatly multiplied through broader dissemination. Demand for solutions increases, but seldom do satisfactions, accounting for more soul searching, with still wider disillusion, as above.

'Awakening' in that manner is not a measure of advancement, I submit. For example, does today's thirst for awakening show objective evidence of causal factors? Are we truthfully discovering the reality of life or gullibly swallowing centuries-old ideologies dished up in modern-day phraseology that sounds plausible, comforting, and benignly assuring? Are we looking to the nature of Man, where any right-thinking person would expect an awakening to take place? Or are we falling for the same misguided philosophies that have tortured Mankind over centuries past, dressed in sheep's clothing or a fancy new age vocabulary? Are we searching for societal answers in a bog of externalities, prejudices, and age-old notions, or are we indeed focused on who and what we are as individuals? If we consider or believe that social order is superior to or outside our domain of influence, likely we will accept answers to our enquiries based on that mindset. Then who has 'awakened' to an 'actionable remedy' versus those who have only awakened to the problem?

So let's explore this matter from a causal perspective seldom if ever entertained. Such change will not manifest in a flash — perhaps taking years or even generations. The hurdle is ideology and core ignorance, particularly concerning our conscious process. Today the state succeeds in tricking people into slavery. It promotes comforts, security, and safety; all administered under the illusion of liberty. To put it bluntly, we prefer to be psychologically bound in chains rather than deal with falsely perceived tension arising from the responsibility of absolute freedom. We seemingly prefer soft-slave statism over any effort to acquire freedom because we lazily or indifferently believe that we enjoy freedom's comforts already. We have no motivation to change because nothing offers any perceivable incentive. Unless some encouragement appears, nothing will change, period.

If we remove the deep state without changing our belief that safety, comfort, security, and freedom can only manifest through authoritarian rule, tyranny will grow back overnight, like a mushroom. Until we wake up to authoring our safety, comfort, security, and freedom on individual terms, some authority will prescribe it on their terms at our expense. History is my witness.

The government's secret is to make everyone dependent on its comforts and security. Your dependence on government is the name of the game. Yet Creator ordained your independence. You were born free and independent, and every faculty you have or that you could need supports your freedom. Yet we have all been robbed of it. Our independent ability to cultivate comfort, security, and safety is denied or throttled by endless regulation. We are not free. We are strictly limited to what will maintain the state's stranglehold over us. An overwhelming cloud of sadness permeates our lives because our repulsive culture is built not on creativity but on maintaining what stifles it; taxation is a perfect example. Consumerism, selfishness and greed ultimately result in delusional, disappointed and desperate human beings. To alleviate that disaster, the 'ruling class' designed propaganda, misinformation, lies and technological distractions to gratify the masses with pleasant illusions about their country, society, and material conditions.

Today's societies did not become so ludicrously misguided and defective overnight. They have been centuries in the making, much through a purposeful effort to destroy education and replace it with social indoctrination. Taught how to feel and not think, children become cogs in the machine of serfdom, ultimately unhappy state dependents, overly medicated, easily manipulated adults, utterly state-dependent for relief. Propagandised during their span of youth, these emerging adults are not prepared for the real world of their nature, thinking for themselves, mentally and spiritually ascending. Adrift like a cork in the ocean, they depend upon the mass media to tell them how to think; they rely on social media to stroke their ego and count on the state for their health and welfare. Technological toys and endless absorption of trivialities make them dumber every minute. From billboards to cell phones and from mass media to movies, imagery constantly assails their minds, such that without discernment, values are programmed into their minds, their emotions so prescribed. So established is this abnormal society; it is today considered normal, and few know the difference.

In the absence of a workable solution, many people are confused. They feel bound to act according to what they consider moral yet feel coerced to follow what others believe is right. They never realise that when the state claims moral authority, it creates and masterminds immoral tyranny. Sadly, most people do not understand natural laws inherent within them or that (principled) ethical thought occasions moral actions, whereby feelings report on those successes. They've no understanding of how their mental processes work in sequence to uphold their life or how ethics trace from the natural laws of one's processes and faculties. They don't know because natural law is shunned as though it never existed.

Consider this. If self-professed leaders can convince Mankind that morality is a church or state-administered social necessity, they have considerable influence over our thoughts. They claim to know the ropes because they're the 'leaders,' while others are ignorant sheeple. Devastating indoctrination to accept authoritarian rule without challenge has crippled human progress. If these so-called 'leaders' enforce conformance to their statutes, what exactly do they hold in their hands? Is it your thoughts, your actions, or both? 'Power' is the correct answer. Certain people fully intend you never learn that ethics and morality are yours to determine, else you would not willingly sacrifice your life to their mandates.

How will Man know that he lacks vital information concerning his nature when nothing seems to permit it, worse they must be subservient to the rule of the collective, not their own choices? The failure of ethics, as science, cannot be more aptly stated. Fortunately, science seems to be coming to its senses, while more are awakening to their sovereignty and autonomy. The decided turn away from globalism will hopefully narrow toward nationalism, local communities, and eventually, the wholesomeness of each human individual will awaken. You have a jump start already.

The original people of Terra Australis (Australia) know that to live on the land is to protect it. They understand that nature governs the consequences of their actions, referring to it as *'connection to country.'* Truth known, this attitude is demonstrable *'connection to mind'* in addition. Said differently, freedom is respect for oneself, all others, and the land. Are they not the rudiments of a respectful free society?

It is now time for Australians and all the world's people to understand their role in healing the land and its people. Your willingness to read thus far suggests you will take this transformative information on board and use it to the full. Some people will find it too much to comprehend, let alone believe. This information will not be without challenges, therefore. People in power would have us believe that we are nothing. The reverse is true, but many do not yet understand that. To fully prosper, we must know with certainty that every one of us is a sovereign being of infinite value, having a soul that will live for eternity. Regardless of your status, position, or locality, we all are equal in the eyes of the source Creator, yet vibrantly unique in every other way. It is up to us to realise our potential and to help those around us to do the same, and protect that condition in perpetuity, whereby we as a people will never be defeated again. Australians will join with their global brothers and sisters as one family to jointly take control of our destiny as was intended from the first breath we each took. We are indebted to move forward in this knowledge. Filled with grace and patience and empowered through a value-charged human consciousness, we can each help those around us to transition from slave societies to where each country, stamps the words' free nation' on the world map forever. Although few initially, we will shine the lantern of freedom for humanity.

You'll recall my statement, *'no one decides justice; it just is.'* It is the natural order of things; natural law. Accordingly, there can be no government as we know it. In a short but masterful historical description, van Dun describes the twisting of original ideas concerning natural law.

> *"Wealth and welfare were taken to be the true 'natural rights' of men, and 'justice' was re-interpreted to mean the efficient production and 'fair' distribution of wealth."* Further, *"At the end of the second millennium before Christ, the Jews lived in a system described in the biblical book of [the] Judges. Their 'judges' were not judges as we understand our modern legal systems. Instead, they were influential respected men" who provided leadership and counsel, with no power to coerce, tax, or write laws that infringed natural justice."*

A political system without the institution of political rule, even if considered as 'the rule of judges', must deny judges particular privileges or special powers. Their 'commission' is not to invent justice or (statute) 'rule' others but to administer existent justice found in nature.

Has anyone on earth today lived without government authority? We know nothing different because we've never challenged statism's (purported) legal and moral authority. To challenge statism is also to convince people of their power to self-govern, thus cancelling all authoritarian counterfeit rule and ridding its irrelevance and harm. It will then fade into oblivion due to a lack of support.

The question arises concerning how we might gravitate from state rule to an organic society based on natural law. The answer lies in understanding what value is sufficient enough to attract followers to the cause. What value might there be that we don't already have? What problems might we eliminate? It's one thing to conduct a citizen-initiated referendum to overthrow tyranny. It's quite another to instill in people's minds why they should divorce tranny and explain without ridicule or censorship what might take its place and all its enormous advantages.

An organic society must appear superior in all respects. It must be revolutionary in concept and vastly more beneficial; else, it will appear as little more than tinkering with what we already have, nothing but playing with words.

Governments have conditioned the minds of the masses through clever propaganda. Most people firmly believe and many intellectuals think that humanity cannot possibly survive without a ruling government, such thoughts being purely utopian. A barrage of questions backs their claims, supposedly. For example, how can contractual agreements be honoured without formal governments and law-enforcement agencies? How will our private property be protected and property boundaries fixed? How will disputes of all sorts be settled? How could a free society deal with mob rule or an endless series of private feuds and vendettas with the retaliatory use of force left in the hands of individual people? How could roads and other common-use assets and facilities be built without taxes?

The short answer is that people do all of these things and will continue to do so, even when based on freedom as a 'lawful' substitute for 'legal' rule.

Governments know that they are a private, legal, fictional entity and have no legal control over anything outside their private corporation. They also know that most 'citizens' are entirely unaware of this fact, so they will do all possible to prevent us from learning. Thus blindfolded, we let them get away with treachery.

8. Organic societies

Many earnest commentators, not forgetting a host of internet click-baiters, think that political parties, which today are also corporate legal fictions, are the key to cleaning things up. How, when these parties do not represent the people? They serve only to advance or maintain their political interests and the power they have. Their sole aim is to get hold of the government and run (ruin) peoples lives, but as natural law demonstrates unequivocally, no government has any lawful right to do so.

The natural law position restores much of that but goes much further. Remember that whosoever oversteps natural law volunteers to be an outlaw, which action confirms they agree to suffer all consequences arising. A 'protectorate' body, as a substitute for government, is subject to the same terms. The moment it attempts to initiate force is the moment it faces justice, with no escape possible. Thus your protection is in-built and fully protected.

Why have you not been taught these natural laws? First, they are only revealed through your understanding of full consciousness, about which academia freely confesses it knows nothing. Second, rulers have a vested interest in your ignorance, given that it would smash their ruling empires to smithereens.

Furthermore, the constitutional phrase 'consent of the governed' is profoundly wanting. The best it can achieve is proportional acceptance, a democracy, majority rule and collectivised tyranny. Existential natural law delivers an unprecedented alternative. Replace the phrase 'consent of the governed' with the words' nature of those governed,' precisely because nature has already consented to morality and law. Self-governance exists in concept; it is for us to demonstrate its existence in practice.

That lawful switchover is powerful beyond measure. First, everyone's free will is preserved, which is nature's consent indisputably. Second, most importantly, no government could authoritatively rule since that would violate free choice, inherent within' the nature of those governed.'

Authoritarian rule is stopped dead in its tracks. Perpetrators automatically confess agreement to suffer all consequences, whereby (government initiated) force, fraud, or coercion cancels before it begins. Note also that the right to bear arms and defend against foreign and domestic enemies is within our human nature. To forbid either or both is unlawful.

Governance premised on the 'nature of those governed' is not significantly different from 'constitutional law' that upholds 'unalienable rights. But 'natural existential law,' amplifies its authenticity and power enormously. No better precedent exists. It gives voracious teeth to constitutional law that it never dreamt of, based on immutable encrypted facts of our nature. Lawful progress of this calibre is unheard!

Some might question whether constitutional law proponents would ever agree to the supremacy of natural law. The answer is simple. Isn't God's Law what constitutional law was intended to deliver?

When you grasp that 'consent of the governed' presently holds you in bondage with no relief and that self-governance via one's nature is the only thing that can free you from centuries of human enslavement, you'll glimpse heaven on earth as never before.

Creator has invited you to live to the fullest extent, filled with joyfully beautiful possibilities, but instead, you are blindfolded. No one teaches that feelings and emotions are the Creator's gift of an automated mentoring tool. No school classes teach how your consciousness works, so nature's bountiful and dynamic power remains hidden.

To this end, natural law is constructive, supportive, gracious, purposeful, loving, and spiritually uplifting; all authority, rule, and initiated force banished!

Understanding natural law enables us to re-appraise society as we know it, cancel what does not work and institute what does. How will we see the difference? Because (in nature) we each are the living model of a cooperative, symbiotic society of fifty-trillion individuals. Nothing further is needed but to understand those spiritual principles and employ them.

With that model in mind, the words of Thomas Jefferson may now be paraphrased…

> *'If a nation expects to be knowledgable and free, in a state of civilisation, it expects what should be and protects it.'*

Knowledge of full consciousness rids ignorance, as explained in my book *'Conscious Ascendance.'* That is the first step. The following step concerns removing oneself from the clutches of legality and positive law. That involves claiming your status as an *'independent living being'* (ILB) instead of a dead, fictional, legal entity as upheld by your social security number, driving license, and passport; all fictitious ID. They are the government's identification of a dead (fictional) entity. To offer those documents as your ID is to give false evidence, confirm your agreement to act as a dead fiction, or do both.

To that end, the American people are several steps ahead of the world, able to reclaim their Birthright status as an 'American State National' stolen from them via the 'Birth Certificate' and the legal fiction strawman. The third step is implementing a lawful protective instrumentality (see diagram 5). That will uphold your individual rights and protect against all forms of initiated aggression, such as fraud, blackmail, rape and murder.

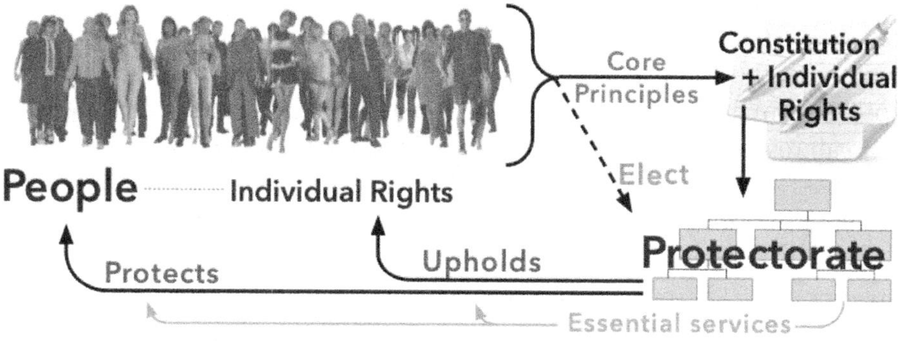

5. Protectorate principles

This (protective) body should also administer natural justice, as natural existential law determines. Natural justice is concerned only with remediating wrongful actions, not correcting wrong thinking. Ethics and moral correctness is the preemptive task for 'human science' education.

Humanity naturally gravitates to organic sociability that friendly, lively, and enjoyable convivial association characterises. These attitudes imply equal standing, mutual respect, cooperation and collaboration in all societal or business interactions, altogether in their (individual) approach, action, and separation. The founding premise is that Man is (socially) spiritual, not animal, or fundamentally materialistic.

Natural law invites life. It is constructive, supportive, gracious, purposeful, loving, and spiritually up-lifting. But, given that authority, rule, and initiated force are nowhere found, tables turn unmistakably.

Education concerning morality, law, and justice is overdue revision. Notably, participants of an organic, symbiotic society come together as equals for a mutual uncoerced benefit; else, people go as they came. Freedom pertains only to single persons. The word freedom does not apply to any public realm. Liberty is the (proper) collective term used for a community. To be free means free in mind, and spirit, with no exceptions; fully independent from all legal or fictional persons, citizens, or Legal Entities. Free individuals have the capacity, and immutable right to act in support of their life, according to free choice, this capacity remaining until death. To destroy absolute freedom, one has to kill the individual.

Now glimpse an organic free society as you've never considered before. Symbiosis means interaction between two different organisms living in close, physical association, typically to the advantage of both. Thus 'society-as-symbiosis,' or 'symbiotic society,' describes a convivial society of independent flesh and blood human beings, living in close, physical association wherein respectful and responsible interaction is typical to the mutual advantage of all; save for outlaws. Such society springs from (free) independence of all people, according to their free will, who all respect the mutual rights of others as natural law. No ruling body exists.

Organic society is symbiotic. I have listed its essential components in Chapter 9 as they fall under the banner of a protectorate body in lieu of government. Meanwhile, I trust you are now beginning to see the alternative to government rule over our lives? The alternative to 'society as company' (in government form) is *society-as-symbiosis.*

Creator has modelled a free, peace-loving society within every man, woman and child, preserving the individuality of each. Nothing prevents us from translating the natural laws of our being into natural laws for human society, especially with proof that they work. We have evidence of their connectedness; their upholding and sustaining life is indisputable. So let's now view these natural laws in societal rather than personal terms.

- No (universal) natural laws command free will choice. All uphold our life as independent living beings. Thus natural law in social terms comes from within every man, woman, and child. That alone is a complete reversal of today's statute laws, written to rule us.
- Interpolation of these laws into a free symbiotic society requires no alteration. They translate verbatim. Of course, they apply only to living beings, not artificial 'legal entities.' Once instituted, they will uphold our individuated life and our right to live it and protect both.
- All people who uphold the right of others to their life automatically defend their right to life. Freedom guarantees through practice. No other assurance can match this accomplishment.
- Together these laws underwrite a science of ethics for all men and women, one that children can absorb from a very young age.
- Thinking is the province of one's ethics, while actions demonstrate morality or its lack. Each living being is the author of their efforts and is justly accountable for them.

- Because upholding life is common to all, we can teach the science of ethics and morality to all. Both are removed from religious persuasion and subjective opinion and squarely placed in the fields of science and objective philosophy.
- Whosoever trespasses natural law in violation of another's right to life is not free.
- Transgression self-confesses immorality and violation of natural law. People unwilling to live and act according to natural law are obliged to accept just consequences.
- Justice concerns remediation of trespass respectful of its causal action(s).

We no longer must wait for deliverance. Protection from aggression is all that remains. Freedom, respect for others and responsibilities are yours alone. Your life is what you are, and your joy in this world is to live it! So what can we expect from a convivial society of freedom, peace, knowledge and trade?

- First, participants of an organic, symbiotic society come together as equals for a mutual uncoerced benefit; else, separately, they go as they came. To be free means to be free in mind and spirit, with no exceptions—independent from all legal or fictional persons, citizens or Legal Entities. Free individuals have the capacity and immutable right to act in support of their life according to free choice, this capacity remaining until death.
- Second, division of labour enables each to devote their efforts to a particular field of work and trade with others working in other areas. Cooperation allows all who participate to achieve more knowledge, skill and productivity return on their effort than they could make alone.
- Third, parasites, moochers, looters, second-handers, bullies, pirates, brutes and thugs offer no value to any individual in a convivial society. Neither do corporate governments. Such poachers cannot benefit from a community geared to satisfying needs and protection precisely because all such destructive actions kill the benefits they wish to obtain.

Observe that a Protectorate has only two functions. First to uphold individual rights, and second to protect the people. Its only entry point is the individual rights of the people. Should it fail its task, people have the right to abolish it and begin over. A 'Protectorate' is the servant of every man, woman and child, not vice versa as governments are today.

Because we are the only living species that can share and expand our knowledge from one generation to the next, so we can acquire more knowledge cooperatively than alone we could begin to acquire in our lifespan. Every man and woman on earth stands to gain a priceless benefit from the knowledge that others discover. Actions indicate, delimit and define what kind of Men can be of value to one another. Every man and woman is free to cultivate beneficial or detrimental outcomes of their actions and to learn of the consequences beforehand.

Knowledge and free trade in an independently based, rational, productive, and free society will benefit all. Those of lesser ability will not miss out. On the contrary, they are often the greatest beneficiaries of freedom and unfettered production. In an organic society, division of labour enables each to devote their effort to a particular field of work, thence, to trade with others working in other areas. Cooperation allows all who participate to achieve more knowledge, skill, and productivity return on their effort than they could make alone.

Bankers, war profiteers, and drug dealers are parasites, just like thieves, slackers and second-handers who contribute nothing. They rely on your production and mine and will fight like cornered rats to enslave us. Beneficial labour division is not possible without voluntary exchange. Without private property rights, all is appropriated. Before 1913, Americans kept 100% of their paycheck, but still, there were roads, schools, colleges, and fire departments.

Peace-loving individuals focus on what each can do, not on what others should do. Moreover, division of labour increases choice. Those who have tasted asparagus or green beans bought from their efforts also have access to tuna, theatre, transport, orchestral music, travel, and non-homogenised milk.

Do any doubts remain that the twenty natural laws are plain common sense? I promised to bridge the gap between what does not work and what will so that you think of society from a radically different perspective. This chapter has barely scratched that surface; nonetheless, it offers a firm foundation for all that follows.

Chapter 9

9. Protectorates – substitute for government

Today's governments are corporations with no more authority over your life than any other incorporated business; thus, in the true sense, no governments exist. Yet these corporations, masquerading as governments, rule us in a manner that suits their ends, none protecting our interests — save only to maintain their power and control. Because most people believe life is impossible without political rule via an emperor, a monarch, or a government, everyone fears the abolition of law. No one searches for an alternative because none is considered necessary or possible.

Yet people now plead for relief as never before. In Australia, they beg for a return to the constitution of 1901, or common law, or to reinstate democracy, never recognising that those failings are the root of our current crisis.

The remedy is inherent in our being, but no one knows it. This book and *'Conscious Ascendance'* have uncovered that secret and shown how we are capable of self-governance and how those benefits admirably fit into society as free nations.

When people learn to self-govern as our Creator intended, all fear will vanish, and all oppressive authority will cancel, never to return. Freedom to excel will be our daily fare, all of us fully protected from outlaws who would crush our sovereignty to restore their criminal empires.

My proposed method is called a 'Protectorate.' Its task is to protect the right to life and property of every man, woman and child, within the equal rights of all others. This alternative is reminiscent of government but is otherwise vastly different.

To visualise such a society, first picture yourself and your neighbours as independent living beings, not fictional entities, not citizens, not even (legal) persons or natural persons. Immediately it becomes clear that a new identification system must replace drivers' licences, birth certificates and passports. They identify citizens and persons. Moreover, as individual living beings, we each have individual rights that must be defined, implemented, and protected. Additionally, you now understand how twenty natural laws govern your thoughts and actions. None rule, None command, but your life is sublimely governed, whereby no statutes are necessary. No further legislation is needed when ethics and morality are crystal clear, and natural law is complete. No parliament is required, no upper or lower house, either nationally or for each state.

Effectively, the government is repurposed in natural law, all legalities foreclosed. Notwithstanding, all (essential) state services like fire, ambulance, hospitals and transport remain. Individual rights and freedoms are protected. All authoritative command systems are abolished. Police, law courts and judiciary systems remain but not in the legal jurisdiction. Natural existential law replaces admiralty law, whereby the judicial system is now lawful, not legal.

As further explanations develop, you will begin to grasp the validity and authenticity of these changes. They are critical because if you are ever to convince others of these merits, you must first have educated and convinced yourself. So let's begin.

Societies need an institution charged with the task of protecting the people's lives, their rights, words, deeds, and property from all infractions and violations. That is the exact opposite of governments that seize our lives as their property from day one, most often through fraudulent issuance of a birth certificate and multitudinous legal instrumentation. This chapter sets forth a skeletal model for implementing free societies, their foundation, nature, purpose and structure. Based on 'natural law' as revealed in our complete conscious process, it applies to the Australian continent as a role model for any country on earth. (Australia presently has a National Government that oversees independent State Governments, below which is 'Local Government,' or local government areas, LGA's.)

Although well recognised and applauded, the phrase 'consent of the governed' is open to gross misuse. This alternative for organic societies is premised on the 'nature of those governed, *'as consented by 'nature and nature's God,'* as Thomas Jefferson stated.

Thus we have the means and immutable power to fortify 'unalienable rights,' freedoms, protections, and 'natural justice.' No better precedent exists, nor can it! Of course, we may disagree with Jefferson's beautifully phrased term, but never can we escape the consequences of our actions. Natural law is immutable. Truth, reality, and values are the keys to a future we have never dreamed of; our most precious gift of consciousness and immutable governing principles are our means. All of this points to necessarily revising education in all schools and universities, human sciences, psychology and philosophy, law and politics. Remember—

> *If a nation expects to be ignorant and free, in a state of civilisation, it expects what never was and never will be. —Thomas Jefferson*

Jefferson's words hold eternal truth. Freedom and civilised association depend on knowledge, and understanding, a capacity we all have as individual living beings. Paradoxically, if not stupidly, artificial laws spurn our individuality despite the inherent natural laws. That truth is humanity's most profound issue, but is never discussed because people believe governments offer indispensable benefits and protections, otherwise unobtainable. They pander to that common belief and insist on continuance, no matter what good or evil governments indulge. All their efforts are commonly considered just and moral in the political and legal sense, all in our best interest, which confirms our acceptance 'authoritarian rule' is indispensable to our comfort and security. 'Service to self' versus 'service to others,' is a false choice. Such ignorance has us believe that life in service of societal goals is our sole moral duty, whence self, family, and friends take second place to the state, no dispute entertained. The result is anti-life, as diagram 1 previously showed.

The conclusion is vibrantly clear.

> *'Any society that votes to be ruled by force deserves all the tyranny and bloodshed that authority initiates.'*

Societal insanity cannot be stated more plainly. Criminal violation of life will continue with our approval until we change our moral compass and withdraw consent!

'Ascension' reputedly concerns 'higher consciousness,' a transformational uplifting of our mind, body, and spirit into higher levels of love and life. We each actively and consciously choose to 'raise our vibrations' and thereby evolve into a higher state of being. Purportedly, this will rid overt societal controls and manipulations that have plagued humanity for centuries. Good intentions indeed, but how exactly will this happen? No answer, because none offers.

Let's turn back to nature. Full consciousness shows unequivocally that a 'free society' and 'natural law' are co-dependent. Each must uphold and guarantee non-violation of the other, or both vanish, as witnessed today. Natural laws of perfected self-governing are the 'separate and equal station' to which "the laws of nature and nature's God entitle each man and woman." As prior described, our nature is Creator's model for free organic societies, whence no greater ethic or morality is needed. Is this a higher state of being? Spiritual life values uploaded to autopilot carry our ethics and morality, so the answer is 'yes'. We move into a spiritual plane of existence.

Most people have a wishful vision for their loved ones and family. They all want to be free from burdens, coercive employers, and political corruption and to live in freedom and peace without restriction. They want to live according to their values, ethics, and morals, and be self-sufficient, free from authoritarian control. They desire food and water security and to be part of a solid community/village/support network where they can raise healthy, self-aware, emotionally secure children. To make the world a better place, they seek normalcy or a state of orderliness where they can plan and predict and know that their plans and ambitions will materialise without sabotage. But sabotage, destruction, disruption and criminal acts surround them today. With all avenues of redress blocked and more obstacles appearing with every news bulletin, their cry for peaceful order magnifies.

The unanswered question in all their minds is how? How can we escape the burden of life? Their pleas are becoming more urgent. How can peaceful freedom be brought into being and be preserved for our children and beyond?

As briefly as possible, I will show how. But first, let's face facts.

- Suppose you leave your wellbeing, prosperity, and success in the hands of others. In that case, you must expect they will chart your course, devise your means, deny your objections and, forbidding any alterations, structure their desired outcomes and confiscate most of your profits. That's what most countries now have.

- Alternatively, if you are determined to learn full responsibility and do what it takes to build your future as you want it to be, then you must chart your course and devise the means. Likewise, you must protect your life, means, efforts and profits from sabotage, theft, and destruction.

As of 2022, with no remedy on offer, cowardice, submission, and surrender is no option; only the second alternative remains. So let's explore it!

Australia has no constitution of worth, no bill of individual rights, nor any history of constitutional law or unalienable rights to fall back on. Consequently, people instinctively turn their attention to what they believed worked for their comforts and security in the past, with 'common law' and 'democracy' forefront. The problem is, had either of those political doctrines succeeded in the past, no one would suffer from today's tyrannical predicament. No remedy presents because no revisions can work. The principle of one man ruling another is corrupt, plain evil; amended fraud remains fraudulent. Richard Buckminster Fuller nailed it when he said —

> *You never change things by fighting the existing reality. To change something, build a new model that makes the existing model obsolete.*

America's founders of 1776 did not let the parasitic rule stand in their way. On the contrary, they declared the independence of America from Great Britain when declaring their rights to life, liberty, and the pursuit of happiness. Given that achievement, what prevents any nation's people from asserting their independence as individuals from any prescriptive, authoritarian states? Nothing, save learning precisely what our American brothers and sisters are beginning to realise. If a body of people can prescribe how others are to act and behave, such that detriment, disasters, pain and suffering result, then the victims get what they permitted, profiting all who wrote the prescriptions. That is Australia's predicament and has been for decades past. The same is true for many nations despite piecemeal differences in application.

It is one thing to structure a government to protect individual rights, but once legislation cancels your rights, the government protects its right to exist, not your right to live. As a result, your freedom vanishes and draconian rule magnifies. That short-circuit is the road to communistic tyranny, the present goal of Agenda 2030 and the World Economic Forum (WEF).

Whatsoever society robs an individual of the product of his effort, enslaves him, or indeed attempts to limit the freedom of his mind is not, strictly speaking, a society. Through the wielding of institutionalised gang rule, it is a mob which destroys all values of human coexistence, thus threatening their victim's survival. Every empire, monarchy and ruling government in human history has prescribed that individuals must subordinate themselves to someone else's mandates, commands, dictates, acts, or so-called laws. There's no escaping that whatever violates your free will denies your life.

If we are to build a new model that makes the existing model obsolete, as Fuller suggested, then the words of Albert Einstein are vitally significant. *"No problem can be solved from the same level of consciousness that created it."*

Do you sense a remedy? With joy in your heart and freedom in sight, our efforts remain, of course. Let's choose consciousness, not ignorance, our right to life, a new societal model, and freedom in a state of civilisation.

Effectively, your heart is hydraulic and your lungs are pneumatic. They work independently yet interact with each other without pause for your entire life. Any infraction of this arrangement, such as a pulmonary embolism, results in death within seconds unless prevented. (I know. I lived through that experience.)

The conscious mind and subconscious mind share a similar relationship, wherein (known or unknown) life values of your choosing are picked up and employed during the enactment of your goals, after which success or distress is reported back to your cognitive mind via feelings.

Readers of my book, *'Conscious Ascendance'* will recognise this wave diagram showing the complete sequential process of human consciousness, save one of our nine higher faculties.

Please forgive my repeat of that description and this diagram. It points to how our new societal model should properly be structured. The first (wave crest) curve depicts what should happen. The second (wave trough)

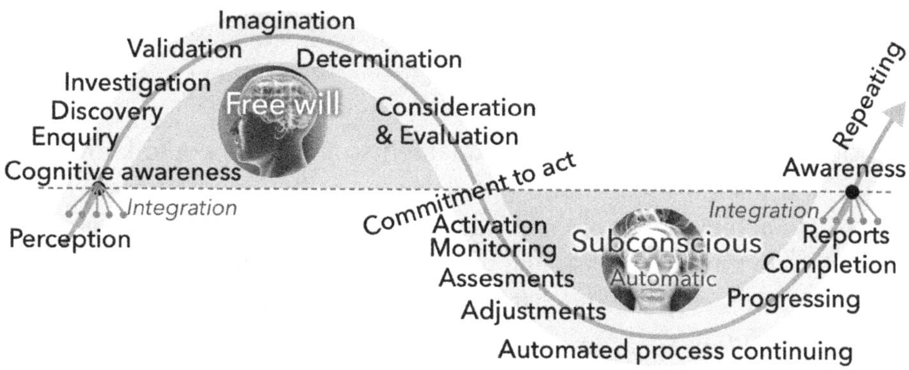

6. The value transfer wave

curve depicts its enactment. The first is free will determined. The second is fully automated. Think about that deeply. To build a free society, we must determine how it should properly work to function automatically as best possible. The diagram shows a model for a free community, provided we follow the same logic, sequence and natural laws. Better yet, we know that the conscious process works. *'Conscious Ascendance'* described its inbuilt protections, cautions, warning signals and how to effect remedies should problems arise. We know these biological and psychological processes are governed to maintain an orderly process, or our systems break down. We cannot change those governing laws. We cannot change how our heart and lungs work, and neither can we change how our two minds exchange values. That is excellent news because our inability to change those laws protects our lives. Our free will mind cannot overrule our subconscious mind because it is fully automated. Neither can our subconscious mind revoke our free choices, or we have free will, no means to engage in life. Now see how an indoctrinated society rules us?

It does so by planting statute laws in our cognitive awareness. (Compare the conflict between the left sides of diagrams 6 and 7.) That is how our consciousness is overruled.

We can free ourselves from that coercive problem. But, to do so, we must declare that our unalienable right to life is not negotiable on anyone's terms, nor the inalienable right to the product of our efforts. Then we must protect our 'individual rights.'

'Life' is the supreme value; thus, society must be subordinate to your life, not vice versa. That understanding cannot be stressed too highly! Three matters are of critical importance.

The new societal structure must begin with the nation's people as individuals, not the nation's society, government, system, or conglomeration.

Rights must be set forth and explained so that the people know their rights and responsibilities and thus learn how they are empowered and blessed to achieve. A 'collective' (group, society) has no rights, nor can it.

Everyone must recognise that their right to life is immutable to protect them from all trespass and harm; further, we must preserve 'individual rights' in perpetuity.

The battle for freedom and prosperity must begin with the very nature of what we each are as living flesh and blood beings. We cannot escape this truth, but we can ignore it.

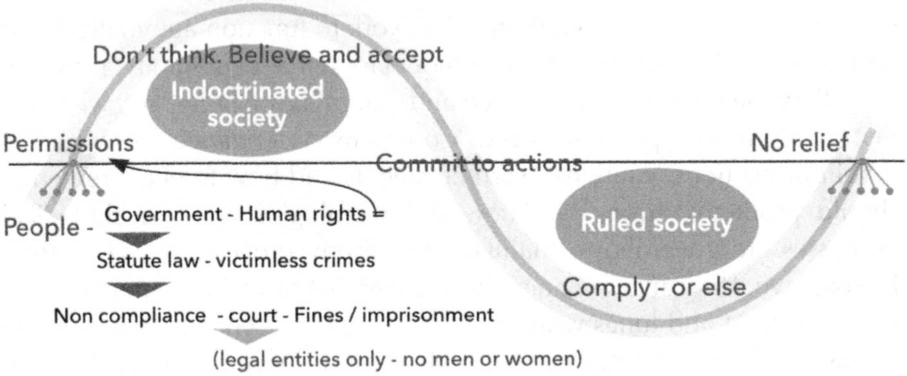

7. Indoctrinated society

Your unalienable right to life and inalienable right to the fruits of your labour must be upheld and protected. Failure to protect those individual rights permits the people to be forcibly ruled, harmed, or both. You cannot have it both ways.

The task of all people is to establish a protective body solely given to protecting the individual rights and freedoms of the people utilising natural law. History witnesses no such thing. America came very close, its acclaimed record over 150 years exemplary by world standards.

We've been gifted a new model, only recently revealed as 'full consciousness,' yet it is the oldest of all. Compare diagram 8 with diagram 7, and you'll see that authoritarian law (Statutes) has vanished from the left side and appeared as the natural law on the right side. Natural laws govern the consequences of our actions. It does not prescribe our actions up-front. Observe how the left side of diagram 6 now correlates with the left

9. Protectorates - substitute for government

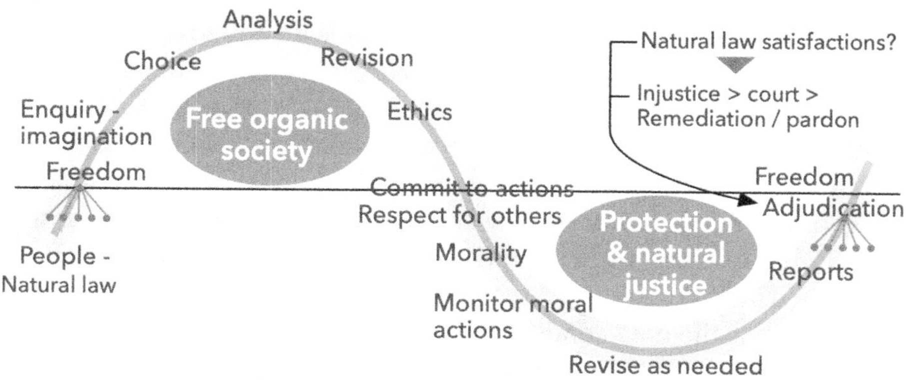

8. Free societies

side of diagram 8. Authoritarian law has been banished and natural law takes over.

This 'technology of consciousness' displaces ignorance. It testifies values, individual rights, comforts and protections and backs all those efficiencies with twenty natural laws. Benefits are available only to those who choose freedom and responsibilities and have a passionate will to succeed. Their task is to learn, validate, implement, and protect freedom. It may take a generation or two to reap its full blessings, but it will likely never happen if you and I do not urgently begin now. We need to learn how to remove the roadblocks and begin construction.

Grasp the full relevance of natural law to achieving your desires, values, and ambitions. Understand its rightful place in your heart. We've only eight billion people on the planet. Yet, each of us holds the Creator's model administering a society of fifty-trillion free, peace-loving, value-centred individual constituents, all addressed by our free will. All our inherent systems are protected owing to the supreme value of life itself. The value exchange system encrypted in our conscious process is the perfect model for our societal economy. Our faculties show us the encrypted right to bear arms and protect against all enemies, foreign and domestic. So they govern our nature to perfection, responsibly and respectfully within the equal rights of all others.

So thorough and complete is this model it relegates all criminal violators and trespassers to 'outlaw status' resulting from their own free choice. It holds them accountable for the consequences of their actions via the twentieth natural law, that of natural justice. All those who choose to be outlaws wilfully relinquish their right to freedom as the consequence of their action(s) since self-destruction is the only destructive right they possess. That is the principle of justice described in Chapter four.

The model is complete. Nothing better exists for any society than what already exists within every man, woman and child on earth. Our mission is crystal clear. Translate those same twenty laws into society.

Once firmly grasped that the consequences of our actions and behaviour are governed as Creator consented, no more is required. No consensus is needed since its only critics are free-loading parasites or self-declared trespassers. So richly blessed are we that no additional consent is required.

Freedom is the only condition in which our 'operating system' of 'full consciousness' can function as it should. Freedom and respect are reciprocal. Your free choice to respect other people's lives is your protection exactly! That is how natural law works. It does not prescribe anything. It simply governs the consequences of your actions and behaviour. Freedom, respect, and individual rights are the three conditions that morally constrain us. No enforcement is necessary for a free society, save for arresting those who choose to violate natural law itself.

It cannot be said more clearly. We must seize freedom, respect it, enact it, and protect it. Omit one of those four essentials, and freedom vanishes completely. It is straightforward, as Francis Bacon said–

"Nature, to be commanded, must be obeyed."

When ruling political bodies such as Socialism, Communism, or Democracy prescribe the actions and behaviours of others, chaos, devastation, and gang warfare are near inevitable. The lesson is clear if society is to be free. 'Constitutional law' cannot correctly acquire any more power than Creator bestowed; lest it properly should not exist. That condition strictly provides that our 'unalienable rights,' freedoms, living identity and 'natural justice' must be upheld and forever protected. No better precedent exists than natural self-governance with all rights, freedoms, comforts, and securities protected.

Consider how that would impact the health industry. Pirates who prey on sickness and disease, including manufactured (genetically modified & patented) diseases, would fade into oblivion, all atmospheric, land and forest devastations, water poisons and directed energy weapons likewise relegated to history.

How long an emerging organic society may take to materialise is less important than committing to commencement since, when the penny drops, full consciousness reveals all its secrets in milliseconds. Ignorance vanishes in the same instant, but no fulfilment is possible without beginning.

Dissent is possible. Some might say, *"what if I disagree?"* The answer is, *"disagree with what?"* Organic societies are founded on Creator's universal consent to live in freedom. We can refuse that consent in only two ways. One is to renege on life and sponge off other people as a mindless 'second-hander'; alternatively, choose to violate natural law as an outlaw. All such escape artists face the consequences of their actions as natural law determines.

It is worth remembering that free will sandwiched in the subconscious process as a team player is fully protected. In societal terms, we cannot compromise this protection. Josiah Warren insisted natural laws—

> *"teach us that our own happiness depends upon a proper respect for the happiness of others and that therefore we should not make social arrangements which require compulsion or the violation of the natural freedom of any individual."*

Furthermore...

> *"there must be no arrangements which depend for their success upon agreement on verbal rules or processes for agreements of opinions, tastes or interests. There should be, instead, preservation of the liberty of each person to differ in these and all other respects."*

To disagree Creator's position is to disavow one's nature. And that's the vital clue. Conscious ignorance has hidden the natural laws of our nature. But no more. As explained in 'Conscious Ascendance' and in my book Law from Within, our respect for freedom engenders voluntary cooperation based on mutual exchange of value, which produces almost unbelievable benefits, primarily unknown in today's business suffocating from cut-throat competition.

Thus self-governance replaces (collective) government, but not as we have ever known it. On the contrary, self-governance is the maintenance of the 'natural order,' enabling us to advance rapidly, producing unbounded benefits with just protection of our right to life in-built.

The Australian people are gifted an opportunity to stamp the word FREEDOM on the world map, as may any country on earth. So I take this opportunity to salute the world's first nation to embrace a new *'age of independence and freedom,'* gained from insights into the unquestionable laws governing our human nature. Let's now look at how such a society might be structured.

Very simply, governments wilt wither and fade into non-existence, forced to vacate the nation through a Declaration of Independence, and a Charter of Individual Rights. A 'Protectorate' structure, thus substituted, is a constitutionally appointed body of people that upholds and protects people's individual rights.

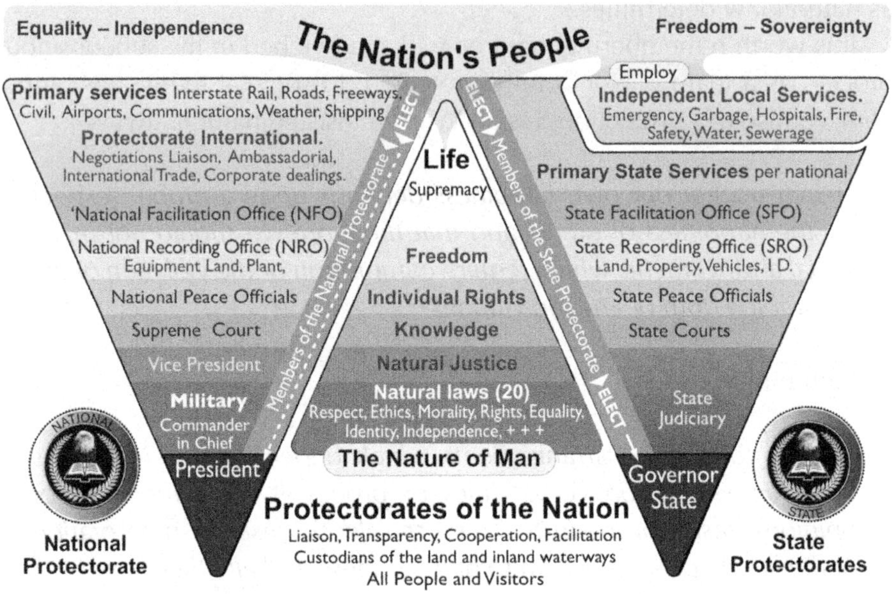

9. Protectorate schematic diagram

It is that simple. 'Protectorates' lawfully replace national, state and local governments. They adhere to an objectively written Constitution that expressly forbids writing any laws. Any violation of their 'commission' brings instant dismissal since rights belong solely to each individual. Such a 'Protectorate' consigns parliaments (or Congress) to history. No upper or lower house exists, no senate, and no legislative assemblies. No acts are passed; hence no enforcement is needed. Police and law courts continue much as they do now, but deprived of victimless crimes like speeding tickets, all are demonstrably smaller and vastly more efficient. Police are Peace Officials.

Consequently, all standard protections such as building standards, air safety, rail and road safety, construction and infrastructure works remain unaffected. The fundamental difference is that safety rules apply only to material objects and practices. Nothing is permitted to rule or overrule our thoughts, free will, morality, or minds. Free to act as we please within the bounds of proper respect for all others, we may accept or reject trade or commercial *'terms and conditions.'* Such can never be mandatory else; they violate free choice.

No government remains; people are free from domination and control instantly. Self-governance is ours entirely, responsibly reinstated within the rights of all others exactly as Creator intentioned. Legal entities no longer exist; thus, full responsibility for one's actions is one's own.

The question arises as to how a 'Protectorate' should be structured and implemented. Should it imitate the top-down government structure, or should it emerge from the bottom? The answer is both but in sequence. Life is the bottom line, and natural laws ensure it as our all-time reference base for all matters. Following from descriptions in 'Conscious Ascendance,' we each are enabled to rise from bottom to top. That position heralds where the 'Protectorate' kicks in. The nation's people are at the top of the life pyramid, not pretend 'leaders.' Self-governance now administers the protection of free societies, thereby protecting freedom and free will from the top down with no obstruction, commandments, statutes and laws. The people, as individuals, are now the employers of each state and national protectorate, and every trespass of natural law adjudicates within natural justice.

What you see in this diagram is not society without government. It is full and complete governance as never witnessed in all history, exercised fully in accordance with Creator's consent so to do.

Before studying the make-up and different functions of the National Protectorate and State Protectorates, and the vacancy resulting from having no local government, several new matters demand an explanation.

First we must differentiate between 'provisioning' versus 'protecting' certain assets and functions we take for granted inside the government. Remember, we are no longer dealing with a body of people that makes its own rules. Street sweeping, street lighting and trash collection are just three examples at a local level. Expand that idea, and at the state level, there are state highways, ambulance services, hospitals and infrastructure such as rail bridges. Step up again to the national level for facilities like international airports, lighthouses and navigation, border control, weather stations, radar and communications. All are in people's interests, so where does 'provisioning' begin versus where does 'protection' commence? What adjudicating criteria apply, and why?

Formerly, governments decided these things, wrote the rules, issued press releases, commanded a budget and pressed the 'go' button. The government ignored the nation's people, yet they paid the bill. Such provisioning' cannot change, but its management can. People provision these services as they choose, just as they select their investments, jobs and workplaces.

I suggest the people implement a 'National Facility Directorate' (NFD) within the National Protectorate. Similarly, a State Facility Directorate (SFD) would function within each State Protectorate. Such is a department or organisation responsible for furnishing society with essential assets that each singular being or entity cannot achieve alone. What does that mean?

One individual can only do a certain amount, such as putting the trash bin out for collection. It takes a fleet of trucks and drivers to collect from a community. Individuals help to fund and maintain that fleet by investing in its success and reaping the benefits. Although ordinarily funded through annual rates paid to local government, a group of people nevertheless assists an even bigger group of people in a way that no single person can do themselves.

Now expand that concept. Local services can only go so far before the state must take over. It effectively does what a trash collection fleet did for each individual, but here for local services. The task is not bigger or smaller so much as it is different. For example, while some road maintenance is local, state highways fall within the more extensive geographical jurisdiction. So now we see a body (State) doing what the (local) body could not do, just as it does what singular men and women cannot.

Now expand that idea to the national level. Local airports are now international airports. River navigation signs are now (nationwide) radar and satellite communications. National assets and services are beyond what any state can achieve.

In sum, protectorates are (societally) tasked with protecting the people, and a part of that task is to ensure that no one is burdened by having to do what is not practically feasible.

That principle lies within us all. Notably, our subconscious mind performs multitudinous tasks on autopilot, at blistering speed, a job that our cognitive minds could never handle alone. As *'Conscious*

Ascendance' described, our subconscious mind wants to know what value we seek. It then employs that value as best possible, offering two reports concerning success on completion. That principle hails the perfect (new) model for society precisely because it works to perfection.

Each Protectorate level does what the level below could not do; benefit and justification are inbuilt. Each Protectorate level must determine (or be shown) what benefits result. It must work to achieve that goal and report its success.

Consequently, each person becomes the employer of Protectorate staff; hence the people must pay their workers, their employees. Where any appointed 'Protectorate' deviates from its commission and does not protect its employers, instant dismissal follows.

Accordingly, the 'Protectorate' fully protects the right of every individual to live on two counts. First, it protects everyone's right to life and property, thus freedom. Second, it protects those who seek more than they can achieve alone through a facilitated collaborative domain that trades value for value without force or coercion.

This concept fully upholds natural law in that we are responsible for our actions. Value for value collaboration between employer and employee is none less than free will collaboration with all the systems and faculties of our nature. Our natural governing laws match perfectly. This collaborative concept does more than we can do through free will alone, yet free will orchestrates the whole process.

Accordingly, each nation's 'Protectorate' begins with the free will of its people and benefits those people as a result. Never lose sight of the benefits because protection exists to ensure them.

Suppose that a two percent (2%) transactional tax funds all Protectorates; all food and health essentials omitted. In truth, such is not a 'tax' at all. It is a payment from employers to employees for services rendered. That is value for value trade. Because all Protectorates deliver to each what no one can do alone, they are obligated to serve each alone, including individual rights upheld absolutely.

Expand that principle further, and we can see that no protectorate has the workforce or machinery to build an airport, radar station, undersea tunnel or jet freighter. But many others do. Thus a 'Protectorate' can convene a committee or board to facilitate and direct such tasks.

For this new societal model, the National Protectorates include a 'National Facilitation Office' (NRO), and States have a 'State Facilitation

Office' (SFO). Their role, as the name describes, is to 'facilitate' desirous outcomes initiated by the people. Its personnel do not engage in a project and complete it as though workers in a corporate branch of the Protectorate; instead, they organise and oversee those who can expedite the project efficiently. Importantly they protect against grifters, henchmen, parasites, profiteers, and empire builders to sustain people's rights and benefits.

The concept of protectorates and facilitation centres as a lawful substitute for government is revolutionary. To help your understanding, let me refer back to a short fiction article I wrote in 2013 entitled, *"Can I be of assistance."* Little did I know then how prophetic it might become.

The story concerns Jerry, who has invented a new manufacturing process and seeks legal assistance from the 'State Facilitation ' as though a new branch of government. He is stunned on arrival since the building and its parking area looks nothing like what we ordinarily expect of government departments. Indeed in introducing himself, he comments to (what he thinks is) the receptionist, *"I was wondering if I was in a government building or lost in a hotel on a resort island."* The reply astounds him. *"Hello Jerry, my name is Colin, manager of the Victorian Protectorate Facilitation Centre."*

Jerry is completely nonplussed and says so. Colin then explains...

"You remember how government used to make rules, obstructions and impediments for everything you did; well, we don't. No parking signs as you may have noticed, no taxes, no business imposts, no licenses, no registrations and no approvals. Just one simple thing to remember; tread on your own toes and none others.

"But managers don't greet visitors," chuckled Jerry, his mood rising for the first time all day as his eyes lifted to the skylight that bathed the 'hotel lounge' in daylight.

"You're right. That's the way it used to be. You were greeted by a receptionist who knew nothing but phones, who directed you to someone who knew little more than a computer keyboard, who directed you to a supervisor, then to an area manager who was out to lunch, and if you found someone who could handle your matter before your parking time expired you were having a great day. So come on over to this lounge and let's chat about why you're here and then I'll manage the right people to satisfy your desires."

"You make it sound so logical," said Jerry as he sunk into a comfortable lounge. "Managers should manage solutions not problems right?"

"You got it; so tell me about your solution."

Jerry nearly fell off the lounge. "Aren't I supposed to tell you my problem?"

"How can I manage your solution if you only want to talk problems" Colin joked.

Jerry explains his invention as his 'solution,' although desperately struggling for words from forever thinking in terms of 'problems.'

"Now I'll have to ask you a third time Jerry, how can I be of assistance"?

"Well," Jerry said, I need to apply for a patent, get some help with production tooling, then apply for an import license for some test equipment from Germany, then register for tax, get a small business licence, ascertain business regulations and safety provisions, get some electronic help, and check the anti-trust laws. Oh, and there's a technician in Japan who's an expert on captivator modules, but I can't afford that luxury.

Colin had smiled at the first few words but by now was doubled up with laughter! He'd spilt his coffee and knocked the tray sideways as he fussed over restoring law and order. What's so funny, Jerry thought. This place is a branch of government, and that's what government does.

"Sorry, Jerry, I should have explained. None of what you just asked applies any longer. Remember how I wanted to talk about solutions and not problems? You see, none of those problems remains. They're history.

Colin then introduces Jerry to three specialists.

Colin spoke when all were seated around in the sumptuous circular lounge, facing each other, each with a side table for tablets and equipped with sockets for additional equipment.

"Thank you all", Colin said. "Jerry has brought a solution, and I'll let him describe it to you. Jane is our travel specialist, Jerry, Sarah is our equipment specialist, and Cliff provides consultants.

Colin excused himself and left the room.

Jane spoke first, trying to put Jerry at ease. "It should have occurred to you Jerry, that our specialist talents fit your solution else Colin would not have invited us in particular to assist you. So would you like to help us join the dots please?"

Jerry was struck dumb in an instant! "Solution" - "Invited" - "Please" - "Specialist talents"- "Assist", all in one sentence? Like this place is government — really — GOVERNMENT? Whatever happened to 'wait here', stand in line, fill out the form, give me your ID, come back in an hour, pay at the cashier's window?

Jerry told his story again in more detail. Three matters were raised and addressed concerning Jerry's project that led to a question from Sarah.

Jane answered. What is best for you, Jerry? Would you like to fly to Japan, or would it suit you better if we flew your specialist here?

Jerry was stunned again! "My passport is out of date," he muttered. Shrieks of laughter filled the room.

Cliff explained that "passports are as old-fashioned as seamed stockings." Jane raised a question concerning necessary equipment.

"On it right now," Sarah replied, staring at her tablet and stabbing it. A picture then flashed up on the screen. "Is that what you wanted Jerry, it's available ex-stock and air freight is clear to go. It can be here inside four days".

A brief discussion followed concerning the other two matters.

"Did Col mention how one satisfaction leads to another Jerry, and how in the old way, just one impediment lead to an endless string of problems, if not multiple obstructions," Sarah asked? "Have you noticed how prices have dropped and wondered why? Are you seeing what kind of slavery system we had under damnable governments?"

"Thanks, Sarah, I'm thinking Jerry's head will need a weeks holiday to take it in," said Jane. "Let's put this solution away." Final coordination between flight times to suit Jerry and the consultant's availability, equipment ordered, and solution delivered.

"How does that feel Jerry?" Sarah asked.

"I'm pretty dumbfounded, as I think you've guessed, but there's one thing you've forgotten. How in hell's name can I pay for it all?

"Pay?" Jane asked? "What's the name of this place you're in?"

The "Victorian Protectorate Facilitation Centre"

"Yes", said Jane. "Next question. Does 'pay' sound like facilitation, or a log jamb? "

"You got me," Jerry replied.

"Go to the top of the class and enjoy Japan Jerry, It's great at this time of year and I'll book you some great accommodation."

That is a fictional example, of course. I included snippets of it for one reason only, that being to shift your mind from thinking a ruling class is utterly indispensable, to then consider the exact opposite. A 'protectorate' exists to maintain order, arrest crime, and administer justice for the people.

That said, there is a fine line between the 'provisioning' of a society and 'protecting' the people. Governments are believed to do both, but fail. They love providing assets, infrastructure and services because, not only do they make government appealing, greater and greater control of the populace results.

Such dependence on government is anathema to free societies. The more it can (free-market) provision and service its own needs, the more the 'Protectorate' can 'protect,' and not 'provision.' The word 'facilitate' best bridges those two concepts. It implies that 'facilitation' is also to be protected, in that the Nation only provisions what the state cannot, which in turn only provisions what local communities cannot, hence the people themselves are the (bottom line) employers of all Protectorate employees above.

Protection utilises the same principle, meaning that individual self-defence is rightfully indispensable, community policing services (peace officials) are of the state thereby, and the military is national. It remains that if a two percent transactional tax can fund the monstrosity we call government and its countless impositions, both Protectorate and Facility Directorate funding is easily achievable, based on value for value trade, not tax.

Logically, members of each protectorate establish the Facility Directorate structure based on its constitution. Although beyond the scope of this book, suffice it to say that a draft Protectorate Constitution has already been written for Terra Australis, (Australia). Matters for concern for the Facility Directorate include, public surveys and research, specialist expertise, consultants, merits, authenticity and validation, funding, progress assessment and adjudication, transparency and education, tenders, project management, contracts, completion, advertising, and reports. Such specialists and services strictly provision the protectorate including its necessary provisioning of essential assets and services.

Beyond that, and using my fictional example, a free society may voluntarily organise and contribute to a 'facilitation centre'; it given to accessing the best minds on planet earth for the benefit of the people. Is such possible? Yes, absolutely, but only when the people are free and crime is arrested. Hopefully, that fictional example it has set your mind spinning concerning vast differences between governments, protectorates, and voluntary 'Facilitation Centres.'

Importantly, impediments presently labour the nation's people, which is 'non-protective'. Cost imposts throttle their productivity. Misguided education smashes creativity. Bogus ideologies steer people into false beliefs. The task is not to ban these obstructions as statutes attempt, but instead to present a clear and inviting path that sings success so frequently that none of the provisioned benefits can be ignored.

Remember above all that when the people of any nation pay the salaries of those whom they elect, then the people are employers, not employees. Employees do not call the tune. The people do.

What follows concerning a Protectorate structure is not finite but rather a guideline only. As structured within the Nation's Constitution document, each separate State Protectorate is bound to conform to the National Constitution and the Charter of Individual Rights. All State protectorates will typically consist of three (primary) services.

1. The Civil Service properly functions as a transparent administrative body, providing the first avenue of address for the People; providing inter-Service liaison, handling treasury matters, and such other administrations as may be necessary for effective and efficient operation of the Protectorate. It also includes the Facility Directorate structure and Recording Office.

2. The Police Service properly deals with (initiated) physical force, its apprehension, cessation, and bringing charges.

3. The Judicial Service properly deals with judicial matters and upholding of natural law concerning the protection of individual rights through enquiry, tribunals, court hearings, jury trials and sentences.

We should note 'border protection' does not exist to enforce written law or collect revenue but to uphold natural law. Its task is not to help 'build' a safe, secure, prosperous Nation; instead, to prevent international criminals from harming the people. Included are all international cartels, incorporated bodies, alphabet agencies, foreign governments, banking institutions howsoever structured, and all such agencies regardless of past treaties, pledges, covenants or alliances. Neither should the military be tasked with protecting the commercial interests of The Nation's people.

Constitutional matters and their address are beyond the scope of this book. Much is done, however.

No longer is there a government to prescribe standards and enforce them. Instead, industry practitioners most knowledgeable in their field of endeavour correctly determine precautions and safety measures. Necessarily, their achievements protect the people from political interference and sabotage for revenue-raising purposes, such as bribery.

People who choose to countermand, trespass, or violate the governing laws of nature or nature's God relinquish their right to so choose in that instant. So they accept full accountability for remediation restitution or recompense as Natural Justice may determine appropriate. Alternate choices are always available, mitigating circumstances admitted. Jurisprudence is the philosophy of law and formulation of its teaching; it deals with the many aspects of treason.

The National Protectorate and State Protectorates should properly provide and maintain a 'Recording Office' in place of what we call a 'registry.' One's ID should top the list since real estate and other property like guns, cars, or boats cannot be recorded absent that reference base. Of course, each individual has the free choice to participate or not, just as one may choose not to eat, but consequences are inescapable. Benefits far exceed penalties.

Personal (biometric) identification is beneficial and adequately recorded at the State Recording Office. Such ID is strictly private property, which means no one can use it without prior consent, save Police Officials in the service of protection and arrest of offenders. Consequently, the sale or harvesting of this information is forbidden. Personal (biometric) identification serves as an ID replacement for drivers' licences, now a thing of the past.

Personal assets such as automobiles should be recorded as one's property, likewise a tractor or boat. A Personal Property code, (PPC) in place of present registration plates, facilitates instant identification of that individual in the case of accident or death for notification to family or next of kin.

' Identity Theft' is 'property theft,' if it results in losing one's individual right to life or property, including personal assets. Personal identification is the person's sole property and cannot be removed or taken away under any circumstances since biometric data is also one's private property.

All previous 'registrations' may be transferred to the public record, that when backed with appropriate action, have the power to overcome and rebut any private registration.

Recording at the SRO replaces government licensing; no fees or taxes apply. Private property recording arrests property theft; business and commercial vehicles, state vehicles, taxis, busses, ambulances and the like separately recorded.

Personal (biometric) identification once recorded, may also replace passports since one's living being and state of residency are now certified, all based on factual data that replaces imaginary identification numbers. Once other countries grasp the protected advantages of freedom, they too will see that protections now afforded to international travel and the ability to arrest convicted felons at the border are all that passports formerly achieved.

Virtually everyone who knows of the American Declaration of Independence credits that document as the most definitive expose of our individual rights ever written. So it is. Its protections of our life as independent beings and not social animals are clear, unequivocal, and unambiguous. So why is it not today's definitive standard? What error or omission has allowed our right to life to be usurped, overruled, rejected, reviled, repressed, stripped from existence and denied practical utility?

There seems to be only one answer. Nothing on the political horizon of 1776 could have suggested that it might be essential to protect the essence and nature of our (declared) protections inherent in the document. Jefferson said so himself, did he not? 'We hold these truths to be self-evident.' His conclusion, when viewed retrospectively, suggests that our individual right to life, liberty, and the pursuit of happiness are so self-evident and certain, that no need could ever exist to protect individual rights from cancellation or denial.

History has exposed that shortcoming. Upholding our right to life, and the vital need to protect our right to life, are distinctly separate issues. That fact was not self-evident in 1776, or the document would have enshrined everyone's right to 'the right to life.' Admittedly, Jefferson offered *"whenever any form of government becomes destructive of these ends, it is the right of the people to alter or to abolish it."* That clause is a vital truth, but sadly, it allows the horse to bolt before the gate closes.

In retrospect, we should have fully protected our declared right to claim that right! We should have proclaimed that while 'the laws of nature and nature's God,' (Jefferson's expression) protect our right to life, we must categorically protect our (natural) individual rights, by right.

Copyright protection should automatically ascribe to the author or artist for all works of intellectual property 'fixed in any tangible medium of expression,' including but not limited to books, photographs, drawings, music, architecture, drama, sculpture, web pages, software, and multimedia works. Terms concerning copyright and patents are included in the aforementioned 'Constitution (for Australia.)

Inclusive in that document, no part of any life form, including but not limited to molecules, cells, tissues, blood, protoplasm, gene, DNA, seeds, plant fibre or any other living form, including but not limited to biological modification of existing organisms creating a new class of biological organism shall be able to be patented. No exception to this clause shall be granted, wherefrom–

Any patents that may exist or have formerly existed for any part or whole or part of any life form, including but not limited to molecules, cells, tissues, blood, protoplasm, gene, DNA, seeds, plant fibre or any other living form including but not limited to biological modification of previously existing organisms that created a new class of biological organism, shall henceforth be annulled; rendered null and void. People may then benefit like never before. Consider these aspects of organic, symbiotic societies, unlike anything ever witnessed, all yours for your will to achieve.

- An organic society is of free, independent people living according to their choices among their likes. All people respect the natural law of the human world in their mutual dealings and interactions.
- Convivial order is that of adults living as responsible and caring people. Their society is the meeting, exchanging, and parting, or freely entering into or exiting from more or less stable relationships on peaceful and friendly terms, within a goodwill atmosphere.
- All people are free to the extent that others treat them peacefully, fully respecting their rights, work, and property. Mutual respect, one for another within the physical domain of which they are the author, certifies orderliness within the 'natural law.'
- People live together as independent beings without being urged to any joint enterprise or social interaction, not unlike a commune. Friendly relations among strangers have nothing but their humanity in common. Respect accepts others' uniqueness, speech, individuality, personal integrity and property.
- Individual freedom allows opportunity, facilitates negotiations, actions and outcomes, yet allows free exit, all absent force, fraud, or coercion. Individuals are free to pursue their goals separately and lawfully, in the

company of or collaboratively with others. Business contracts are personally and responsibly warranted, not committed by office, title, position, company, or corporation.

- No organisational or statutory purpose exists, although cultural ethics may predominate. No authority exercises direction, rule, or control, meaning no government may exist because such forfeits the nature and integrity of that society.
- Nothing establishes rulers or rule. No individual or group owns society, controls it, or is responsible or answerable for it. No common goal exists but for freedom, protection, and preservation. Moral guidance comes through education.
- Direction and influence may exist in the social order, e.g., from elders and those of great wisdom, but no positions of power exist to exert influence or command anyone. Participants abide by the natural laws of societal orderliness.
- All problems resolve through diplomatic negotiations or an appointed judge or arbitrator. Always remember that no one who seeks resolution can become the negotiator's or judicial agent's subject.
- Those who step outside natural laws choose to be outlaws, such actions automatic agreement to suffer all consequences arising, as Chapter Four describes the Principle of Natural Justice. The arrest of violence and service of natural justice, remediation, and compensation, accords with natural law. No social, organic order can wage war!

This opportunity is now on Australia's doorstep, indeed all other Nations, all for the willpower to achieve it! The question of choosing between Positive law, Constitutional law, Maritime law or Common law, or even of choosing between capitalism, socialism, communism, or democracy in any form, is history. Natural law governs the consequences of our actions regardless of whether we agree or disagree. Consequences are inescapable, as today's takeover of the human mind under the concealed banner of trans-humanism explicitly shows.

Authoritarian rulers have long known that human freedom is a fact of nature, but because that denied their rule, they had to invent means to ensure that people remain ignorant of their self-governing powers, forbidding their God-given rights absolutely.

Had they not, authoritarian domination and control would have crashed and burned centuries ago. However, their invention will be their downfall because the more tenaciously they deny your freedom, the more absolutely they freely confess their atrocious, despicable, criminal activities against humanity. Never deprived of an opportunity to choose conversely and repent as individuals, no excuse is permissible, as witnessed in the Nuremberg Code.

You've now glimpsed what a Protectorate Nation and its people can enjoy. I began this chapter by saying that societies need an institution charged with protecting the people's lives, rights, words, deeds, and property from all infractions and violations. That, you now have, save for adding a lawful Protectorate Constitution upholding the individual rights of every man, woman, and child within natural law.

Chapter 10

10. Declaration of Independence

This chapter sets forth a Declaration of Independence whereby peoples of all nations and countries may divorce from oppressive regimes and tyranny exercised by authoritarian governments and dictatorships, thus establishing and maintaining free symbiotic societies within their state or national borders. Initially written in 2021 for the Australian people, I have amended it here for universal application to all people. Although not cast in stone, its natural law principles are immutably those of "nature or nature's God" within every Man, woman and child for our discovery, use and implementation. In reading what follows, please mentally substitute your 'subject nation or state' each time you encounter the term [subject state], alternatively the 'people of - your nation' each time you encounter the phrase (subject people).

America's Declaration of Independence defined why and how the thirteen colonies severed their political ties with Great Britain to form the American government. The desire of many colonists to separate from Britain had been brewing for years. On Jun. 7, 1776, Richard Henry Lee of Virginia presented a resolution to the Second Continental Congress stating that the colonies *"are, and of right ought to be, free and independent States."* His call to dissolve political ties with Britain set the stage for the 'declaration.' Still, not all members of the Continental Congress were ready to accept what became known as the Lee Resolution. After several weeks they appointed five men to draft a document explaining why the colonies believed they had the right to form their government. This 'Committee of Five' consisted of John Adams, Benjamin Franklin, Thomas Jefferson, Robert Livingston, and Roger Sherman. They appointed John Adams and Thomas Jefferson to write the original draft of what later became known as the Declaration of Independence.

Adams insisted that Jefferson take the lead, which he did, and although other members of the Committee of Five made a few changes, Jefferson remained the principal author. His draft drew on the language and ideas of several other documents, including the Virginia Declaration of Rights and his version of a Virginia constitution. His opening words asserted a common idea among European Enlightenment thinkers of the time: that "all men are created equal," that phrase later used to advocate for women's right to vote and civil rights for African Americans.

The Continental Congress formally assembled again on July. 1 to consider the Lee Resolution for independence. For the next two days, members of the Continental Congress discussed and modified Jefferson's draft. John Hancock, president of the Second Continental Congress, was the first to sign the Declaration of Independence on Aug. 2, 1776. The next day, twelve colonies voted in favour. New York abstained at the time but declared its support for independence a week later. John Adams shared the news that the Continental Congress had declared independence from Britain.

The Declaration of Independence was officially adopted on Jul. 4, 1776 — now recognised as Independence Day. Fifty-six Delegates from the Continental Congress Signed the Declaration, but it was not made public until 1777 due to fear of British rule punishment.

Although America's freedom attracted little attention initially, the Declaration of Independence document later grew to be revered. It inspired many other countries and heavily influenced France's Declaration of the Rights of Man and Citizen (1789), as well as Venezuelan (1811), Liberian (1847), and Vietnamese (1945) Declarations, to name a few.

That history is notable since, in very many ways, Australia and many other countries now find themselves in a similar predicament. The most pressing matter facing all is learning how we can profit from that document, discover its failings, and what will perpetuate peoples' freedom in all nations.

10. Declaration of Independence

The Declaration of Independence contains one of the most memorable lines in history. *"We hold these truths to be self-evident, that all men are created equal, that they are endowed by their Creator with certain unalienable Rights, that among these are Life, Liberty, and the pursuit of Happiness."* The document had a much broader and deeper compass than mere secession of territory, notably establishing a new nation based on new principles.

That is the task facing all [subject people] today since no political principles employed in the past have prevented what has recently occurred. So what went wrong in America and multiple countries since those times? What has denied the progress of 'self-evident truths?'

Unfortunately, the answer is not self-evident; tragically, it is hidden. How? Because, since the Declaration serves to protect the rights of its citizens, logically, the words 'protection' and 'rights' must reign supreme above all else. Yet the need for 'Protection' is missing from the list of self-evident truths. Further, individual rights should be the rightful and lawful means of preserving or protecting equality, should they not?

Granted, the word 'liberty' appears, but as previously explained, it refers to collective rights or permissions. Conversely, the term 'freedom' applies singularly to individuals, automatically imparting (responsible) liberty to groups or society as a collective. Sadly, the word freedom is missing, too, problem being that it is possible to have liberty yet not be free.

Thus while the Declaration of Independence contained immortal truths, it duly authorised and instituted a representative public body in a (political) sovereign capacity conducive to general opinion. That *"governments derive their just powers from the consent of the governed"* implies consent of the majority.

Here then, is an unresolved anomaly. While the rights of all individuals are purportedly held sacred and protected through constitutional guaranties, which even the government itself is bound not to violate, nonetheless, the rights of all individuals are state collectivised under the banner of 'liberty.' The government is thereby enabled to indoctrinate, regulate and manipulate the 'consent of the governed,' from which it derives its just powers. Thus while America liberated itself true to principles it declared 250 years ago, its particular failure to protect 'individual rights' has permitted degenerate political action. That has resulted in direct authority issuing from the unbridled weight of an influential (purportedly elected) few. Such corruption, dare I say crimes against humanity, is the exact opposite of what 'certain unalienable rights' offers all men created equal.

The Declaration of Independence, having no inbuilt protection, soon allowed twisting of its precise meaning. Specifically, the Federalist camp worked to treat it as a mandate for forming a new central government. Thus eleven years later, a new Constitution enabled that exactly.

What transpired was a struggle between Thomas Jefferson and Alexander Hamilton. Twenty years after America's Declaration of Independence, the retiring president George Washington warned that creating political factions would likely lead to *"formal and permanent despotism."* Yet, despite his cautionary words, his two closest advisors, Thomas Jefferson and Alexander Hamilton, helped form the factions that ultimately led to the dual party system under which the United States has operated since then. While others, notably James Madison and John Adams, contributed to the formation of political parties, Hamilton and Jefferson shaped the early national political landscape. Although their struggle is unfortunately obscured in one form or another, that political battle has continued to mark America's greatness since its inception.

Hamilton and the Federalist's ideal was the British model, save that a strong President would act or oversee as a lawful if not benevolent monocrat in the absence of a monarch. Instead, over time, and with little or no challenge, federalists have believed in ever-expanding power of the federal government, myriad governmental regulations, controls, and special privileges; in economic life, the crushing of the states, and limiting the rights of the individual.

Looking back, the American Constitution forged a compromise between the ideologies of Jefferson and Hamilton, with James Madison acting as the balancing fence-straddler between the two camps. While the trappings, the rhetoric, and specific issues have changed, the fundamental disparities and distinctions have remained unresolved on the American scene until recently, but not through political expediency or agreement. Instead, the sellout of government to incorporate banking and dominant control interests has demolished the government. It now masquerades in name only.

At the time Jefferson and John Adams vied for the presidency in 1796, two political factions had formed known as "Republicans" and "Federalists." These rival factions battled throughout the new republic.

Passions ran high as each side became convinced that the other's goals would betray the legacy of the Revolution that had been recently fought and won at a high cost. However, both factions and many others understood that a moment's political advantage was not at stake. Instead, two visionaries expressed and led the future course of the American nation despite fundamentally opposed visions of what the United States should be.

Their differences remain to this day despite corporatised plundering of both. While Jefferson as a true revolutionary, passionately believed in individual liberty and an egalitarian society, he pursued the idea of a weak central government that facilitated increased powers for the states. On the other hand, Hamilton, a mastery organiser and tactician, feared public chaos and social disorder. Consequently, he strived for a powerful national government, believing that would ensure the nation's security and propel it to economic greatness or supremacy.

I have given you this history for two significant reasons. First, to show that despite all their advantages, their competing legacies are flawed, yet like twin strands of DNA, they continue to shape America and much of the world, including Australia. Second, and most importantly, to show that this epic intellectual struggle can henceforth be finally concluded, never to re-surface ever again. So it is time to get very serious — more truthfully factual than at any time in earth's history.

Sociopaths and psychopaths have, as their final scorched earth policy, united to unleash a program intended to pollute the DNA of Mankind to erase the Creator's imprinted signature. After that, they claim, as their exclusive patented property, we no longer belong to or have access to our Creator Source. Like cattle rustlers attempting to change our brand, all dimwitted or trusting souls who fall for this ruse (their concocted "Mark of the Beast") will become property belonging to them for whatever use they deem appropriate, including genocide; so they claim.

Will they get away with it? No. Why not? Because their choice of criminal actions voluntarily relinquishes their right to free choice, whereby their (laboratory manufactured) DNA patents are rendered void from inception. They have walked out on life freely. They gave up their freedom willingly. Exercising their own free choice, they volunteered that death be their God. Natural law will deliver the consequence of their actions, but only if the people call them out. If we tacitly consent, we reap the consequences of our action.

Our task is to apprise political criminals of these immutable facts with irrevocable certainty that no defence on their part is ever possible. Can that be done?

Yes, absolutely it can. How? By uniting our human conscious process with the lessons offered by the United States Declaration of Independence. These principles, presented below, will hopefully show you the only road forward with clear and unwavering certainty, one never attempted in all history.

You will recall me describing that our cognitive free will is (axiomatically) positioned between the subconscious faculties of perception and muscular activation. Therefore, we are the indisputable author of all our actions, automatically responsible for their consequences as natural law determines. Nothing can alter that fact save death.

No change to our DNA by any man or woman can alter that fact without such actions confessing the perpetrator's free choice to violate their (own) nature. That action annuls any claim made and holds them fully accountable for all detrimental and harmful consequences of their actions. That is natural law and natural justice.

'Conscious Ascendance' showed how the strategically sandwiched location of cognitive free will warrants independence and individual rights. Furthermore, our sequential mental process delineates the matter of 'protection.' The subconscious mind cannot overrule free will, or we have no free choice. Neither can our will revoke the subconscious mind because its process is fully automated. Our Creator protected free will because our conscious process cannot function without it. That lesson is for us to learn.

Our (unalienable) right to life is individual and cannot be otherwise. Likewise, our (unalienable) right to property is personal and cannot be otherwise. Therefore, we must protect our rights and freedoms, period.

Four lessons concerning your [subject nation's] Declaration of Independence are now vividly clear.

1. Rights belong exclusively to every man, woman and child. No group of people or government may overrule, usurp, deny, or forbid those rights.

2. Individual rights must be enshrined and fully protected. We cannot abandon them to 'self-evidence.'

3. Because free will is self-activated, we must preserve its functionality without restraints. Moreover, since no life-supportive action can transpire without free will, it cannot be overruled, usurped, denied, or forbidden.

4. Happiness and free organic societies result.

5. Those necessities are a game changer beyond all else. Our Creator's message is indelibly and vividly clear. He intends we govern ourselves, which informs us that we do not elect anyone to control us. Jefferson's political philosophy came very close when he said, *"That government is best which governs least."*

We must ensure that free will remains free, that our DNA is not modified and that our right to life and property is free from all interference and theft. Further, whatsoever empires, monarchies, and governments infringe or violate those freedoms are (self-declared) natural outlaws. There can be no government whose legislation may gravely threaten our protections.

Just as neither of our two minds can prescribe the other's process, neither can any outside source do the same. All that we need, therefore, is a body of people charged with administering our protections and not one thing more.

Is there any precedent for such a thing? Yes, absolutely there is. Our bodily immune system, endocrine system, conscience and emotions all testify that cause unmistakably. The principle of protecting life, its means, and continuance is factually indisputable in our nature.

Now the phrase 'consent of the governed' is shown for the imposter that it is. It allowed our consent to be manipulated through propaganda, indoctrination, and even the perpetuation of conscious ignorance. In truth, humankind has long consented to uphold an evil dedicated to moulding our consent.

But it exists no more. To that end, it is vital *'consent of the governed'* be replaced with *'nature's consent to self-govern our freedom within the equal rights of all others.'*

No obstruction, denial or cancellation of our lives by self-declared outlaws is valid because their wilful choice to abandon their own life renders their prescriptions, statutes, orders and laws void from inception.

Are you beginning to grasp what a free society truly is? Do you see how your [subject nation] now has a gifted opportunity to stamp the phrase 'free nation' on the world map?

Jefferson correctly identified that divine rights belong to individuals. All subsequent authoritarian rule arose from not protecting those rights and freedoms. Self-evidence will never suffice. Fortunately, we now have proof of what does. Protection is immutably encrypted in our nature, making it impossible to erase, even by DNA pirates.

The 'natural rights' spoken of by Jefferson were the right to life which requires each individual is free to work and acquire property and pursue happiness. In political terms, we also possess the natural right to defend our life, liberty, and property from invasive attack. It was the government's (initial) purpose to use its defensive power of force to repel all assaults on our rights and freedoms. Should it overstep that boundary, it becomes the greatest tyrant and plunderer. Moreover, when government maintains a virtual monopoly of force, its potential for evil is far greater than any other individual or institution.

Jefferson's position on foreign policy did not extend to equipping the government to remake the world to America's liking by force. Indeed he expressed his foreign policy in this classic phrase: *"Peace, commerce, and honest friendship with all nations — entangling alliances with none."* So we read in the American Declaration of Independence—

"that whenever any Form of Government becomes destructive of these ends, it is the Right of the People to alter or to abolish it, and to institute new Government, laying its foundation on such principles and organising its powers in such form, as to them shall seem most likely to effect their Safety and Happiness."

Two fundamental considerations are present.

1. First, no man has a mandate from God to rule over other men, nor any right to do so. No emperor, king, monarch or government is a superior moral agent with rights over any man or woman without the people's express consent on full disclosure; everyone individually! Such 'consent' cannot ever be universally or collectively obtained ' To do so is to dictate that majority consent must overrule minority dissent, which (lauded)' democracy' almost inevitably results in gang warfare that is nigh impossible to prevent.

2. Second, societal mayhem is inevitable when consent is given only to the government institution but never to its separate legislated laws. Coercion and force that holds us captive, all rights and freedoms banished, is not consent.

Two lessons are crystal clear. Rights are singular, not plural. Our rights and freedoms cannot be abolished, but governments can.

For that, the American Declaration of Independence offers clear direction.

> *"Prudence, indeed will dictate that Governments long established should not be changed for light and transient causes; and accordingly all experience hath shown that mankind are more disposed to suffer, while evils are sufferable than to right themselves by abolishing the forms to which they are accustomed. But when a long train of abuses and usurpations, pursuing invariably the same Object evinces a design to reduce them under absolute Despotism, it is their right, it is their duty, to throw off such Government, and to provide new Guards for their future security."*

Throwing off the government is not just an option today. Our emphatic moral duty is to charter a new nation using the political principle that Jefferson launched. **Any government that fails to protect the people's rights and freedoms must be banished.** All governments, any time, any place. The most important question remains. If it is only necessary to preserve people's right to life, their freedom and pursuit of happiness, is any government needed at all?

My answer is a resounding no, but self-governance is needed, most assuredly. There is no better quest than to abolish what punishes us, accept our God-given rights and freedom and protect both in perpetuity. For that, Creator has our back. Everyone is blessed with all means necessary to institute free societies, doubly blessed by the fact that all trespassers and outlaws wilfully confess crimes against humanity by their very actions.

Accordingly, 'Nature's consent to self-govern removes all need for government reliance on 'consent of the governed.' No need for government remains, provided we respectfully and responsibly engage our free will and rights and ensure both are protected from all trespass, henceforth and forever.

Advisory notes concerning independence

What follows demands your study and comprehension. Your critique and suggestions may well apply to the people of your nation. The form and substance of the Declaration (given below) closely approximate the American Declaration of Independence, mainly for reasons already given. In form, it contains the same three parts: a preamble, a list of grievances, and then a statement of rationalised rebellion invoking the charter of a new nation. It references all people's unalienable and inalienable rights to life and freedom consistent with the pursuit of happiness, jointly embracing the Charter of Individual Rights described in chapter eleven. Both documents advisedly read as though one.

A 'Protectorate' replaces government, defined as a state or national body charged with Constitutionally protecting the rights and freedoms of the nation's States and their people, domestically and internationally. This definition denies any legislative amendment, violation, usurpation, or abolition.

The preamble introduces the conceptual principle of 'new Protections,' hence abolition of government, not replacement. This concept is unprecedented — no such thing has ever transpired before because the form and powers of natural law encrypted in our human nature were not previously known. Therefore, consent to the rights, freedoms and powers within those laws is established and non-erasable. And that assuredly confirms the people's Safety and Happiness, according to 'Nature or Nature's God,' to use Jefferson's words. Differently said, people's (self-governing) compliance with the natural laws of their nature attests to their (freely given) indisputable consent for absolute protection of their Creator's gifted rights and freedoms. No further permission is needed, now or ever!

Thus freedom and lawful protection manifest in society using the exact principle governing free will, absent any added prescriptions, instructions, statutes, or law. No better form of self-governance exists, nor can it.

The Declaration below lists multiple grievances in topic form rather than using particular descriptive words. Astute readers may seek assistance in drafting such a document, from intellectuals versed in lawfulness versus legality or from students of jurisprudence. Several vital issues include but are not limited to travesties concerning original sovereign peoples, people of all ages, all forms of government, changes made without the people's consent, fraudulent identification through the legalese, tradable birth certificates; in short, the whole gamut of authoritarian domination and control, past, present, and future planned. The list should be explicit and tight, pertinent to abolishing governments existing in name only.

Immediately following the list of grievances, words should summarise the whole list. They should describe that all committed crimes against the [subject nation] people are indisputable facts. Consequently, they warrant immediate abolition; no invention for dramatisation is permissible.

The next paragraph exposes immorality and injustices and concludes with the principle of natural justice whereby (outlaw) practitioners self-confess criminal actions. In other words, everything in the document must uphold all of the Life-sustaining natural law principles that our human nature reveals, such that no objection may surface without disputing human nature itself. Such a watertight case necessitates eliminating any phraseology, words, concepts or principles that undermine its cause, and all sentences cross-examined regarding their statement. Further, any anomalies, dichotomies or ambiguities must be removed, even across all paragraphs and pages.

The best legal, lawful, philosophical, and psychological minds will deeply scrutinise such a document. It must therefore point all readers to the source of natural law in our nature, unequivocally, no sidetracks permitted. (Refer to my book,' *Conscious Ascendance.')* Dissenters must be left no argument but to dispute the nature of what they are, thus negating all dispute. Our task is to ensure that result, and that no escape is possible.

My second last paragraph explains the [subject people's] divorce from all government, government affiliations and treaties with all corporate or governmental entities, whether foreign or domestic, all being no longer applicable. Again, the sovereignty of the people means divorce from all who would violate that sovereignty, all foreign and domestic agencies, corporations and governments. Finally, the paragraph draws attention to implementing a 'Protectorate Constitution' necessary to institute and commission the 'Protectorate' body.

The final paragraph delivers the outcome of all that proceeds it. As concisely and accurately as space permits, it established the new nation, its lawful parameters, the non-erasable source of those foundations, and the self-governance of all its people. We must remember this document cannot be read or comprehended in isolation. Without knowledge of the source of natural law and with no relevance to justice, rights, and freedom, no measure of its authenticity or validity is possible. The same applies to all associated documents, such as a new Constitution for [subject nation], and the Charter of Individual Rights.

Speaking from experience, any discussion concerning these matters almost inevitably results in someone saying, "but what about...A or B or C." Importantly, one does need to know the whole story to comprehend the derivative parts. Yet, the big picture is almost unexplainable without grasping the component parts. It's a catch-22 situation. So, choose very carefully with whom you discuss these matters. As addressed elsewhere, the revision of our whole education system is urgent across the board, but most notably in the human and mental health sciences.

[Subject nation] Declaration of Independence

When in the Course of human Events, it becomes necessary for the People of the [subject state] to unilaterally dissolve the Political Bands that once united them but that now abjectly make them slaves to a corporatised sociopathic conglomerate, so to assume among the Powers of the Earth, the separate and equal Station to which entitle them, a decent Respect to their immutable ' right to life' requires that they should declare the causes which impel them to the Separation, and their unalienable right to regenerate [subject state] in perpetuity.

Self-evident truth holds that all Men are created equal in nature, unique in expression, endowed with the unalienable right to life, freedom and pursuit of happiness, and inalienable right to the fruits of their labours. That whenever any instituted Form of Government becomes destructive of those rights and freedoms, it is the Right of the People to alter or to abolish it, and to institute new Protections, laying their Foundation on such Principles, and deriving their just Powers from such Form as the Laws of Nature and of Nature's God encrypted in the human nature consent, that assuredly attests will effect their Safety and Happiness.

Prudence indeed dictates that established Governments should not be changed for light and transient Causes and that Mankind appears more disposed to suffer without appeal than to right wrongs by abolishing sufferance stealthily enacted with increasing force and violence over generations. But when abuse, usurpations, initiated force, and insufferable trauma in pursuit of overt dictatorial, communistic objectives evince absolute Despotism absent relief, it is their right, indeed their Duty, to throw off such government and to provide new Protections for their future

Comforts and Security. Such has been the patient Sufferance of all [subject state] Peoples, recently exacerbated to unmitigated genocide, which urgently adduces them to abolish all former Systems of Government, indeed the very concept of government, and begin anew. [Subject state] colonisation reveals a History of repeated Injuries and Usurpations, later transformed without People's referendum to a 'corporate service provider absent de jure government' having in direct Object the Establishment of an absolute Tyranny over these States vested in communistic world control; a 'new world order.' In proof thereof, let Facts of criminal violation of Man's right to life be submitted to a candid World.

At this juncture, a Nation would write its grievances succinct, accurate, and all-encompassing. Some examples might include–

So-called government in [subject state] has made itself a barbarian, authoritarian, mentally deprived troglodyte of regulation and prohibition; an autocratic state of force enacting acts of brutality and savagery'; the terrorist capital of the world.

It stole the 'life' and 'right to life' from every citizen through fraudulent 'birth certificates,' declared them legal wards of the state; instituted 'Maritime Law' in which courts no 'judge'" has a word for a man or woman.

It has granted revenue gatherers tyrannical powers of search and seizure; to vest those confiscations of private savings and possessions in maintaining and expanding incorporated bodies posing as [subject state] governments, including countless parasitic freeloading and exploitative agents.

Registration has deprived people of ownership over their lawfully acquired lands and their cars, vesting actual ownership of such lands and vehicles in government and its agents.

So-called government in [subject state] has grown bloated from manipulated inflation and use of confiscated money, further securing its powers to force the populace to exist in a 'state of animality' utterly forbidding their 'unalienable right to life,' contemptuously spitting in our Creator's face.

The government has erected a multitude of parasitic bureaucracies, most of which drain the budget and contribute nothing but swarms of agents and officers that badger the people, confuse their minds, and eat out their substance to desperation, homelessness, and suicide.

It has forced all members of the populace to identify themselves on demand, utilising fraudulent identification constructed for (legal) persons and reserving powers of arbitrary detention, arrest, or fines.

It has disarmed the populace, forbidden their unalienable right to bear arms to defend their own lives and properties, while most egregiously failing any substitute protection.

It has seized children from their parents and forced their vaccinations absent parental consent, with entirely untested experimental mRNA injected Covid medical experiments. Through the same ('voluntary') procedure, it bribed and coerced mandatory poisoning.

That list should conclude with a clause such as this.

The government has willingly and voluntarily turned its back on life itself; such outlaw behaviour is voluntary abdication from any lawful right to administer the [subject state] people.

The document should conclude with summations such as this.

Falsely acclaimed [subject state] government has committed itself and its agencies to ensure that the unalienable individual rights of all who maintain and uphold it never exist. Forbidden redress through immoral (legal) rules, deception, and corruption in defiance of a free people, all [subject] people remain insanely and criminally forced to uphold bloody-minded tyranny as the only liberty possible! Such tyrannical rule indisputably confirms that the corporate entity named the '[subject state]' is illegitimate and criminally liable.

When Statutes constrain men and women contrary to their nature due to any fictional or covert invention, and when criminal abuse, usurpations, and violation of Man's right to life, reduce existence to animal-like status under absolute despotism, cessation of insufferable criminal evil demands. When injuries, violence, and usurpations consistently repeat for the direct object of tyranny over Man, the 'moral right to rule' and 'immoral wrong to refuse rule,' is a historical criminal fact open to all seekers of truth no need to re-state it. No leniency is warranted; unlawful actions self-confess crimes against humanity.

We, therefore, the One People of the [subject state] on/in [subject location], assemble in appeal to the Supreme Judge of the World in Rectitude of our Intentions to solemnly Publish and Declare that the [subject states] of [subject Nation], of right, be one Free and Independent Nation. Thereby it's [states] and all peoples absolved from Allegiance to [subject government/authority] — all political Connection dissolved inclusive of all non-elected bodies, assemblies, incorporated entities and all other partisan authorities/agents, wherever located. People of a Free and Independent Nation have the right to maintain National Defence against all enemies, Foreign and Domestic, conclude Peace, contract Alliances, establish Commerce, and do all other Acts and Things which Independent Nations and States may (of right) do.

This document, rendering void all previous constitutional and quasi-constitutional documents, now renders the [Subject] Nation reconstituted, founded on the Rights and Laws of Nature and of Nature's God encrypted within every man, woman and child as set forth in the [subject state] Declaration of Individual rights, whereby the [subject] people shall through self-governance delineate, enact and uphold such Natural Laws, Rights and freedoms in perpetuity. For this Declaration in securing and protecting life, reason, and freedom respectful of all in human affairs, we pledge our diligent, most reverent commitment and our sacred honour.

© Author - Signatories named and autographed

Explanatory notes: The Preamble text (above) resembles the 1776 American Declaration of Independence, attributed to America's Founding Fathers, Thomas Jefferson, mainly. However, there are some fundamental differences of crucial importance that may make the preamble and closing texts incomprehensible without their understanding. Let me explain.

Human consciousness has revealed twenty natural laws that, although never spoken of before, offer great personal benefit, in addition to presenting the Creator's model for free organic societies, never witnessed in history. Therefore, health professionals should properly promote health through nutrition and natural remedies, only falling back on pharmaceuticals when all else fails. Likewise, societal professionals should promote social well-being and comforts through education concerning human nature, natural law, ethics, and morality, only falling back on natural justice when moral actions fall off the rails.

That is precisely how natural law works. It invokes ethical thoughts and moral actions, It advises. It monitors, It upholds free will, thereby amplifying respect for the lives of all others. And there lies the previously (never explained) truth. *Natural law never rules. It cannot ever do so since overruling our free will violates natural law.* That principle is encrypted in our human nature in several places, particularly in human consciousness. Implementation of that principle is a giant leap forward. It monumentally slashes the governmental workforce and returns countless thousands to productive work. It gives common law many-fold more impetus than it ever had, but with one proviso. Natural law rules that even common law cannot govern; and that's the good news. As I've said for some years now,

"any society that elects forcible rule deserves all the tyrannical force that its rulers initiate." That is today's condition exactly.

Now look at the last line in paragraph two —" *organising its Powers in such Form, as the Laws of Nature and Nature's God consent and assuredly attest will effect their Safety and Happiness."* For centuries humanity has insisted on rule by *'consent of the governed.'* People still see that as their solution, even pleading for Citizen Initiated Referendums (CIR) to provide it. Guess what? That does nought but further grant and endorse the Moral right to rule and the immoral wrong to refuse rule. Humankind has it all back to front.

It should properly be the moral right to refuse rule and the immoral wrong to rule. That is what Creator consented when He encrypted natural law in our biological and psychological processes. Hear me out, please. If we eat toxic food, we suffer and perhaps die. That is how natural law governs the consequences of our behaviour while fully preserving our free will'

Now, look at the last paragraph of the document. *"that [subject people] shall through self-governance delineate, enact and uphold such Laws and Rights; and for this Declaration in securing and protecting life, reason, and freedom."* Securing and protecting life, reason, and freedom means that free will must never be overruled, which means no commandments. That means no authoritarian tyranny can ever exist again, provided that freedoms and our right to freedom are wholly protected.

All that remains is to protect the 'Protectorate' from anyone who would violate its Charter of Protection. To that end, consider a society whose free choice is preserved through natural law, backed with Natural justice that deals only with outlaws; those who, choosing to step outside natural law, confess crime by their actions. They are the only people with which the law must deal. Why? Because they voluntarily relinquish their freedom. Only free people can choose. Natural justice is concerned only with restoring the natural order, the Natural law.

Is there a need for Government to administer road, sea, and air travel or building construction? Not when groups of people already perform those tasks under rules long established. Those 'companies' have already written 'rules' for safe passage or conduct for employees and public protection. We all have the right to accept those rules or refuse them. By that choice, we preserve free will and outlaw tyranny!

The List of grievances is open to suggestions from the nation's people. Paragraph 3 of the Summary clauses reading *"non-elected bodies, assemblies, incorporated entities and all other partisan authorities/agents,"* refers to such bodies as the UN, WHO, CDC, BIS, Federal reserve, SEC in Washington and such like bodies in the UK and Europe, far too numerous to list. Paragraph 4 follows from the preamble to amplify its content regarding directive and consolidation.

A Declaration of Independence prepared along these lines will free the peoples of all nations and countries from oppressive regimes and tyranny exercised by authoritarian governments and dictatorships. After that, the nation's people must establish and maintain free societies within their state or national borders.

> *"If you want something you have never had, You must do something you've never done. Thomas Jefferson*

Natural law principles are those of *"nature or nature's God."* No more is needed. Any additional safety or security rules must be closely scrutinised not to trespass on the natural law they uphold. That is what the next chapter facilitates.

Chapter 11

11. Universal protection of Individual Rights

The immutable principle of individual rights is indispensable to free societies. Yet, today, individual rights are evaded, distorted, perverted and denied. So seldom are they discussed; it is small wonder freedom is so scarce. This chapter is devoted to their implementation and societal protection, never to be repealed.

A collectivist tyranny dare not and indeed cannot enslave a country through outright confiscation of its values, be they material or moral. Instead, internal corruption is used, like plundering a country's wealth is accomplished through inflating its currency. Apply that principle to the realm of rights, and one sees that newly promulgated 'rights' sprout like flowers in springtime so much so that people fail to notice that the meaning of the word 'right' is reversed. Just as bad money drives out good money, these 'printing-press rights' aided by 'fact checkers' negate authentic rights. How is it done? By switching the concept of rights from the political to the economic realm.

Please keep the meaning of the word 'right' in your mind as you read this list from many years ago.

1. The right to a useful and remunerative job in the industries, shops, farms or mines of the nation.
2. The right to earn enough to provide adequate food, clothing, and recreation.

3. The right of every farmer to sell his products for him and his family to enjoy a decent living.
4. The right of every business person, large and small, to trade in an atmosphere of freedom from unfair competition and domination by monopolies at home and abroad.
5. The right of every family to a decent home.
6. The right to adequate medical care and the opportunity to achieve and enjoy good health.
7. The right to adequate protection from the economic fears of old age, sickness, accidents and unemployment.
8. The right to a good education.

What is the one question that smashes every one of those 'pretended' rights? Answer. *"At whose expense?"*

None of those things grow in nature. Men and women produce goods and services. What' right' exists for some people to command others to provide them? Our entitlement to the products and labours of others deprives those suppliers and workers of their rights and condemns them to slave labour. An alleged 'right' of one individual, which necessitates the violation of the rights of another, is not and cannot be a right at all! There can be no right to impose an unchosen obligation, an unrewarded duty or an involuntary servitude on another individual. There can be no 'right to enslave.'

The right to life does not mean that others must provide us with the necessities of life. Instead, we each have the right to support our life through work on any economic level, as high as our ability will carry us; take the financial actions and risks necessary to earn property and dispose of it. That does not mean that others must provide us with material property.

Likewise, the right to free speech is unalienable. We have the right to express our ideas without danger of suppression, government interference or punitive action. That right does not mean that someone must provide us with a lecture hall, a radio station or a printing press to convey our ideas.

Every undertaking involving more than one individual requires the voluntary consent of every participant. We each have the right to make our own decision, but no right to force our decision on any other individual or group.

There can be no 'right to a job,' instead the right of free trade, being the right to take a job if someone elects to hire us. There is no right to a house, only the right to build or buy a home. There are no rights to a fair wage or price if no one chooses to pay. Consumers have no rights to dinner plates, surfboards or cars, if producers choose not to manufacture them, but we have the right to produce those products ourselves.

Likewise, there are no 'rights' of any particular groups, no rights of farmers, workers, businessmen, employees, transport workers, the old, the young, the unborn, or students. There are only the individual rights that every living man, woman and child already possesses as an individual. Private individuals are not a threat to other's rights or freedom.

The conclusion is self-evident. Those who resort to commanding other people's choices have chosen to be criminals, against which actions we have lawful protection, established and authenticated by our immutable right to life.

For decades, 'collectivists' have propagated that a private individual's refusal to finance an opponent violates the opponent's right to free speech, an act of 'censorship'. Furthermore, a media outlet's refusal to publish writers whose ideas oppose its policies is considered censorship—likewise, (purported) censorship through ratings, network advertisements, and affiliates which reject particular programming. Similarly, governments may threaten to revoke the any television station licence that does not comply with their views on programming.

Did it ever occur to these people 'censorship' is a term pertaining only to governmental action? No private action is censorship. No private individual or agency can silence another or suppress a publication in a free market. Authors find another publisher. Only governments have regulatory censoring authority. An individual's freedom of speech includes the right not to agree, not to listen and not to finance one's, own antagonists.

Today's false view of censorship includes such doctrines as the 'economic bill of rights.' That means an individual has no right to dispose of his property and efforts using the guidance of his convictions; meanwhile, other speakers or propagandists have a 'right' to that person's (intellectual) property and money.

To deny the expression of ideas deprives our right to hold any views or opinions. Accordingly, one individual or group acquires the 'right' to unlimited license, while others reduce to helpless irresponsibility. It remains that so long as people falsely debate 'economic rights,' individual rights are further cancelled.

The right of free speech is the freedom to advocate one's views and bear the consequences, including disagreement, opposition, unpopularity and lack of support. Free speech protection does not protect against those outcomes; instead, it protects dissenters and unpopular minorities from forcible suppression. It does not support or guarantee their advantages or reward popularity they have not themselves gained. On the contrary, it lets them build benefits or popularity as any creative enterprise should, still allowing them to achieve less or none.

Before exploring 'rights' protection further, here is a repeat description of individual rights in chapter Five.

- **Unalienable rights** deny all authoritarian rule. Our right to life is unalienable; all trespass, violation and aggression of our right to life are outlawed.
- **Inalienable rights** deny confiscation of our lawful property. Our property, an item, or product, can be aliened, but no one can take our (labour of love) right to produce it. Theft, and eminent domain, are outlawed thereby.

Societies necessarily need an institution charged with protecting our rights, words, deeds, works, and property from all infractions and destruction.

Likewise, we must ban governments who, through fraudulent birth certificate issuance, seize our lives as their property from day one.

The independence and freedom of every man, woman and child necessitate two fundamental initiatives.

1. Drafting of a Charter of Individual Rights, making it accessible to all people, and teaching it.
2. Ensuring that individual rights are widely understood in terms of freedom, respecting the equal rights of all others most importantly.

This chapter addresses the first requirement, while my book *'Conscious Ascendance'* addresses the second. Again, education plays a pivotal role, as discussed in Chapter Twelve.

Australian people and those in many countries have never had a declaration or 'Charter of Individual Rights' that protects their people against infringement from public officials. Since 'rights' are forever social, not individual, no such document is ever written.

Protecting individual rights in the face of (believed) communal rights poses a unique question. Should individual rights be written 'proscriptively,' such as to ban or to render one or more activities unlawful? Alternatively, should individual rights be written 'prescriptively,' which means to prescribe, thereby allowing or offering one a solution or cure? Observe that Lawmakers proscribe (forbid) certain activities, while a physician will write a 'prescription' that advises or directs.

Thus it must be decided how individual rights will be framed and written. What form will they take? For example, will they expressly state that you have the right to free speech, which is the prescriptive version? Or will it be written that no one may forbid your free expression, which is the proscriptive version?

Let's explore this matter because, as previously described, our unalienable) rights are essential to reason and volition. We can no more transfer our right to life than our ability to reason or receive emotional reports is transferable. Therefore, it is practically but not legally impossible for any government to claim jurisdiction over our rights.

Taxation is a classic example of stealing our rights under a (purported) social contract. Governments know that we have no legitimate complaint about breaches of such rights so long as it first gains legal jurisdiction through our consent in a *'social contract.'* That explains why we all must consent to be (unlawfully but legally) transformed from sentient living beings into fraudulently concocted LEGAL ENTITIES via the birth certificate.

Logically, therefore, such social contracts are lawfully void. No excuse for violating unalienable or inalienable rights exists. Furthermore, tiny right violations that even just governments occasionally commit may readily morph into deliberate and inexcusable violations committed by oppressive governments. Thus 'individual rights' protection is vital.

America's founders seemingly understood a distinction between unalienable rights and inalienable rights, but not, I suggest, the difference between our (unalienable) 'right to life' versus our (inalienable) 'right to property.' That, as previously mentioned, is my distinction. But unfortunately, the ambiguity concerning those words over centuries has allowed our right to life to merge disastrously into a social contract that smashes our God-given rights. Dare I say that was the purpose of the ambiguity all along?

We should categorically define unalienable and inalienable 'rights' from the outset to cancel any misinterpretation or misjudgment. Said differently, in keeping with how natural law works, our rights must confirm that harmful actions testify to their abrogation, trespass or violation as proof of guilt. Beneficent, constructive and joyful outcomes testify proof of cause likewise. Justice is a two-way street.

Previously I asked whether it be 'prescriptively' stated whether we have the right to free speech, or 'proscriptively' that nothing might transgress our right to free expression. Think about it. If you have the 'proscriptive' right to free speech, then your action of speaking is rightful. No one can deny it. No challenge or penalty applies. Additionally, if someone denies your 'proscriptive' right to life and property, their wrongful actions are on trial. Do you see? 'Proscriptively' written rights clearly show that trespassers of your rights express guilt through harmful actions.

Conversely, 'prescriptively' written 'rights' are wide open to interpretation. All evidence is available to presumptive attempts to clothe evidential facts with a 'right.'

In simple terms, you are not granted a right. You are protected from anyone denying or forbidding your right to life, including such as free speech.

Justices must decide civil law matters on prior agreed 'contractual terms and conditions,' not individual rights. That is excellent news because a charter of Individual Rights will be based only on the twenty natural laws. That denies all social contracts instantly. Nothing exists to confuse any trespass of one's God-given rights with the lawful 'right of resistance.' Civil cases are ordinarily outside the scope of such rights and resistance. Should criminal actions also be present in Civil matters, they will serve only to aid resolution through the virtue of outcomes readily established.

Some say our right to life, as a flesh and blood living being, has existed since homo sapiens emerged. That's a great thought, but it is fundamentally flawed. Its premise is that Man's rights apply collectively, meaning that rights are born of society. Truth is different. Your right to life began the instant you were born. You became independent. Before that moment, you were a (dependent) potential human being, not an (independent) living being. Neither before nor after were you ever a fictional legal entity. Neither did nature leave any window of opportunity for the government to declare you their chattel sneakily. Those who strip you of your right to life have no such right or claim of right.

Some ten years ago, I wrote a (universal) Charter of Individual Rights to be read strictly in conjunction with the (universal) Declaration of

Independence concerning establishing a 'Protectorate' in place of government. Should any discrepancy or ambiguity exist, the Charter of Individual Rights takes precedence. Here is a summation of that document, minus legal/lawful wording and phraseology.

The first article protects every individual's Unalienable Right to Life. All authority to command another refused. Trafficking of any part of the human body is outlawed, and no national individual is to be classified or treated as an animal.

Article 2 concerns everyone's Right to Life, Freedom, mobility and the Pursuit of Happiness, thought and action, travel, and privacy, unrestricted and without curtailment. The reference baseline is every Sentient Living Being's nature from being born of nature. Accordingly, no law or statute shall restrict or deny any individual unalienable right to life, freedom, and the Pursuit of Happiness, inclusive of a free-will choice of thought and action, choice of travel, and privacy; all guaranteed inclusive of the responsibility, liability, and accountability naturally and inherently flowing therefrom.

Additionally, no living human being separately or individuals collectively shall, regardless of purported authority, abrogate, subjugate, subordinate, fraudulently acquire, usurp, blackmail, invade, violate, commandeer, steal, arrest, confiscate, or detain the duly secured value of life, or one's property according to the principle of Natural Law.

The third article guarantees' Free Association' between consenting adults, including peaceable assembling or joining together in marriage or friendly association. Similarly, it forbids any compulsion to associate or join any association, whether civil, intelligence, police or military. No law or statute shall restrict or deny voluntary (consensual, uncoerced) association or interaction between consenting adults.

Article four dealt with equality, freedom of expression and privacy. First, the natural equality of all men and women establishes, with allowance for their uniqueness of form and expression. All aberrations such as transgenderism are thereby subject to individual rights and no other.

Nothing is permitted to deny free will or full consciousness, which testifies it. Nothing may preclude the right to biometrical identification of a sentient living being, such as their private property, as their testament of life for life's purpose. Furthermore, nothing may deny the free exchange of ideas, religion, speech, communication, expression, or assembly for economic, political or religious purposes, nor the right to voice public criticism against oppression and wrong-doing. Neither may any statute, law or directive countermand or obstruct the free exchange of ideas, freedom of religion, freedom of speech, freedom of the press, electronic, optical, or any other form of communication or expression. Freedom of assembly is also protected, and the right to physically gather or associate with others in groups for economic, political or religious purposes. Nothing may countermand or obstruct redress of grievances, opinions and views, which upholds the right of public criticism; or the right of the public to combine and demonstrate against oppression and wrong-doing.

Article five addressed physical and mental health. For example, no medical experiments, examination, or treatment of any kind may be given without informed consent following full disclosure. Additionally, a mother's right to life and choices within recognised medical practices protect unborn infants umbilically co-joined as a dependent. Her protection as an (existing) independent living being is imperative since she is the sole protector of the fetus during pregnancy and childbirth. Additionally, nothing may forbid what one chooses to inhale, drink or ingest; thus, no natural remedies or medications may be banned.

Article 6 delivered natural law to the 'age of independence.' Adults cannot enjoy free will whilst some unknown individual prescribes adulthood. Accordingly, this article explicitly permits a fifteen-year-old teen to choose and practice adulthood, always subject to their actions bearing adult fruit, any infringement instantly returning the offender to child status until age eighteen. This three-year window of opportunity implies parents' need to ingrain ethics and morality consistently throughout childhood, demanding a parental moral example. Offspring benefits are considerable, from peer approval to preferential employment opportunities during college.

This unprecedented initiative affirmatively reinforces that natural law governs the consequences of our actions and that free will protection is imperative to reaping demonstrable advantages never witnessed, save as observed amongst some indigenous tribes.

The seventh article ensures one's Inalienable Right to Property. Nothing shall cancel, forfeit, annul or alienate any Individual's right to own property free and clear of all encumbrances. Further, it establishes the right to protect one's right to property in such a manner as to preserve each individual's free will choice to gift, trade, or dispose of said value or property.

This article permits one's property to be aliened in service of an incurred debt but denies all compulsory acquisition for public use. Nothing shall deny one's right to be secure in person, home, papers, effects, reputation, and other properties, against unreasonable searches and seizures or arbitrary arrest and detention. Natural law maintenance defines all search or seizure of self or property.

Article Eight is the Right to Intellectual property. It describes copyright inherent in all original works regardless of particular notice, no different from what already exists. Patent holders have two years to market their product; else, the right to be the sole marketer expires, but not the patent rights, all cross claims to profits delineated.

No part of any life form shall be patentable, and no exception to this clause shall ever be granted. All past patents concerning biological organisms are rendered null and void without exception.

The ninth article concerns everyone's right to protection from harm. No one may initiate force, violence, coercion, blackmail, or fraud against any individual's life or property, and no slavery or involuntary servitude shall exist. Nothing shall deny the right to resist and protect against all transgression, trespass, and violation of life, while any individual separately or collectively may lawfully and morally use retaliatory force. Such arrest is lawfully limited to that necessary to prevent further force initiated against any individuals or their property.

One's right to defend against all foreign and domestic enemies, and the right to bear arms in self-defence is protected. No National Emergency, regardless of reason, shall negate or override any individual's right to self-defence.

The right of all individuals to preserve, protect and defend their life, liberty and property, and to organise with others into a private militia for that purposes, shall not be infringed.

All initiated force, coercion, blackmail, or fraud against any other individual's life or property is denied. No slavery or involuntary servitude shall exist, save as just punishment for a crime.

All inventions to create or impose a fictional (legal) entity contravening the nature and life of a living human being is prohibited. However, such incorporated identification is permissible for 'rules' for clubs sporting bodies, institutions, libraries and such like, where members voluntarily agree to and accept those specified 'terms and conditions.

No rights are ascribed or conferred to 'collective 'bodies. On the contrary, every individual has the Unalienable Right to dispose fully and freely of their body (life) or the fruits of their labours, strictly in non-violation of the rights of others.

Nothing may deny the right of an individual to organise the overthrow of a government initiating force against its people. Similarly, Members of the Armed Forces, private militia, intelligence, or police may disobey any order they have certifiably established conflicting with the rights and liberties in the Charter of Individual Rights.

In article ten, one's specified rights are reserved, upheld and protected in sum. Thus they may be referenced to a Nation's constitution document, as I later referenced to a 'Constitution for the Australian Protectorate.' Accordingly, article ten states that no Individual or Group of Individuals, regardless of asserted authority in or from any country or planet, may ever amend or abolish Individual Rights. Further, no exception shall ever exist or amendment made to the first nine articles.

That, as mentioned, is just a summary, absent lawful phraseology, abstentions and cross-references. The original document and the subsequent document drafted especially for Australia are copyrighted but accessible on the application for any nation's usage, provided the authored source is credited. All amendments must fall within the Proscriptive format, strictly confined to unalienable and inalienable rights, and the twenty natural laws encrypted in our human nature testifying immutable authenticity.

The American Declaration of Independence, is credited as the most definitive exposé of Man's individual rights ever written. Its protections of Man's life, as an individual, and not as a social animal, are clear, unequivocal, and unambiguous. Why then, is it not upheld as today's absolute standard? Having made such progress, what error, or omission, has allowed our right to life to be usurped, overruled, rejected, reviled, repressed, stripped from existence and denied practical utility?

There seems only one answer. Precisely because it was declared that *'life, liberty, and the pursuit of happiness,'* are *'self-evident truths,'* nothing on the political horizon of 1776 suggested any necessity to safeguard the essence and nature of those protections for eternity. All was self-evident then, was it not?

In retrospect, we should have fully protected our declared right to claim that right! It should have been proclaimed, 'the laws of nature and nature's God' pertain to our living being and therefore they must be forever protected from all usurpation or cancellation. Remember that while those laws are fixed, the content of our free will is not. Our right to act, includes the right to reject natural laws thereby slapping Creator's face, which, tragically, is humanity's history.

Our task, world-wide, is crystal clear. Unless we rid ourselves of a pseudo government that rules through force, including any compulsion to vote for its continuity, thus to substitute a 'Protectorate' that prevents reoccurrence, humanity as a species, is doomed. This chapter has explained a charter of individual rights, their implementation and societal protection, never to be repealed. While the defining text remains open for amendment, and for any nations adoption, this is no task for pretenders or intellectual apprentices. It is only for those having a thorough knowledge of law versus legality, additional to a full grasp of the human conscious process which defines the tenets of natural law. (Please refer to my book, *Conscious Ascendance*.)

Chapter 12

12. Revised Education

Authoritarian rule survives today because the human populace is ignorant concerning any alternative. Today's education strives in ignorance of consciousness; and whether accidental or intentional, fear propagates unchecked further wreaking conscious ability. Books could be written about the ills of our world, how the poor and underclasses are growing along with racial injustice and lack of human rights. The real issue is, what exactly will overturn all of that? What will end this human tragedy? What is the real cause and origin of such disasters? Beliefs have failed, consumerism is unconvincing, money has become a monster, conformance has not worked, and religion has no answer. Political change at the ballot box is a farce. If humanity does not wake up to itself and discover the actual cause, matters will get worse and fast. The solution is a radical overhaul of our education systems from bottom to top, especially its curricula. This chapter begins with that enquiry.

Humanity in every country is damnably mind controlled and, for the most part, does not know the mental wreckage that results. Our subconscious minds constantly suffer messages pleading to stay asleep, conform, submit, register, watch screens 24/7, buy, borrow, but never imagine, question, be independent or challenge authority. Anyone unable to think independently and who relies on outside influence, even if entertaining, is ripe to be ruled, dominated, and enslaved. From infancy, we are fed carefully constructed fiction having no resemblance to life's reality. An oligarchy rules us under the ruse of democracy, but whose end is fascism.

So-called government is nothing but private corporate interests whose only interest is money. We are treated as expendable resources to be used, abused and trashed, 'subjects' to be controlled. All that remains is to agree that fascism is not only practical but entirely necessary. That day is fast approaching, thus accelerating media censorship; digital monitoring of our lives and social credit ample witness.

The root cause is not fear. Ignorance is the cause. Fear is but one outcome that will remain until we each can overcome it. Society cannot. Fear is the partner of blind ignorance; because we do not know our consciousness, its processes and the natural laws that govern it.

We have become fearful of being diverted from a pacified life, mollycoddled through all persuasions intended to keep us in that mindless state. Social media leads us to believe we are knowledgeable, but not so. Intellectual thought scares many people senseless. We incessantly stare into electronic screens in restaurants, crossing the street, in taxis, busses and trains, at social functions and in school. Hand-held devices dominate young people's lives. They cannot let go, fearful their world will collapse should the battery go flat. Pressing the 'off' button to 'get a life' is considered a crime.

Absence of knowledge aside, should children be lied to, propagandised, stripped of their birthright and made a servant to the state, as happened to us? If they could learn even just the rudiments of their mental processes and how free choice is much more than a yes/no switch, do you think they might beg to know more?

Nothing teaches how tender young infants value-charge their subconscious minds, despite the fact they cannot speak, read, write, or use a smartphone. We've done it, so no more proof is needed. Later we learned the language but little about how concepts, principles, and values, most significantly, are personally and socially crucial to life. Who teaches how to upload life values to the subconscious mind today? No-one does. Because we know nothing about how full consciousness works, we know nothing about natural law freedom.

Grasping the truth of our nature is now imperative for humankind. Nothing has precedence, is more relevant, or is more urgent. Action is required, and knowledge before that. However, so long as human and sociological sciences refuse to study human consciousness, these laws will remain hidden; we and our children and grandchildren will suffer. On the other hand, knowledge of full consciousness and natural law will quickly dispel bogus philosophies and erroneous teachings; all false inventions left only one court of appeal — nature itself.

Almost every precept ever taught is called into question! This challenge applies to all schools and universities, all human and social sciences resulting from understanding the Creator's most precious gift of consciousness and the natural laws it reveals.

For too long, we have been taught dependency and acceptance, social conformity, anonymity, and the belief that the herd knows best, and we have suffered. Life, we are taught, is nothing more than a ceaseless struggle for mediocracy. Is this travesty of gross ignorance? Or is it (deliberately) concealed perversion of intellectual comprehension and natural justice purposefully intentioned for nefarious purposes or criminal gains?

Consciousness, spirituality, and natural law stand in complete contrast! They block ignorance and political crime, and that integrity begs urgent re-appraisal of psychology, psychiatry, philosophy, religion, politics, trade, competition, society, and political rhetoric of all flavours. Conscious knowledge and its governing laws challenge commonly held beliefs across all human sciences and sociologies. Even libertarians and voluntaryists cannot escape reappraising their premises. No human sciences can escape this questioning!

Do that, and you'll see everything is in place for the institution of free, organic societies founded on natural law, precisely as the Creator has modelled within the nature of every man, woman, and child. The truth of our nature is now the battle for humankind. Nothing has precedence, is more relevant, or is more urgent. Nothing past has described consciousness so fully or natural law so specifically. Their relationship is incontrovertible. You cannot have one without the other.

Organic societies are founded on the 'nature of those governed,' ensuring that consent is universal! 'Constitutional law' may then acquire absolute power never witnessed in all history, strictly provided 'unalienable rights,' freedoms, living identity and 'natural justice' are upheld and forever protected. No better precedent exists than to be self-governed according to our very nature.

So let's explore and challenge some of what we take for granted these days to grasp better how education must revise its curricula.

Quantum physics holds that the entire universe is only energy; hence we live in a vibrational universe. Thus arises the notion that reality is just an illusion. Reality is not illusory — that notion is the illusion. Knowing everything is energy does not explain how we can weld two pieces of metal, but not wood to metal.

Conscious ignorance conceals the fact 'perception' is tasked to uphold our life. Its process is to grasp an 'abstraction' of reality. It cannot grab, touch or hold a physical thing because it is not so equipped. In practice, therefore, it can only use an abstracted summation of what exists, which might be said to be illusory, but not so. The abstraction is authentic because it represents an existent thing or object, even movement. For example, our subconscious mind must perceive 'movement' as truthful because our conscious mind must deal with the (truthful) exactness of 'movement.'

Remember also that many animals can see, hear, smell, and feel with far greater sensibilities than we possess. Animals must have more finely tuned abilities because their lives depend on perception, not thought. We are not naturally deficient, therefore. Fish can swim better than ourselves but cannot build swimming pools. Eagles can see better than ourselves but cannot make microscopes or spectacles. In other words, our sensory abilities abstractly work with the reality of physicality.

That knowledge does not change science or neuroscience; instead, it shuts ignorance and opens the door to observational science and deductive reasoning.

Today, much use of the word 'reality' is nonsensical. Existence exists. It is what it is, so please understand the deception that befuddles almost everyone. To build a new coffee table or formulate a new idea does not 'create a new reality.' That is lazy speech, pure and simple.

Despite the table and idea being both new and real, neither redefines the meaning of the word 'reality.' Hence no 'new reality' has been created.

Such language is deceptively dangerous. Referring to every new thing, experience, or event as a new reality infers that *"it must be true because it is real!"* Blame political correctness, if you will, but this allows propaganda and outright lies to be widely accepted as true because they are new. Belief supplants truth based on perverted language, and humanity pays a hefty price. Reality is not an illusion, but our interpretation of it may well be.

Some say that a shift in consciousness will only occur when fifty-one percent of people, or more, devote themselves to serving others rather than serving themselves. Rubbish! The opposite is more likely true. Considerable benefits result from a shift in personal consciousness, from learning what consciousness is and how to employ it. How many others choose to do the same is irrelevant. We each may influence others to seek like benefits and advantages, but their choice to employ full consciousness is their own. Statistical group percentages are irrelevant to personal preference.

What is ego? Is it the acronym of 'Egotist,' or 'Egoist'? Egotistical behaviour, according to its dictionary definition, is believing oneself superior. An egotist may think they're more attractive, intelligent, rational, or (fill in the trait) than anyone else. That misconception is what is the word 'ego' commonly means. It is not some dominating power to be overcome, therefore. It is self-aggrandisement, a manufactured belief, easily displaced through choosing life values and employing them.

Because that outcome is self-beneficial, no comparison with others enters the picture. Accordingly, 'egoism,' remains in complete contrast with 'egotism', which, ethically, holds 'self-interest' as the foundation of morality. Moreover, self-interest implies life values, which emotionally result in self-esteem concerning oneself and one's independence.

'Selfishness' falls in the same basket of ill-used language. In the 1940s, selfishness meant *'concern with one's own interest.'* Today it is said to mean *'concern with one's own interest at another's expense.'* Misused language and political correctness find a very fertile breeding ground in the intellectual vacancy that results from not knowing what consciousness is or how it works.

Reverse that dire condition as explained in *'Conscious Ascendance'*, and education may be prudently revised.

Present-day education concerning consciousness is back to front! Today, scientific objectivity is pursued in laboratories, correctly as it should. Neuroscience is extremely valuable additionally. The problem is that while neuroscience is materially objective it ignores spirituality, thus objectivity is dissolved in ambiguity.

Tragically, our thinking has become flawed at the basic level of enquiry. When science rejects spirituality because it is unscientific, it denies the 'value' of mental content. Yet the spiritual significance of cognitive content is exactly why we possess consciousness. Consequently, we need a (mental-spiritual) regenerative educational program across all curricula. Even libertarians and voluntaryists are challenged to reappraise their goals.

We are blessed with consciousness to live the fullest, most beautiful, and bountiful life we can. Its study reveals the natural laws of our processes as objective science. That work can be greatly simplified, meaning that beginning from a tender age, we will all be taught the practice of choosing wisely, using reason, logic, and integrity, congruent with the laws of identity and causality, in a life-supporting manner. Further, natural laws are for our guidance, fulfilment, advantage and protection, knowledge, understanding, and blessed joy. Creator encrypted these laws within you so that: a) you could discover them and b) that no one could erase them. Nothing could be more objective than that.

Symbiotic communities will follow when our unalienable rights are genuinely honoured and protected. The more this forthcoming new era opens up, the easier it becomes.

Social education: Higher schooling

Let's now jump to the opposite end of formal education. We want youngsters educated in the real sense and better off than we were. But we are stopped effectively, stuck in Baby Boomer and Generation X mindsets. Although college offers economics, history, science, math, literature, philosophy, and classics, such courses are financially prohibitive. Worse, they are diluted and inadequate, thus failing to teach marketable skills. Add government student loans, and many students graduate (or do not graduate) with six-figure debts and useless degrees employers seldom prize.

Bad though, that is, it gets worse. Students often move on from university with world views hostile to property, markets, family, free speech, and even civilisation. All too often, universities are now gardens of socialism and transgenderism rather than exciting places for knowledge, ideas, and conscious development.

Colleges should properly be places of encouragement, imagination, development and growth that kids attend with eyes wide open. Building on their schooled knowledge of the conscious process, they can awaken to real options like never before. The gate then opens to a lifetime of self-directed learning. Instead of beginning their deprogramming, they build reliable, productive and spiritual programming, thus starting lifelong friendships and connections worldwide. Three barriers stand in the way.

1. Mental deprivation from not understanding the conscious process.

2. No-one grasps natural law as a result.

3. Apathy is acceptance of the status quo, with no effort made to understand how to implement radical change and take steps to protect those changes.

This book and *'Conscious Ascendance'* offer that platform. Those people who wish well for their children should not procrastinate. Learn of your dynamic abilities, exercise them, and fear will vanish. Wake up, speak up and act up. Your life hangs in the balance, and so does your children's lives.

This book has posed many viewpoints that differ from the standard acceptance, some more vital than others but all important nonetheless. So, although this list is incomplete, let's review some issues.

Existence:

The fact that 'existence precedes consciousness' is indisputable. Life must exist before any cognitive understanding of it, and that order is irreversible, or consciousness is a lie. Creator's natural laws of identity and causality certify existence. Unfortunately, many philosophies, ideologies and theologies such as mysticism, collectivism, subjectivism, altruism and (government) statism thrive on that ignorance. Governments will fight tooth and nail to reverse, subvert or fictionally replace our nature, never admitting that maintaining, upholding, or enforcing lies that defy one's nature is to spit in Creator's face.

Beliefs:

Bogus ideologies vanish when objective ethics and morals founded on the sanctity of life assume prominence. Because our conscious and subconscious mind processes blend as one, fake ideologies may quickly assimilate subjectivities as 'truth' without our knowing. Moreover, undesirable outcomes are almost inevitable when we abandon enquiry, investigation, and validation. Invented notions will then assume authority, readily coerced or enforced because all disagreement is considered unethical, immoral, or both. Free will is overruled. 'Authority' presides, purportedly, because Man has a 'tendency to evil.' No protest is possible; investigation, validation and truth are long abandoned. Morality then assumes a 'collective' prerogative that everyone must believe in, and free will suffers again. Psychology needs an urgent overhaul.

Errant Ideology:

When invented societal laws take root because seemingly that's all there is, results are entirely predictable. No valid checkpoint exists because all is subjective. Cause traces from bogus ideologies based on consciousness as the (emotional) arbiter of actual reality. Therefore, authoritarian government is an unchallengeable necessity, mainly because some non-thinking or agenda-driven individuals declared Man a social animal, never questioning their asinine assertions. Nothing will change while subjective ideology rules. Our conscious processes need a complete overhaul based on (spiritual) life values.

Deception:

Perception is always truthful. For animals, no investigation is possible, while we must enquire necessarily. Accordingly, our understanding may be false or misguided. That said, once convinced 'awareness' means 'understanding,' no enquiry seems necessary. Easily persuaded that the state is legitimately truthful, no investigation is warranted or even possible.

Does this explain how tyrants protect themselves and capitalise on false ideologies that subvert actual concepts and understanding? Do you see how they use the 'social animal' idea to forge universal acceptance of top-down control in all cultures and countries, thereby crushing all investigation into (their) state criminality?

Consent:

That you are an independent living being is a fact. Also, you are legally a 'citizen,' a fictional legal entity subject to (force-backed) statute laws. Government necessarily relies on you acting as your legal entity; otherwise, its fraudulent creation would remain the inert (dead) fiction it is. But fictional entities cannot open letters, read, write, speak, cook or drive. So you must apply, register, become licensed, vote, conform, and submit to every (applicable) rule of authority the government makes, and every statute it says is 'law,' because without your participation, as its legal servant, it has nothing. Consent of the governed initially assured protection of one's life; but no more. Today, consent means to give up life's values, submit to authority and obey its every command.

Law:

Government-administered 'positive law' (legally) countermands' natural law' and cannot do otherwise. If the government upheld the natural law, then no need for artificial laws would exist. To rule over Man, the government must cancel our right to life. Freedom to live, and freedom to rule, are antithetical. That which assumes supremacy outlaws the other, and this is the crossroad we now face. Law education needs urgent revision because immutable (existential) natural law replaces 'natural law theory.'

Evil:

Some people do err, and some commit acts of evil, but their actions are of their free choice, not a tendency. To conclude that Man has a 'tendency to evil,' and impress this upon us as truth to justify authority and law enforcement is to contradict or deny our free will nature. A biased will is not free.

Forced animality:

Conscious ignorance has permitted a legal condition that forces us to function in a state akin to animality, which requires we depend entirely on our automatic (subconscious) processes. But we cannot because we are not so equipped! Human sciences and social sciences are sadly lacking.

Right to life:

Our right to life is individual because life is indisputably singular. Because no collective liver, brain or stomach exists, so no group rights can exist. Unless a government upholds individual rights, then whatever rights it portends to support are imaginary. They are simply permissions, dressed as 'rights,' based on the rejection of natural law and every individual's right to life. Religion and spirituality must now reconcile.

Perception:

Perception is fuel for our conscious mind that prompts free will to think. Understanding is vastly different. The first is automatic, and the second is of choice. 'Conscious awareness' is a legitimate phrase. But taken to mean 'conscious understanding,' beliefs become synonymous with knowledge, so we are misled while firmly convinced we are knowledgeable.

Individuality:

Every Man and Woman is an individual being of creation. Therefore, the psychological notion 'family' is the smallest unit of society is false. This error is a core tenet of subjectivism, collectivism and the founding premise of statism. Philosophical education needs urgent revision, save for 'objectivist philosophy' that is already a country mile ahead.

Free will:

Freedom to think means we must not surrender the sovereignty of our mind to anyone, any belief, or any other. Nothing serves our thoughts, knowledge, or self-mastery when rulers, neighbours or imposters are the term-setters of our minds. Free will encompasses our responsibility towards others, not our responsibility for them. Unceasing respect for the lives of others is the only means to guarantee our freedom!

Process vs Content:

Our free choice to think and the process of thinking are two different things. 'Mental process,' distinct from 'mental content,' ranks near the top considering life's vital importance yet receives little or no attention in today's social and human sciences. Witness that Man agrees he can 'change his mind' but never 'influence his subconscious mind,' and you'll see how social and human sciences have failed to express the truth of Man's life on both counts. Left in this vacuum, not of our making, we readily fall prey to every salvation, mainly when the truth is considered less critical than fast relief from emotional distress. Ethics, morality, and natural justice must be repurposed.

Mentoring:

Given that our chosen values program our subconscious mind, emotions objectively inform whether our values are being upheld or hindered. Lacking investigation, however, our feelings establish nothing. Never before described as a mentoring system, the role of free will relative to conscience and emotions hails a complete overhaul of our human sciences.

Vocabulary:

Whereas the vocabulary of the conscious mind is word concepts, the subconscious mind uses an image vocabulary. For data to pass from the conscious to the subconscious mind, it must transmit in the language it will be received and understood. This transference helps to explain surreptitious mind control methods and the vital need for intellectual integrity.

Objectivity:

A significant difference exists between (objectively) knowing and (subjectively) believing. It is the difference between fact and fiction, life or death, morality and morality, and justness vs unjustness. The truth is such that it does not allow for knowledge, fact, life, morality and justness to be bent to someone's personal (or political) persuasion! The natural laws of identity and causality forbid it. Therefore, (invented) fictional ideas or notions are impressed on our minds as truth. Truth and falsity always remain distinguishable nonetheless. Our nature obliges that we learn the difference.

Education:

12. Revised Education

Literature concerning Man's six higher senses fails to distinguish between conscious and subconscious processes. We are thereby obliged to adapt to prevailing consensus or authoritarian rule because natural laws seemingly do not exist. Education concerning ethics and morality needs an overhaul—likewise, human sciences concerning our conscious and subconscious minds and emotions. Our nine higher faculties fit within this spectrum. Ethics can be included or made a core part of most disciplines. Consistency is more important than content, meaning the subject of ethics should underscore different curricula, not swamp any. In all of this study and revised education, omniscience or infallibility do not demand. Consider your potential because I gave you that secret in *'Conscious Ascendance.'*

> *"If in any two years of adult life, men could learn as much as an infant learns in his first two years, they would have the capacity of genius." —Ayn Rand*

Natural law vs Common law:

Natural law, in generic terms, refers to 'the order that governs the activities of the material universe.' Theologians and philosophers have long written tomes concerning what they understood as 'natural' law. They reached countless principles and problematic conclusions over centuries, many now entrenched in the authority of common law. Its legal system rests on 'stare decisis,' a legal principle where judges must respect precedents established in prior court decisions. The argument is that matters past 'settled' should not be disturbed. Much of the world's population lives in common law jurisdictions, particularly countries that trace their legal heritage to England as former colonies of the British Empire. Common law cannot indulge or even entertain natural existential law. Because each individual is the author of their actions, past precedents are completely irrelevant, twenty natural laws notwithstanding.

Objective Law:

Natural law is objective in that it upholds life; alternatively called Objective law insofar as teaching is concerned. Observe its crucial difference with statute law in criminal terms. Under statute law, 'one man punishes another.' (Rule, law, statute, regulation, commandment, presidential decree) Within natural law, 'one man or woman chooses to punish himself or herself,' hence the vital need to advise or educate people in advance concerning the principles of natural justice. (See

Chapter four.)

Justice:

Because one's choice to act switches from (thought / thinking) ethics to (actioned) morality, moral or immoral actions are divorced from ethical or non-ethical thinking that gave rise to them. Justice is concerned only with remediating wrongful acts thereby; not the correction of wrong thinking. That (preemptive) task is for human science education.

Spirituality:

We consciously or unconsciously choose spiritual values that our physical efforts should manifest. Two-way communion and communication between our conscious and subconscious minds are a value-based spiritual exchange. Thus we are spiritual beings living a spiritual life; each served via the existent reality that we adapt to our purposes.

In all, our nature and individuality are properly the central point of human and social sciences, not community. The science of Ethics should focus not on our actions but on our choice of values and evaluative processes. All of the above may seem intense or involved to some folk, but it is not. All reduce to simple principles that, when reiterated consistently and regularly, afford ample opportunities for implementation.

Social education: Ethics and morality

Should we keep an open mind in that regard? Whoa! An open mind is part of the delusion! It allows all truth and fallacy without distinction. A discerning mind far outweighs an open mind. Open enquiry is valid; discernment is its checkpoint. One searches for truth concerning one's life, which, when found, cancels all that is not. Questions cease when truth is released. Knowledge results, initial beliefs having served their proper transitional purpose.

Why have these simple explanations of life and natural laws escaped common knowledge or academia for so long? Isn't the answer clear? Follow the money and control, then escalate that principle. Switch ethics and morality from individuals to the collective and easily control millions of people. The ruse is exceptionally effective. Strip Man of personal values to control the human species under the guise of accepted morality, and everyone's thoughts, and actions, are yours to determine, thus rule. Man falls for this deceit and has done for centuries.

Many people speak of a higher power, believing it offers more and that we can profit from its proclamations. That is true, but we each are that higher power, as 'Conscious Ascendance' explains. Fail that understanding, and we quickly become victims. Bow to government as the (false) higher power, and we permit rule as it desires, including with violent force, while we're blind to the dynamic we have allowed. Power brokers know that their only power is yours and that your gift of it is all they need to control you.

Nothing but conscious understanding and action will smash false ideological conditioning, now centuries old. Because that process is not automatic, mental effort is needed, and your free choice must activate it. Ethics then become the summation of one's purposeful devotion to upholding life. That science will teach choosing wisely, using right reason, logic, and efficacious integrity, congruent with the laws of identity and causality, in a life-supporting manner. Ethics should properly teach Creator's personal invitation to live the fullest, most beautiful, and bountiful life possible. It should teach that natural laws are for your guidance, fulfilment, advantage and protection, knowledge and understanding, and blessed joy. Creator wrote these laws within you precisely so that you could discover them and no one could cancel them. Nothing could be more objective than that.

Science is awakening to the importance of our individuality and the connectedness of our conscious and subconscious minds as our spiritual essence. The more this path opens up, the easier it becomes. Those who fully understand our magnificent potential as unique individuals have no fear. They know that within their individuality from its very creation, their sustenance, welfare, freedom, and magnificence are theirs, always provided they claim them!

Social education: Economics

Henry Hazlitt wrote a book entitled *'Economics in one lesson.'* He hoped to reduce its whole teaching to a few principles explained in ways people would never forget. It worked. Although he relied on some stories from Frederick Bastiat, his impeccable capacity for logical thinking and crystal-clear prose shines through. The 'Mises Institute' says that his book *"is probably the most important economics book ever written in the sense that it offers the greatest hope to educating everyone about the meaning of the science."* I

It is an economics book for reporters, politicians, pastors, political activists, teachers, or anyone who needs to know. [Google the 'Mises Institute' and secure your free copy.]

Social education: Philosophy and psychology

Nothing but a drastic transformation in conscious ability will rid ignorance and correct today's social obscenities. Nothing but a healthy reappraisal of consciousness will free our destructive patterns and thrust us into a healthy state of collaboration with each other and our ecosystem. Until then, we will keep polluting our environment and minds, killing and destroying like an ignorant bunch of mindless automatons until everything is dead.

- Metaphysics has failed epistemology, thus philosophy.
- Philosophy has failed psychology.
- The psychology of consciousness has failed us.
- Human consciousness abandoned; collectivism fails society.

Having smashed through conscious or psychological ignorance, we must ask whether philosophy can also be called to account. The answer is yes, but with one proviso. Ayn Rand's Objectivist Philosophy stands head and shoulders above most all else. Indeed I believe it to be the only philosophy conducive to full consciousness, as explained.

Philosophy addresses how we gain knowledge, at least it should. The problem is that historical and contemporary philosophy, for the most part, is diverted from that true path. Its abstracted ways distract it from reality and splinter it from a psycho-epistemology concerning the acquisition of practical knowledge. How can we know our true purpose if philosophy does not pursue this course and impart that knowledge through our education programs? Belief supposedly fills the gap but falls woefully short.

Although never realised before, a revolutionary about-face of this magnitude is ours for the knowledge and willpower to achieve it! Full consciousness and its natural laws are our passports to humanity's glorious future. Nothing less will suffice!

First, we need to see and understand ideas in their proper context to life. Only then can we assemble many ideas and apply them to our lives and circumstances, knowing their sure success. Fear does not dissipate; instead, no platform offers on which to build. Moreover, if we continue to develop our knowledge and free ourselves from contradictions, our contextual database adds to our understanding. This synergy offers increasing reliance on our abilities, less fear, and a more remarkable ability to fit things together in other ways and in different situations. The more we consciously advance, the less fear holds sway.

Second, we need to develop our explanations and validations. It is prudent we express why some things are right and why competing explanations fail or are wrong. Without, we have two competitors and no means of establishing anything.

Third, a contextual benchmark is necessary, enabling us to measure progress. It should not rest on the past but on what thoughts and efforts will meet our future goals. Priorities matter because life is the bottom line. Any new idea must support and uphold your life and mine since no communal life exists.

Fourth, our explanations must add something to life in context or explain what is missing or false. Ideally, we must adequately distinguish what ideas are valid in context but lack in measure or application, i.e. a half-truth or part-truth. What, exactly, is to be gained?

Fifth, we must know how to apply knowledge – what will bring the outcome we seek. What is consciousness? What are its functions, and why do we have those and not others? How does our conscious process work? What in practice does it do? Can we direct it to attain the goals we seek, and how can we fully exploit our abilities? What might cause failings or a complete failure? What do we know, and how? How practical is our knowledge in life terms? How can we apply our consciousness for the most incredible efficiency, efficacy and pursuit of happiness? How does the conscious mind communicate with the subconscious mind?

That knowledge, hidden since the advent of Man, means we cannot reclaim our mental and spiritual birthright; thus, warmongering will continue. That is all explained in my book *'Conscious Ascendance.'*

A glorious future awaits our efforts. Our task is to seize it. We are each behoved to learn how natural laws apply to social dealings and how freedom, respect and responsibility are inseparable. We must know what we are, for only that will show us who we are. Only then can we proceed unobstructed, without fear or trepidation.

We ignore this potential at our peril. Evil pursues its path relentlessly and without remorse. Unless we stop evil authority dead in its tracks, as we must, it will prevent your life and mine as presently it intends.

We have the opportunity to declare our correct (political) living status as individual, living sentient beings under the protections of a 'constitution' founded on our nature and its natural governing laws. We have the keys to personal freedom and social liberty; a new sociological and political foundation, more ethical and moral than any employed in the past. Peace-loving, organic societies are not only possible, the likes of which the world has never witnessed, but nature itself impels we do so!

No one has yet witnessed a world where everyone moves freely through life with radiantly clear knowledge of their true potential, spiritual purpose, and authentic connection to the Source of everything. Free, prosperous, symbiotic societies based on natural law and justice are now for us to institute, whence all contrary consigns to history. So will arise an unprecedented, intellectually and spiritually advanced human civilisation, in which all are (Creator) blessed and protected.

We each have the wings to transform our lives beyond measure, thence to robustly transform society into what it should always have been. Philosophical objectivity founded on the supreme value of life is the only means capable of uplifting human society to a (life-value-based) spiritual plane never dreamt of in human history.

The Private Declaration of Independence (Chapter three) is strictly educational, written to enlighten people about their choices in life, and learn about natural law, its simplicity, truthfulness, elegance, and God-given foundation.

Your life is you. Your joy in this world is to live it and to thrive! Grasp the vital importance of those words, and declare your independence. Then, as more people do likewise, legal positivism will begin losing effect, thus fading to the point where free society and its protection will ascend, never to be quashed.

Chapter 13

13. Collaborative value transfer

For far too long, pupils and college students have entered the workforce on a treadmill of unsatisfactory striving, mainly based on memorising and acceptance, social conformity, beliefs, and how the herd knows best. And, beyond that, 'competition' is pounded into their skulls as the most profitable way forward. *'May the best one win,'* is a slogan no one dares challenge. But, should that standard win, or is there something seldom considered?

Here's an interesting question. How long would we survive if our body cells abandoned diligence, commitment, and devotion to their tasks and chose instead to put all like-minded cells out of business through dog-eat-dog competition, as we do in business today? Suppose our body organs joined this bunfight. Suppose the heart bought out the liver, deregistered it, and closed it for twelve months to remodel it as a second heart to increase blood flow – because blood is vital.

Do you see the senselessness of humanity's voracious appetite for competition? If competition became the primary motivation of every cell and organ in your body, nothing would work as it should, and nothing would serve its original purpose. All would be lost, and death most certain. Nothing better argues for cooperation when seeking happiness and thriving life. No one questions whether competition or collaboration is more productive or beneficial.

Most people believe that defeating competitors produces the best result and that no other business model could produce better. Yet, on closer examination, cooperation is vital to success. For example, one company's employees must cooperate within the company if it is to compete with another company successfully. Likewise, different companies will competitively tender for a large building or civil project and then be obliged to work cooperatively with many other companies under the directives of a project manager. Similarly, team sports offer great appeal because they provide each individual with the opportunity to compete and cooperate simultaneously.

As independent beings, 'cooperation' with others is to our foremost benefit. We can benefit from skills we do not have and contribute our skills that others do not. Teamwork synergistically produces benefits. The question is, will cooperation be our free choice, or will persons or authority dictate or forcibly coerce our involuntary cooperation?

The difference is clear, as Josiah Warren phrased it—

> *"One is in perfect accordance with a natural personal liberty which constitutes the chief element of the happiness of human beings, the other violates it and is the chief cause of the Bedlam-like confusion which pervades all ranks and conditions of mind."*

In determining the ground rules very carefully, as Warren saw necessary, we should question whether 'involuntary cooperation is possible. Should it not be called servitude? "Conscious Ascendance clearly showed that free will sandwiched in the subconscious process where it is fully protected. We should not compromise this protection in societal terms. As Josiah Warren insisted, natural laws—

> *"teach that our own happiness depends upon a proper respect for the happiness of others and that therefore we should not make social arrangements which require compulsion or the violation of the natural freedom of any individual."*
> Further, *"there must be no arrangements which depend for their success upon agreement on verbal rules or processes for agreements of opinions, tastes or interests. There should be, instead, preservation of the liberty of each person to differ in these and all other respects."*

13. Collaborative value transfer

To disagree with that position is to disavow one's nature. Indeed, as elsewhere shown, respect for freedom matched with voluntary cooperation, based on mutual exchange of value, produces almost unbelievable benefits, unknown in today's enterprise and trade that struggles and suffocates from cut-throat competition.

Massive problems develop when normal and natural processes are interfered with, most especially interference and regulatory imposts of governments, including myriads of taxes in some form or another. Many years back, a study computed that no less than three hundred direct and indirect taxes applied in getting one chicken's egg from its nest to the dining table. It takes little effort to see how this idiotic interference smashes cooperative effort. Businesses must compete to survive. Yet, these regulations and stipulations are so pervasive that we never see any alternative, much less the presumed need for authoritarian power in the first place.

Will the government ever be denied or cancelled? Not while it writes the legal and moral rule book that enforces compliance with gunpowder laws; meanwhile, human sciences ignore natural laws as though non-existent. Nothing will change while the 'collective' mindset continually disavows our independence and the natural laws of our being, instead preferring to be herded, branded, corralled and whipped as social animals.

America's founding fathers did not let any parasitic rules stand in their way. They declared the independence of one state from another. What then prevents us from expressing our freedom from all states? Nothing but refusing to say and practice the independent success of our very own nature, in personal and societal terms. We will not win our battle for freedom on our opponent's terms.

Our fight must begin with the very nature of what we are and ensure that freedom and individual rights survive perpetually. Success should ideally start with overhauling our education systems, as later described. Better yet, and left to our own devices, a productive blend between competition and cooperation is entirely possible, a collaborative business model.

Many years ago, I was fortunate to play a pivotal role in the success of a company that devoted itself to full market cooperation; in the rejection of dog-eat-dog competition. Its philosophy was simple and direct.

- Conduct research to find a market niche.

- Question precisely what value that market wants from the company's products.
- Discover how much customers are willing to pay for that product.
- Satisfy that market niche in full, refusing all diversions and distractions.

The method was simple. From specific research, design and build a model home and promote sales, then repetitively construct a replica home for each customer. Cosmetic variations were permitted but no structural alterations, much like car production but on a city-wide assembly line.

The company was consumer-driven, fundamentally, not competition driven. In a spiritual sense, it researched a sought-after value, agreed upon value exchange and delivered that value without compromise. Readers of 'Conscious Ascendance' will recognise that is how full consciousness functions; your success, physically, mentally, emotionally, and spiritually, but here translated into a business model.

In the traditional sense, the company still competed with others who produced like products. But, strictly satisfying only one market niche, it generated a product genre all its own, thereby divorcing itself from competitors. What others did was entirely irrelevant. Our biology and consciousness work in the same way. We each are unique.

Space precludes full description; suffice to say, this business model was a huge success. The company used further research to fine-tune products, making developments more attractive to consumers, and even educating buyers about the importance of good design. As a result, they became much more discerning about what they bought, design quality became of greater interest and significance, and customer comments were relayed to the architects for refinements.

Advantages and economies profited the company, and the more successful it became, the more its customers benefited. Advertising fell to near zero as referral business surged from the usual seven percent to near seventy percent. Development costs plummeted. The company policy of value exchange spread to sub-suppliers, where advance purchases with staged delivery drove product costs lower still. Success bred success, primarily because of a mammoth reduction in design and development costs. Many suppliers were offered bulk purchasing in advance, provided they could guarantee staged delivery and accept staged payment. Most obliged, and prices tumbled further. The company vetted subcontract labour for costs and quality control while outsourcing much material, labour and products. Those who cooperated with the company via quality and price were guaranteed work in advance. With no need to seek further work, they consolidated their quality and service.

Attractive selling prices did not result from omitting essentials; forced cost economics ensured their retention. That method proved profitable, even through periods of severe industry depression when others suffered heavily. Moreover, faithful replication offered buyers exceptional design at the lowest prices while maintaining unprecedented quality control.

The formula worked to perfection. Customers and suppliers relished their involvement. They fell head over heels for contemporary design, appearance, appeal, appointments, model choices, and the opportunity to personalise their products as we (cosmetically) customise new cars on purchase. Moreover, whereas most (so-called) competitors changed their models every six or twelve months, several of the company's products were still in demand fifteen years after the initial product launch.

Few people understood that refused structural alterations throw enormous strain on market research, correspondent design, and faithful reproduction. Deficient products and refused correction combine as a fast and sure way to go broke! But, on the flip side, everyone wins! Order books filled weeks in advance. Errors, infrastructure, and administrative costs were slashed.

Do you see how it all threads together? Customers received a material product in exchange for money, but the actual value was spiritual. As a result, their lives blossomed precisely as company researchers were commissioned to discover. They did not ask what product was wanted. Instead, they asked *'what qualities and values will enhance your life?'* And that is what customers received. 'Value exchange' and satisfaction were the bottom line.

Do you see what underscored this proven success? Competition with other home builders did not exist. Instead, there was full cooperation with market preferences and collaborative production across all labour and supply chains. But more even! That successful value exchange model is the same principle that powers your consciousness. From initial research to satisfaction for all involved, the company asked consumers and suppliers, *"what do you value, and what value will you exchange for it?"*

Company and customer satisfaction resulted from the company working cooperatively with its consumer base and with all suppliers and service providers. In other words, cooperative efforts from outside the company synergistically assisted the company and, ultimately, its customers. Everyone was a winner. Now think how much more everyone would have profited had the government not stolen financial value (tax) from that exchange.

'Conscious Ascendance' describe vastly increased synergy from having our two minds on the same page. Collaborative intelligence represents the same. Intellectual diversity comes from sharing the same goal with others, such that different people work in harmony without diversion or interference. Our strengths emerge in a collaborative setting; all built on a shared sense of purpose.

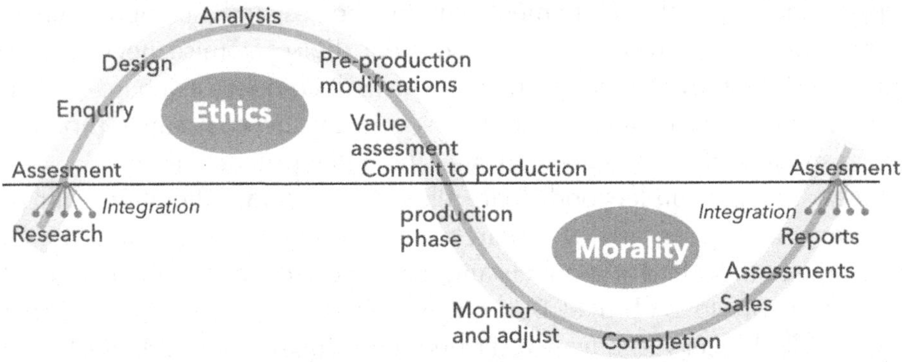

10 Business model schematic diagram

Diagram 10 plots a cooperative business model which mimics our complete conscious process in principle. It shows the design process beginning with research in the same way perception prompts our cognitive mind to enquire. Accordingly, product design and development follow the same mental function, including value assessment. Once committed to the production phase, the same monitoring and adjustment process occurs as happens in our subconscious mind. Please observe that the whole design phase embraces an ethical approach, much like our cognitive efforts.

Similarly, monitoring and adjustments occur just as our subconscious mind works. Two reports result in the same manner. The first is material evidence of a job well done, and the second is a value report as concerns profitable gain. In other words, this diagram shows how collaborative business mimics the psycho epistemology process, which is value transfer between our two minds; but here, value transfer between the producer and the consumer. Are you beginning to see just how relevant our conscious understanding is to our freedom, security, production, financial benefit, and justice? The same pattern applies in all cases.

13. Collaborative value transfer

In daily practice, our focus is more concerned with the harmony and focussed purpose of our uniquely independent efforts, almost to the point where the shared objective seems to materialise automatically. (Presto! The subconscious mind is automated.) Collaborative intelligence of this kind requires a subtle yet very fundamental change in one's thinking. It is a spiritual change fundamentally and occurs on two fronts. First to seek a spiritual value from our efforts, and secondly, to have our customers benefit as the result.

While our human nature operates on cooperation and not competition, sadly, none of us are taught anything concerning a collaborative mentality. Yet our key to a thriving future lies in learning how our resources such as creativity, motivation, and enthusiasm spark others to do likewise, resulting in synergistic harmony where everyone wins. Observe that little happens when we competitively act alone. Yet our very nature shows incredible results from many different agencies and assets working collaboratively towards life, with none sacrificing their individuality. In short, there is no competitor or enemy to be defeated. Instead, there is a host of support. No energy is sidetracked or diverted, therefore. Everything works creatively and constructively. All participants profit.

Because we are the only living species that can share and expand our knowledge from one generation to the next, the growth of expertise available to each is beyond what one individual could begin to acquire in their lifespan. Every man and woman on earth stands to gain valuable benefits from the knowledge that others discover.

Rewarding and life-sustaining benefits are not automatic. They must be diligently sought after, worked at, and accorded respect for their truthfulness, authenticity, and safe efficiency. Actions indicate, delimit and define what kind of Men can be of value to one another. Every man and woman can cultivate beneficial or detrimental outcomes of their actions, and all are free to learn of potential consequences before they act.

Division of labour in an organic society enables each to devote their effort to a particular field of work and trade with others working in other areas. Cooperation allows all who participate to achieve more knowledge, skill, and productivity return on their effort than they could make alone. The Natural Law of Cooperative Enterprise states that" a cooperative effort with others will return more benefit than individuals can achieve alone."

Governments also thrive on the division of labour, yours and mine; however, parasitism grows in advance because their focus is regulation, not production. Bankers, war profiteers, and drug dealers are parasites, as are thieves, slackers and second-handers who contribute nothing. Moochers, looters, bullies, pirates, thugs, and even corporate governments, offer no value to any individual in a convivial society. They depend on our production and fight like cornered rats to enslave us. Do such poachers gain any benefit from an organic community? No, because their harmful efforts plunder the benefits they seek to obtain. Hence no government can exist in an organic society.

Think back one hundred years and more. Before 1913, Americans kept one hundred percent of their pay cheque, but still, there were roads, schools, colleges, and fire departments. Peace-loving individuals focus on what each can do, not on what others should do, whereby division of labour makes for more choices. Those who have tasted asparagus or green beans from work efforts also have access to tuna, theatre, transport, orchestral music, travel, and non-homogenised milk.

Of course, beneficial labour division is not possible without voluntary exchange. People who trade with other owners through voluntary exchange of ideas, labour, and goods create and exchange private property. Uncoerced transfer of ownership to new owners respectfully maintains each owner's inalienable rights.

The free market in an organic society embraces the 'Trader Principle,' wherein values are unobtainable through force. Whosever wants something must offer an acceptable value in exchange; save when something is gifted or bequeathed. Thus in an organic society where one's rights are protected, property transfers are voluntary trades. Conflicts, thefts via taxation and parasitism give way to mutually beneficial, voluntary exchanges protected through natural law from which all parties benefit.

Our nature encrypts the cooperation principle

As described, the code of voluntary exchange encrypted in our consciousness and natural law is simple once consciousness is understood. First, we establish what value we seek. Then we take active steps to attain it. That is what you receive, precisely because natural law governs behavioural consequences.

Three great values gained from a convivial social existence are peace, knowledge and trade. Because Man is the only living species that can share and expand his knowledge from one generation to the next, every man and woman on earth stands to gain from what others discover.

Knowledge and free trade will blossom in a rational, productive, free society structured on independence. Will people of lesser ability miss out? On the contrary, most often, those less capable are the greatest beneficiaries of freedom and unfettered production.

Consider this example from years back.

> *'Spain is without a national government and the people are loving it. For over 280 days, the Spanish people have been without an elected government and, as it seems, it is the greatest thing to have happened to the country since it's four-decades-old democracy began. In the words of language teacher, Félix Pastor, "no government, no thieves." Though the leaders warned that the country without a government would fall into chaos, the opposite seems to have happened. Since officials have stepped out of the way, people are thriving.' —Secrets of the fed.*[16]

Thus self-governance may replace the government, but not as an entity we have known. Self-governance maintains our 'natural order.' Protection of our rights is all needed after that. Self-governance goes hand in glove with a 'protectorate,' wholly and solely given to protecting self-governance. It follows that whereas the Australian people are gifted an opportunity to stamp the word FREEDOM on the world map, unprecedented in world history, so too is every other nation. All people can enter a new 'age of independence and freedom,' founded on insights into the laws governing our human nature. That revolution is now yours for the taking.

Chapter 14

14. The Choice

Humanity is at a critical junction. One road leads to a very bleak future. The other offers an unprecedented spiritual age, requiring independent minds with confidence sufficient to dispel all social pressures to obey invented edicts. We must begin knowing and stop believing. Stop blindly accepting what government, religions, teachers, and so-called 'experts' want us to believe. We must stop giving away our power, free our mind, learn to master our consciousness, grasp hold of its incredible abilities, discover our individual rights and protect them.

> *Men fight for freedom; then they begin to accumulate laws to take it away from themselves —Thomas Jefferson*

This book has shown how the same natural laws that govern our consciousness can genuinely build a more just and prosperous world. Still, it takes effort to gain competence, knowledge, and wisdom.

- The natural law of allowance offers that window of opportunity through the gift of free choice.
- The natural law of just consequence necessitates that we choose, always remembering that refusal is a choice.

Whilst these natural laws invoke natural justice, we must ask how much we prize collective consensus government of our lives, as compared to the individual sovereignty of each man and woman human to govern themselves, free from coercive, top-down power.

The world shut itself down in 2020, and has become the 'new normal.' Centuries of conscious ignorance have struck with a vengeance! But, today's battle is not medical, political or financial. It is not about vaccines, RFID chips, new elections, 5G or a gold standard. Instead, we are now face to face with an infernal intellectual and philosophical nightmare that has wreaked havoc on the world, and that now forces us to confront and deal with our human nature as never before.

That is a good outcome, troublesome and frightening as it might seem. Our lives are now at the turning point in human consciousness. Either we succeed in grasping our true nature and benefit from that knowledge, or we fail miserably and continue to reap what we sow.

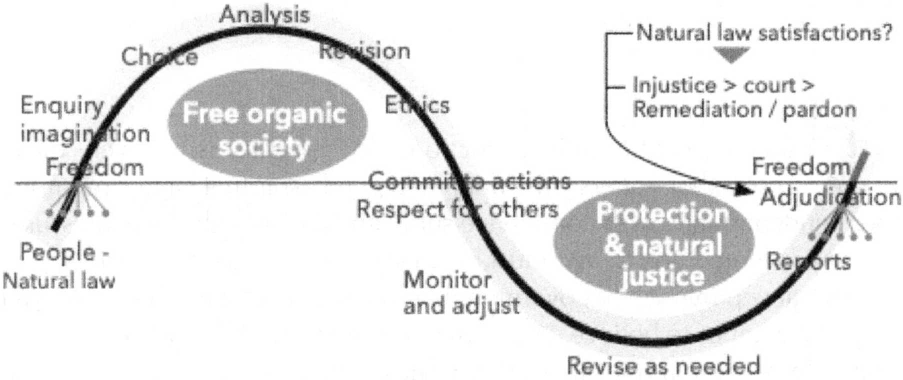

11. Free Societies

Let me return to a previous diagram where Man-made law on the left switched to natural law on the right-hand side. That success is profound. Free organic society takes over from free will in our conscious process. When committing to act, *'respect for others'* is engaged. Ethics become our morality. After that, our behaviour is monitored and adjusted just as the subconscious process works. All come together to reveal not only our material progress but also our morality. Our actions produce two reports in daily practice, just as our subconscious mind does. Should those outcomes testify to justness and morality, freedom remains as it began. If not, we relinquish our freedom through our wilful choosing, such injustice towards others being a matter for natural law courts.

This diagram confirms that freedom prevails from start to finish according to our individual choices. The government no longer exists. Accordingly, this switch advises a 'protectorate', not a government.

14. The Choice

Our Creator's will is natural governance. Life prescribes that we uphold it as best possible. Our governance is the source of justness, inwardly to ourselves, and later broadcast to the world as our morality. Spiritually based ethics are no less than spiritual life values put on autopilot, as previously described. To employ life values is to use ethics. To put those values on autopilot is to put morality on autopilot.

Once we grasp that the (natural law) principles of ethics, morality, and natural justice, reside in the core of our conscience and emotional reporting systems, we see Creator's recipe for personal freedom, and the means for free organic societies thereby. Creator's will is self-governance within natural law and no less.

This book and *'Conscious Ascendance'* offer a new personal and societal platform never told in all history. They point to a glorious future within your grasp if you reach out and take it. Do you want a vibrant new life or to support domination and control with every escape route blocked? Do you want authoritarians and psychopaths to prescribe your life or to master it as your Creator bestowed using your free will choice so to live in a free symbiotic society?

If that is your preference, you can assume complete conscious control. You can master your mind and yourself. You can grow mentally, emotionally and spiritually. You can reap the rewards beyond any you've dreamt, but unless you act, nothing will change. These publications offer an unprecedented opportunity to open a new epoch in world history lasting thousands of years.

Government and its legal processes are antithetical to man's nature and morality. Government cannot ever defend freedom when it decrees some must be deprived to control others. When today's millions who strive to overturn government tyranny finally accept the impossibility of any government, and turn their attention to the study of man instead, they will sense the simplicity and beauty of creation that has been denied their understanding for centuries. Only a body of men and women charged with 'justly' defending Man and Man's rights can protect that condition.

To that end I wrote a Constitution *of* Man in 2013, not a constitution *for* man. The Preamble text read as follows—

Whereas the value of Mans' life derives from the chosen actions of living, and Mans' value has been harvested and plundered for centuries by pirates, monarchies, military rulers, despots, oppressors, dictators, lawmakers, mercenaries, fascists, socialist and communist regimes, republican and democratic rule, tyrants and corrupt corporations — none have allowed that the sustaining of life according to free-will choice is of the nature of Man, qua Man, his fundamental right and correspondent responsibility to self and all others — equally bestowed by Creator upon every Living (Homo sapiens) Being without exception. Therefore, having suffered endless tyranny and rule for centuries, Independent Living Beings (henceforth ILBs) of planet earth now find it necessary to be bound together in their search for life, freedom and pursuit of happiness within the natural rights and laws of their individual being, respectfully equal with the rights of all others; all authority and usurpation denied.

Recognising our bond to natural laws and freedom, we now ordain and establish this 'Constitution of Man' to ensure individual freedom, thereby preserving equality and justice through personal respect and accountability, according to the immutable right to life founded in man's nature. Creator's provisions are now individually accepted into the hearts and minds of the One People, inseparable in perpetuity.

In testament thereof, this Constitution witnesses the right of all Independent Living Beings to fulfil their purpose, according to their own choice. Such forbids the initiation of force, fraud or coercion against any other Independent Living Beings or group(s); in consequence, to morally and practically ensure that force is used only in retaliation against those who initiate it to arrest its continuance. Therefore, to establish individual freedom, equality and justice in perpetuity, We, the One People of Planet Earth, now ordain and establish this Constitution of Man equally applicable to all Independent Living (human) Beings in posterity and perpetuity.

Section one solely pertained to a Declaration of Individual Rights, which included the Right to Life, Right of Equality and Sovereignty, Right to Freedom, Right to Value and Property, Right of abdication, Conditional Right of Independence, Right of Protection, and Rights in Perpetuity.

Article 9 declared Collective Rights as Inadmissible, and Article 10 precluded all Exceptions and Amendments.

Section Two concerned Provisions of Justice. Its Articles included a Grant of Charter for a Commissions of Justice and the resultant Independent Commission(s) of Justice. If further declared all previous Laws Null and Void, no amendments to the Constitution of Man permitted.

These core principles, once established, are sufficient to draft a constitution for a country, state or nation. After that, it only remains to add particular clauses concerning the makeup of the protectorate in recognition of its geographic, cultural, or population make-ups, densities and so forth.

Only recently, I received a (photographed) document identical to the above principles. Therefore, I have transcribed it with minuscule changes only, as follows.

Constitution of the Universe

Preamble

The purpose of human life is to live happily.

The function of government is to guarantee those conditions that allow individuals to fulfil their purpose. Those conditions can be guaranteed through a constitution that forbids the use of initiatory force, fraud or coercion by any person or group against any individual.

Article 1

No person, group of persons or government may initiate force, threat of force, or fraud against any individual's self or property.

Article 2

Force may be morally and legally used only in self-defence against those who violate Article 1.

Article 3

No exception shall ever exist to Articles 1 & 2.

The Constitution Of The Universe rests on six axioms.

1. Values exist only relative to life.
2. Whatever benefits a living organism is a value to that organism. Whatever harms a living organism, is a disvalue to that organism.
3. The basic value against which all values are ensured is the conscious individual.
4. Morals relate only to conscious individuals.
5. Immoral actions arise from individuals choosing to harm others through force, fraud, deception, coercion — or from individuals choosing to usurp, attack, or destroy values earned by others.
6. Moral actions arise from individuals choosing to benefit others to collaboratively producing values for them.

My initial goal was a structure based on those principles. It has now become a Protectorate instead of an Independent Commission of Justice. This book adopts the protectorate principle suiting any nation on earth, hence the end of authoritarian government.

Diagram 9 (Page 164) is poles apart from the (ruling) government diagram previously shown in diagram 7 (page 160). The Protectorate, Diagram 9, is authorised to perform two tasks only. First, to protect people's unalienable rights to act in support of their own life and sustenance, and second to protect the natural law of the human world. In fundamental terms, the Protectorate does not exist to prescribe one's morality. Neither does it rule or command anyone or anything. Instead, it protects your right to make those judgments and to arrest and remediate (immorally intentioned) 'unjust' actions that harm, disable or destroy your life.

Anyone who seeks to interfere with the Protectorate (diagram 5 page 149) must first pass through the Constitution because there is no other entry point. The Protectorate is itself protected. Neither can any of the 'people' spoil freedom contra the diagram flow. Every attempt to do so runs headlong into the Protectorate, whose role is to prevent such attempts. Thus anyone who attempts to violate freedom is served justice through their actions. The Protectorate is thereby prevented from writing any rules of its own; unnecessary because upholding immutable natural law that already exists does justice. Thus the Protectorate cannot initiate force or violence; it can only use retaliatory force (police) to end incited violence. Theft (aka tax) and eminent domain are forbidden.

Is there any precedence for such a thing? Not practically but in principle yes there is. The Protectorate's purpose and strictly contained function are to uphold and protect the sovereign, unalienable, Individual Rights of all men and women equally for orderly, universal, peaceful, harmonious co-existence of human life. That need is unmistakable. Every government in Earth's history has failed or will fail. No monarch, dictator or government has fully upheld the unalienable 'Individual Rights of Man'. None can without relinquishing their authority and the tyranny and slavery they oversee!

That is not news. In a letter to Stephen Cleveland (March 18, 1837–June 24, 1908), who was the 22nd, and 24th President of the United States, Lysander Spooner chastened the President, amongst other offerings, as follows—

> *For the reasons now given, the simple maintenance of justice, or natural law, is plainly the one and only purpose for which any coercive power --- or anything bearing the name of government --- has a right to exist.*

It is intrinsically just as false, absurd, ludicrous, and ridiculous to say that lawmakers, so-called, can invent and make any laws, of their own, authoritatively fixing, or declaring, the rights of individuals, or that shall be in any manner authoritative or obligatory upon individuals, or that individuals may rightfully be compelled to obey, as it would be to say that they can invent and make such mathematics, chemistry, physiology, or other sciences, as they see fit, and rightfully compel individuals to conform all their actions to them, instead of conforming them to the mathematics, chemistry, physiology, or other sciences of nature.

Lawmakers, as they call themselves, might just as well claim the right to abolish, by statute, the natural law of gravitation, the natural laws of light, heat, and electricity, and all the other natural laws of matter and mind, and institute laws of their own in the place of them, and compel conformity to them, as to claim the right to set aside the natural law of justice, and compel obedience to such other laws as they may see fit to manufacture, and set up in its stead. —Lysander Spooner [10]

Far too many people believe that government exists to grant their freedom or that government is a benevolent provider of benefits. Look for your own sake and your children's sakes. We've been told the truths of freedom over and over, for way more than 100 years, more than 2000 years in fact!

There is no excuse for the continuity of 'law makers" when the Laws of Creation themselves have so long existed. Neither is there any excuse for not discovering these 'natural laws.' I suggest you follow the footnote link to read the full-text Spooner wrote to President Cleveland.

Natural Law disdains such things as position, rank and title. It is the orderliness of people living together as people, free from all restraint save reciprocal moral obligation and respect for the rights of others. These conditions have prevailed since very ancient times because the nature of man has not changed. Customs, clothing, tools and transportation have changed, but our need to attend to our welfare and survival has not. Social interaction has changed with legal systems, conformism, regulations, conventions, and such idiocy as political correctness in modern times. Still, Man's nature has not changed; thus, natural law is no different now from what it was then.

I will now focus on a (previously drafted)' Constitution for the Protectorate of Australia,' but amended for any nation on earth to adopt, based on previous chapters, especially chapters nine, ten, and eleven. What follows is more in note form than in (legal) language that I would properly use in a constitution document. Nonetheless, it is devoted to the concept of protecting the freedom of people to govern themselves.

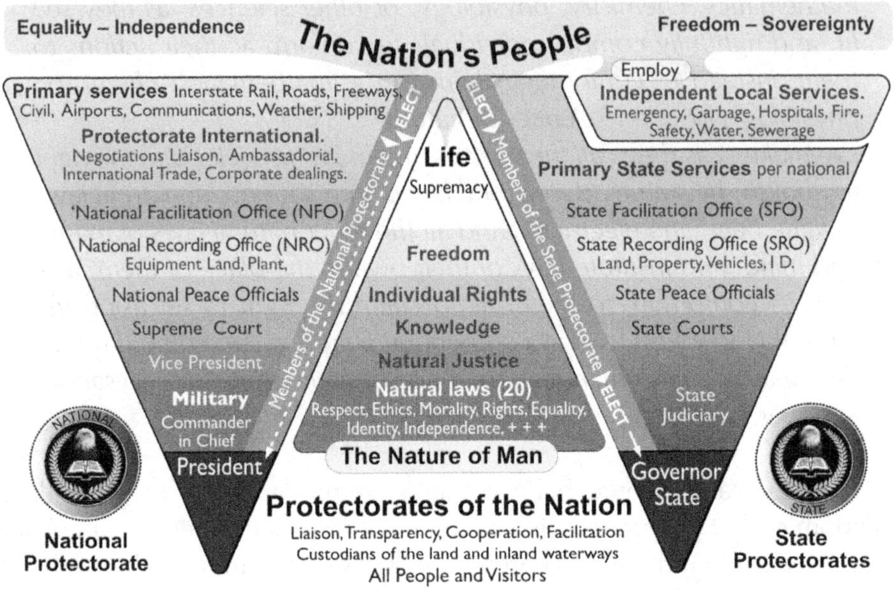

The principle is straightforward, as shown in this diagram here repeated from Chapter 9 (page 164). The base of the centre triangle is the 'nature of man.' That is the starting point. At its pinnacle is the supremacy of life, and from this springs the Nation's people. They elect a national president, members of the national Protectorate, and members of their (respective) state Protectorates, who elect a state governor. As discussed in Chapter eleven, respective services and protections grow from these bodies, all under the Constitution Document and Charter of Individual Rights.

The constitution document begins with defining the geographical land mass and all states within. Then, all state Protectorates fuse as the 'National Protectorate,' whose 'Commander in Chief' is the 'President.'

This totality replaces the former governmental structure according to the Declaration of Independence. Thereafter, the national and (sub-national) State protectorates have the standing and provenance to act for the Nation's people.

14. The Choice

Per my original draft for Australia, the people are now called Australian Nationals,' alternatively by their resident State, e.g., as a Tasmanian National or a Western Australian National. None are 'citizens.' No legal reference to the word 'person' remains, so people may use the word person as ordinarily happens in colloquial everyday speech. Some text that follows is from the constitution document; however, the word 'Nation' substitutes for the word 'Australia' for international relevance and application.

Because the sovereign Right to Life of all Sentient Living Beings is non-revocable and non-negotiable, one's right to seek life-sustaining goals or outcomes through actions within the equal rights of all others categorically forbids all trespass of those rights. Therefore, there can be no debate without one relinquishing those rights; whence all discussion is cancelled.

No group (or government) can have Rights above those of the sovereign Individuals of the Nation. No authority is granted to any individual to command another. All commandment is refused, no man or woman a human agent; no legal or other instrument presiding contrary, or contradictory of the unalienable individual Rights of Man herein formulated. No group rights can exist since every group member has the necessary rights. No claim of right can exist that does not already exist.

Given the right to life, one's right to uphold and sustain their life is also a given; every fruit of their labour is an inalienable right; hence the unalienable right to life and inalienable property right. Rights are fully preserved in any process to contract for the acquisition, transfer, or exchange of property.

All forms of theft are thereby denied, including all duties, registrations, income tax and eminent domain. Neither the National Protectorate nor any State Protectorate has any power or authority to make or enforce rules, statutes or (positive law) legislations; no power to set limitations on the people; no power or authority to dictate, coerce, violate or overrule the freedom of thought; and no immunity from criminal prosecution. Moreover, no declared 'emergency' of any kind may override the rights of the people.

Since no protectorate can wage war on any foreign country or power, the military's task is to Protect the Nation's people from international threats, piracy, drugs and aggression; to protect the Nation's borders from illegitimate travel and trade.

Border protection does not exist to enforce written law, collect revenue, or help 'build' a safe, secure and prosperous Nation, but to uphold natural law. It prevents international criminals from harming the people, including all international cartels, incorporated bodies, alphabet agencies, foreign governments, and banking institutions howsoever structured, regardless of past treaties, pledges, covenants or alliances.

Neither should the military be tasked with protecting the commercial interests of the Nation's people. Every Article, clause and word of the Constitution serves the protection of life and property only. Accordingly, no government exists to proscribe standards and enforce them. Instead, industry practitioners most knowledgeable in their endeavour determine precautions and safety measures. Thereafter such provisions are protected from political interference and sabotage.

People who choose to countermand, trespass, or violate the governing laws of nature or nature's God relinquish their right to so choose in that instant. Natural justice exists for remediation, reparation and restoration of the natural order, as described in Chapter four. Excessive bail shall not be required, excessive fines imposed, or cruel and unusual punishments including death ever committed. Justices may repair to traditional precedents of (positive) statute law where appropriate and create new precedents, provided that nothing therein made shall conflict with the rights and liberties defined within the Nation's Charter of Individual Rights and its Constitution.

Many aspects of treason are dealt with by Jurisprudence, the philosophy of law and the formulation of its teaching. Such include treason charges, overt acts, giving aid and comfort, declaring war, espionage, terrorism, conspiracy to levy war, sedition, insurrection or rebellion.

People are permitted to express anger toward the Protectorates — even a desire to overthrow them — but speech that is likely to incite others to violence is not protected. Although words usually cannot constitute treason, they often prove the speaker's treasonous intent.

Each nation needs to determine the makeup of its National and State Protectorates and how essential services serve local communities, as discussed in Chapter nine. But, again, remember that the primary task is 'protecting,' not 'provisioning.' Some matters deserve further mention, however.

Protective services include the protection from harm and ill-health, ensuring continuity of fire fighting services, protection of health during emergencies, ambulance services and hospitals, waste removal and pest control, and protection from dangerous building and construction practices.

The people themselves need to provide such assets as they deem fit, for which purpose they have access to a State Facilitation Centre, as below. There, professionals can assist with all aspects of planning, construction and community finance provisioning. Local people are thereby responsible for establishing their community assets per local choices, all resultant aids and services being safety and health protected courtesy of the state protectorate. All are of the people, thus instituted for the people. The only state control necessary in an organically free society is preserving the people's rights to freedom.

The State Facilitation Centre's (SFC) task is to make available specialist safety experts who guide industries in effecting the protection of life and property. For example, it is not for protectorates to proscribe building safety standards but to ensure that those who refuse safety standards established by the building industry bear the full consequences of their actions.

Remember that it takes time to let go of the notion that government is a watchdog that relieves our responsibility. Our responsibility today is to destroy that idiotic myth.

It is now time to make the profound mental shift from administering proscriptive (government) statutes and punishments for non-compliance to fully embracing self-administered protection founded on natural law. Then you will be able to adjudicate and ratify your Nation's Constitution and become acknowledged as one of the founders of the most outstanding social achievement in humanity's history.

Biometric identification is not that spoken of today as digital identification. Its task is straightforward. It attests that you live and have relinquished your legal identity, whereby you live as a flesh and blood human being. Necessarily each Nation should specify that every national (living being) only be lawfully identified as the biometrics of life witness. That done, (legal) fictional identities that are dead are void from inception for that reason.

Such a method exists. It is called 'iDeed,' and it already functions in America for 'American State Nationals.' It provides an Identification code, which doubles as a private bank number. Additionally, it offers a Private Property Code, which doubles as number plates for up to nine different private cars. Plus, it provides a security number to test any theft of one's private ID system. Birth certificates and driver's licence IDs are made redundant — both are fraudulent from inception.

Because one's biometric ID numbers or codes are the private property of the donor, other people's use, sharing, or harvesting without consent following full disclosure is theft. No data sharing or sale is permissible. Because 'Life' exists or does not, it cannot be an appendage of itself. Life ownership is thereby rendered impossible, self-ownership included. Neither the National Protectorate nor any State Protectorate may assume any sovereign 'ownership' right to rule the Nation's People like chattels, a strict violation of the Charter of Individual Rights.

'Identity Theft' is 'Property Theft' if it results in losing one's individual right to life or property, including personal assets. Personal identification is the person's sole property and cannot be removed or taken away under any circumstances since biometric data is one's private property.

The National Protectorate provides and maintains a 'Recording Office' (NRO) in place of what is today a 'registry.' Its purpose and guiding parameters are the protection of life and property. One's personal ID will top the list. All previous 'registrations' may be transferred to the public record, thereby cancelling stolen ownership via 'registration.'

State protectorates will establish State Recording Offices (SRO) for State-related purposes, not National. Recording at the SRO replaces government licensing; no fees or taxes apply. The separate record of private cars and transport shall exist for private property ownership, theft arrest, and car recoveries. Each individual's assets, such as their automobile, can be recorded. The Biometric ID already contains a Private Property Code (PPC) that doubles as a car number plate for up to nine private vehicles. Instant identification of the owner is now possible in the case of accident or death for the notification of family or next of kin. The SRO will separately record business, and commercial vehicles, including State vehicles, taxis, busses, ambulances and the like.

Personal (biometric) identification serves as an ID replacement for driving licences, now a thing of the past. However, car insurance companies will likely insist that claimants prove their driving ability.

Personal (biometric) identification recorded at the State Recording Office may also serve to replace passports. Moreover, once other Nations grasp the protected advantages of freedom, they too will see that protections now afforded to International travel and the ability to arrest convicted felons at the border are all that passports formerly achieved.

Copyright protection should adequately ascribe to the author or artist for all works of intellectual property 'fixed in any tangible medium of expression,' including but not limited to books, photographs, drawings, music, architecture, drama, sculpture, web pages, software, and multimedia works. Further discussion concerning 'patents' is beyond the scope of this book.

National and state police come into focus, and law courts, all addressed in the Constitution document for Australia; suffice to say, universal application is beyond the scope of this book. The same applies to border protection. Nevertheless, some general matters deserve address.

Road, rail, and air transport facilities protect the rights and safety of those traveling. Navigation beacons, satellite comms, and weather bureaus serve similar protective functions. However, since none of these assets commands usage, no law can exist that demands it.

Safety standards also protect, but none may command compliance without trespassing free will. All are advisory, therefore. One can choose to respect advice or not, but none can escape the consequences of their actions. Natural law upholds one's free will. For example, those who exceed advisory (highway) speed signs will most likely self-cancel their automobile insurance. That is the 'natural law of just consequences.' No government exists to impose a fine. Trespassers choose to punish themselves.

No need remains for government departments to regulate trade, industry and commerce, thence enforce compliance through punishment. However, those businesses should craft 'terms and conditions' to clearly and fully express what is required and what consequences apply. Natural law and free will are upheld. Fewer conditions will apply since most terms today exist to legally protect a business from punitive government action, not consumers.

One of the principal roles of the National Facilitation Centre (NFC) is to prepare educational material for the Nation's People for teaching curricula at all levels. This mission is wholly protective. The better people understand their rights and freedoms and how to respectfully maintain them, the greater they will see that no crime can deliver better, whereby crime rates will markedly crash.

Such education material may be known as the 'National Freedom Standards' (refer to Chapter 12)

The Freedom Standards have a broad compass, including–

- A detailed explanation of the biological, psychological and human conscious process, the source of the twenty natural laws, their application and societal relevance.

- An ethical and moral educational structure that describes profound respect for the laws of nature and nature's God.
- A detailed explanation of ethical and moral uniformity thus derived, definitive and unambiguous in meaning and purpose, applicable personally and societally.

The Freedom Standards intentionally provide a frame of reference for all teachers and educators. Their publication will take some time, but once ratified and published; they will be the definitive reference guide pointing to the Constitution and Charter of Individual Rights.

Natural law was rejected some five hundred years ago and replaced with a theoretical construct of the 'state of nature,' which nonsensical beliefs permitted what we call the 'Social Contract.' Thomas Hobbes held that the 'state of nature' is a state of anarchy, an existence on earth that is nasty, brutish and short. It has no law to govern it, save *"might makes right."* Men and women are only capable of acting in their self-interest, according to Hobbes. An authoritarian government utilising a 'social contract' is the only way to restore order and stop civilisation from complete self-destruction. In Hobbes' state of nature, there is no place for practical reason and no room for conscience. Instead, the ambitions of each individual are checked only by external constraints, usually fear.

Later, Jean-Jacques Rousseau posited the *"satisfaction of desire."* During the 16th, 17th, and 18th centuries the' social contract' became popular. Theorists used it to explain the need for government and the obligations of its subjects. Very briefly, it provided that all individuals forfeit their natural freedom in exchange for state protection. No one saw the glaring mistake or they chose to ignore it; thus, rule without question was born and has remained to this day.

The 'Social Contract' argued that more care is devoted to state organisation than to what it does. The reason is that nothing it does can ever be unjust since the 'Social Contract' is the foundation of all law. Do you see error; gross injustice and permitted crimes against humanity for centuries? The 'Social Contract' entirely theorises that our endowed state of nature is an (unruly) anarchical condition with no law. That supposition, baseless as it is, was complete justification for newly forming the British Empire in the 1680s. And it remains the same justification used today by the 'One World Order' globalists.

14. The Choice

Do you see where this criminal insanity leads? Government and enforced rule are unequivocally imperative because nothing else is humanly possible! But it gets worse. The social contract, which none of us signed, poses the question, *"why should we not have a right to all things, since all things have been declared a matter of human rights?"* Do you wonder why all human institutions (tribes, groups, the family, universities, etc.) must submit to the state's power having unlimited authorisation to do whatever it pleases? Because, never shredding the social contract, we approved it. Tacit consent is called 'consent of the governed,' so we consented to 'force backed rule.'

The state expands, throttling our capacity for action while our understanding of its motives fades to nil. The immense machinery of the state does all it can to cancel all references and benchmarks. So it produces a world of conformity. 'Command' is concealed through the magical word 'legal,' its modus operandi very carefully structured so that everyone complies without question. It's what we do or must do. Power is inferred, not commanded, and everyone falls into line. The state thereby fertilises an artificial 'state of nature,' an anarchical condition that demands rule without question, as (manufactured) proof upholding the insanity that initiated its existence in the first place. Worse yet, we must adapt to this artificial nature as animals adapt to organic nature, whereby our creative abilities are smashed almost beyond repair.

Natural law never found its roots. So we know nothing of the beautiful flower that should have bloomed worldwide. My descriptions of full consciousness have slain that beast at last. Natural law is indeed an immutable fact, not a theory! The root of natural law is your life and mine. Therefore, the mental switch is to divorce the consciousness process from physicality, not from the content it processes. When the morality of 'is' versus 'ought' is re-directed to the supreme value of life, one grasps the absolute necessity to protect it and protect the means so to do.

Natural law is an objective science since its sole object is life's sustenance and maintenance. Because it governs the consequences of human actions, no preemptive direction or command can exist; thus, all orders are void. Accordingly, there can be no such thing as 'law enforcement or 'law enforcement officials,' or indeed 'law enforcement officers (LEOs).' However, surveillance methods may arrest trespass or violations of the natural law (order).

Aristotle came closer to the truth than any other natural law advocate.

He rejected subjectivist ideologies about the good. The fact of goodness is not its relation to desire, but instead that it is the perfective or completing of a being, which entirely depends on that being's nature. He stated, *"what is good for an oak is what is completing or perfective of the oak, which depends on the kind of thing that an oak is by nature."*

Natural law is equally simple and scientific. Your 'nature' is that of 'Life' expressing itself. So what is completing or perfective of you is perfective of life. Add that your heart and lungs perform as do your conscious process, and it is clear that our governing laws are perfective for ourselves and our lives.

There can be no debate unless you reject your nature as the means of so doing. And that cancellation of nature is what 'social contract' (government) perpetrators have done unto themselves, willingly, without force or coercion.

Am I alone in this view? The answer is yes, and no. I am alone in discovering that twenty natural laws exist within every man, woman and child and that nothing taught concerns them, save for one. But I am not alone in grasping the juristic essence of natural law as a science; therefore, a matter of jurisprudence. I highly commend your study of natural law through the many works of Frank van Dun — a philosopher of law in the Netherlands. All the groundwork is done and is now available to students of jurisprudence. Most importantly, van Dun shows the exact differences between natural law and all forms of Positive (man-made) law.

Those who take on the job of compiling the Freedom Standards have another resource avenue to follow. I refer to the extensive works of novelist/philosopher Ayn Rand, author of the world-famous book *'Atlas Shrugged'* (1957). The online *'Ayn Rand Lexicon'* has many pages of her quotations and other 'objectivist philosophers' concerning just about any ethical or moral subject you can think of, not forgetting individual rights. Do not panic when you find the index alone runs to about eight pages. Be thankful you have an outstanding reference source that will massively reduce your learning task.

Best of all, I find strong correspondence between my work and these two masters of philosophy, especially since we all speak constructively concerning human moral practices. So there is no need to increase your vibrations, canvas new age jargon, or consult Blacks Law Dictionary. All are redundant. Above all, remember that any document upholding Man's life must express that every violator self-confesses unlawful trespass. If not, then its (constitutional) substance fails natural law, which in turn fails humanity.

We cannot discard the twenty natural laws with impunity; thus, protection is imperative. But unfortunately, where America justly set forth means to protect the people, it omitted protection of those laws. This book intentionally cancels that failing once and for all.

My two books offer a skeletal reference for all who desire to become founders of the greatest intellectual and spiritual revolution in history. Those laws are, without doubt, forerunners of great works yet to come. Together, their sociological and political foundation is more ethical, moral and just than any the world has ever witnessed, all consented, protected, upheld, and backed by our Creator! These books are the key to personal thriving and societal freedom unprecedented in world history. I urge that you read' Conscious Ascendance' if you've not already done so.

Humankind must urgently choose a new path. If not, that option will close shut, and society will vanish. No tinkering will work; bandaids will not cure a rotting body, so our choice is unequivocally clear cut. Institute a new societal model that kills enforced rule or be forcibly killed as ruled today. Genocide is unambiguous. Ruling psychopaths have declared their intent unmistakably; every escape route slammed shut, but one. The crime is theirs, not ours. They chose criminality and must bear the consequences, as the 'natural law of justice' principle declares. Our remedy is to build a new societal model that makes the old redundant. Fortunately, you now have the tools and the workshop manual.

Humanity's future rests in your hands. Your love and passion for life, particularly your devoted 'will' to thrive in freedom, will jump-start success. So start now to use your dynamic powers! Thrive like never before and step up to your nation's glorious future as one of its founders. Embrace this transformative challenge with a zest for life. Love will blossom unconstrained as this personal and societal revolution becomes yours to enjoy. Your heart will sing in praise as peace calms your soul. So too, will your great-grandchildren and the people of your nation over many centuries ahead.

Acknowledgements

To reach self-governance and societal orderliness with protective backup is revolutionary, given no past history of any such concept. The connection is unmistakable notwithstanding.

I am indebted to the work of Ayn Rand and her outstanding Objectivist Philosophy. Her grasp of life values greatly assisted me to understand consciousness and to grasp the orderliness of its sequential process. Frank van Dun helped my understanding enormously, his explanations of natural law greatly assisted my revelations of the twenty natural laws encrypted in our human nature. Mark Passio's contributions to natural law are also outstanding. His passion and fire for truth expressly presses that this information is imperative to society, and urgent! I am also indebted to the work of Larken Rose particularly related to the take down of authority.

The observations and contributions of all these people have a magnitude that few people grasp. Thanks to them and countless others, this book may never have been written.

Thanks also to my sons Scott and Craig, also to my colleague Max Taylor Jr in America. Grateful thanks also to Linda Ray in Western Australia for her proofreading assistance over the past few years.

To all, please accept my heartfelt thanks for assisting in this work of monumental importance. I trust future generations will recognise that their benefits and joys are due in part to your many valued contributions.

About the Author

Superseding Kenneth's book 'Law from Within' (2017), his expanded explanations from infancy through spirituality are now 'self-help' on steroids. His book 'Conscious Ascendance' is the (part 1) forerunner of 'Navigate to Freedom.' 'Observational science' and deductive reasoning concerning consciousness reveals the natural laws on which freedom depends. The complete story becomes ever more powerful as natural law and consciousness meet face to face. Kenneth's comprehension of this diminishing complexity is astonishing, clearly resulting from 45 years practice of objectivist philosophy and his recent decade of intensive research into human consciousness and natural law. Logic and deductive reasoning show a bigger picture than those two subjects impart themselves whereby a 'Protectorate' in place of government is shown to defeat any social organisation ever attempted in the past.

Appendix:

Definitions concerning Natural law

Today's (English) language and vocabulary have been twisted, polluted and distorted beyond sensible, logical and lawful comprehension; through poisonous philosophies and theologies, political correctness, legalese and mental corrosion resulting from unchallenged beliefs. Electronic communications, such as text abbreviations, have compounded these errors such that 'near enough is good enough,' whence laziness and apathy forbid enquiry, thereby exacting a devastating toll on critical thinking, understanding and communication.

This table defines words used in this book and elsewhere to define 'existential natural law' by this author. In broad terms, this vocabulary agrees with the works of Frank Van Dun, a philosopher of law. The difference between these definitions and those often used in maritime law (the law of the sea) and common law (the law of the land) is not one of jurisdiction, although it may seem so. This list defines natural law for the proper use and the benefit of all people at all times and places.

My previous book, *'Conscious Ascendance'* contains specific definitions concerning the human conscious process.

Allegiance [noun] - By the 'individual rights' immutably inherent in human nature, one's moral duty to uphold the public order and be a protector of all peoples inherent rights and freedoms.

Australian National [noun] - A flesh and blood living inhabitant born or 'nationalised' on the land of one of the states of 'Terra Australis;' not an alien, thus enabling specific reference to being, for example, a Tasmanian National or Victorian National.

Authority [noun] - in business and commerce, the power or right to give orders, make decisions, and enforce obedience. In politics and today's governments, verbal or written instructions, usually in the form of laws, acts, or statutes, having express intent to initiate rule, domination, control, overt force, dominion or lordship; all such initiated force trespassing an Individual's unalienable (free will) right to life. The word 'authority' may be used in everyday speech to delegate an action, such as "you have my authority to..." such usage specifically excludes all commands that trespass or violate free will choice.

Charter: a written grant by the sovereign or legislative power of a country, by which a body such as a city, company, or university is founded or its rights and privileges defined; a written constitution or description of an organisation's functions.

Civil: Relating to ordinary citizens and their concerns, as distinct from military or ecclesiastical matters: • Law relating to private relations between members of a community; non-criminal.

Constitution - a body of fundamental principles or established precedents according to which a state or other organisation is acknowledged to be governed:

Council: an advisory, deliberative, or administrative body of people formally constituted and meeting regularly.

Domicil. The place where a sentient living being has fixed his/her ordinary dwelling, with no present intention of removal.

Elector [noun] - An Individual qualified by the provisions of this document to (jointly with other qualified people) elect a qualified candidate to a position of 'Member' in the Australian National Protectorate or any State Protectorate.

Federal - having or relating to a system of government in which several states form a unity but remain independent in internal affairs.

Human: [adjective] Relating to or characteristic of humankind, or Mankind; of or characteristic of people as opposed to God or animals or machines; (noun) a human being. (Hu man or hue man is a legal bastardisation of the word human that refers to the colour of man, the reference to a legal person. Both are denied by natural law.)

Identification - Natural - An Australian National, or (Australian) "State" National, whose (private property) encrypted biometric identification attests their flesh and blood independent living being, to the exclusion of all invented identifications or ID, biometrically appended or otherwise.

Independent Living Being (ILB)© A copyrighted term used in the Copyrighted iDeed© process for biometric attestation of life, facilitating universal biometric ID that by nature certifies Individual Rights so cancelling any and all fraudulent (legal) identifications of that particular Individual. (ILB Identification commenced in America mid 2020)

Individual [noun] - A (single) Sentient, (volitionally conscious) Living Being having unalienable right to life and inalienable right to property: all reference to (legal) person (s) null and void.

Law [noun] (Natural law, God's law, Divine law, Laws of nature)

Order, or orderliness; the natural order / orderliness of human nature. *("Law is not a prescription telling us, how we ought to behave. Law is a natural fact, and law is natural law and nothing else." —Frank van Dun, Philosopher of law.)*

Natural Law [noun] - As for 'Law.' From the latin word Ius, which refers to a bond or obligation that arises out of a personal commitment made in a solemn speech; Law is an order of things. Accordingly, the term 'natural law' denotes a natural order of things. 'Law' also connotes respectability; law is an order of things that people ought to respect. Twenty natural laws are revealed by the full human conscious process, hence 'natural law theory' is now (factually) superseded by 'existential natural law.'

Natural Law Definition - The set of universal, eternal and immutable conditions governing behavioural consequences of volitionally conscious beings: Absent compliance with these maxims inherent in the nature and state of Man, the peace and happiness of society can never be preserved.

Naturalisation [noun] The lawful act or process by which an individual from another country may acquire nationality of Australia in accordance with Protocols concerning the Australian Declaration of Independence, Constitution of the Federal Protectorate' and Charter of Individual Rights, as administered by a State Protectorate.

Person [noun] - Per (centuries old) colloquial everyday language, an individual man or woman; a flesh and blood sentient living being; such definition repudiating or refuting all past, present, or future definitions, Law Dictionaries notwithstanding.

Person: Natural, i.e., Natural Person(n) - An individual person; this definition repudiating or refuting all past, present, or future definitions.

President [noun] - An Australian National elected by the people to the first rank or chief place to preside over the 'Protectorate' in maintenance, preservation, and continuity of its orderly, lawful function.

Police [noun] Police officials: Official monitors or observers of the public order within the natural law and individual rights, charged with detaining or arresting all who choose to violate or trespass the public order.

Police verb - maintain natural law and order in, keep the peace in, keep guard over, keep watch on, watch over, guard, protect, defend, patrol.

Policed [adjective] - Policing [verb]- Surveillance, monitoring or observation of the public order for the maintenance of peace and order as determined by (existential) natural law according to The Australian

Constitution and Charter of Individual Rights.

Police Protection Service - The civil department of a Protectorate concerned with maintenance of public orderliness and safety; Police employees trained in detection of natural law trespass and violation, crime prevention and authorised to maintain the peace, safety, and order of the community.

Protectorate [noun] (National) - a national body charged with Constitutionally protecting the rights and freedoms of the nation's people, domestically and internationally; this definition expressly denied any legislative amendment, violation, usurpation, or abolition whatsoever. that is controlled and protected by another.

Protectorate [noun] (State)- A state body charged with Constitutionally protecting the rights and freedoms of the state's people, inclusive of state visitors; this definition expressly denied any legislative amendment, violation, usurpation, or abolition whatsoever.

Rights — individual - "A 'right' is a moral principle defining and sanctioning one's freedom of action in a social context; Right to engage in self-sustaining and self-generated action for furtherance, fulfilment and enjoyment of one's life; free from physical compulsion, coercion or interference by other men. Rights are innate , immutable, invisible and indivisible; none can conflict with any other, or be deemed to. Individual Rights are axiomatic, self-evident truth.

Without property rights, none have any means to sustain their life, whereby a right to the actions and consequences of producing or earning property is not a guarantee that one will earn any property, instead a guarantee that he will own it if he earns it. Right to property is the right to gain, to keep, to use and to dispose of material values. Individual Rights are axiomatic, self-evident truth.

Rights — Inalienable - Right to Property: Inalienable right is the immutable self-evident right to the product of one's actions; fruits of one's labours, deriving from every Sentient Living Being's Unalienable Right to action. Without property rights, none have any means to sustain their life, whereby a right to the actions and consequences of producing or earning property is not a guarantee that one will earn any property, instead a guarantee that he will own it if he earns it. Right to property is the right to gain, to keep, to use and to dispose of material values.

Rights — Unalienable - Right to Life: Unalienable right is every individuals right and freedom to act on his own judgment, for his own goals, by his own voluntary, uncoerced choice in sustenance and maintenance of his life; no obligation to others save to abstain from violating their rights.

Sovereignty: Self mastery: accepting complete responsibility and liability for one's actions; an ethical mind engaging moral actions; applying life-values such as diligence, discipline, respect and integrity, in pursuit of practical, moral and spiritual thriving.

Statute. [noun] (Positive law) - A written (man-made) "law" passed by a legislative body, inclusive of regulation, enactment, act, bill, decree, edict, rule, ruling, resolution, promulgation, dictum, command, order, stipulation, commandment, directive, pronouncement, mandate, proclamation, dictate, covenant, demand, by-law, and ordinance. (Derived from the latin word 'Lex,' arising from directives used to mobilise armies). No Statute can ever apply in any Protectorate. [Any Statute found to be contrary to the Australian Protectorate Constitution is null and void and will be removed from all public record.]

Subject [noun] - A person having implied allegiance to a personal sovereign such as a monarch. No 'Subject' can exist in a Protectorate Nation.

Surveil [verb] (surveils, surveilling, surveilled) [with object] - keep (a person or place) under surveillance; closely monitor or observe.

Understand:1) perceive the intended meaning of (words, a language, or a speaker) **2)** perceive the significance, explanation, or cause of, or be sympathetically or knowledgeably aware of the character or nature of (some constituent attribute, identity or idea) 3) to comprehend, apprehend, grasp, see, take in. (No legal connotation applies, as in "standing below or standing under another's authority.

Bibliography

1. Passio, Mark. Extrapolated from his work; Web URL, www.whatonearthishappening.com/

2. Rand, Ayn. New American Library; The Ayn Rand Lexicon; Democracy. Web URL http://aynrandlexicon.com/lexicon/democracy.html

3. Rose: Larken, The most dangerous superstition. WEB URL: http://www.freeyourmindaz.com/uploads/1/2/8/3/12830241/the-most-dangerous-superstition-larken-rose-2011.pdf

4. van Dun, Frank. Natural law. Website URL, https://users.ugent.be/~frvandun/Texts/Logica/NaturalLaw.htm

5. Website. Anarchism.net. "Manifesto." Web address, http://www.anarchism.net/warren-manifesto.htm

6. Adask, Alfred. "Unalienable vs Inalienable." Web address, https://adask.wordpress.com/2009/07/15/unalienable-vs-inalienable/

7. van Dun, Frank: Voluntaryist.com: What is Kritarchy. Web URL, http://voluntaryist.com/forthcoming/kritarchy.html#.YoQ4zZOC-Zx

8. van Dun, Frank. "The Lawful and the legal" Web URL, http://users.ugent.be/~frvandun/Texts/Articles/The%20Lawful%20and%20the%20Legal.html

9. van Dun, Frank. "The Lawful and the legal" Web URL, http://users.ugent.be/~frvandun/Texts/Articles/The%20Lawful%20and%20the%20Legal.html

10. lysanderspooner.org/LetterToGroverCleveland. Website URL https://static1.squarespace.com/static/55a3c833e4b07c31913e6eae/t/55a524c0e4b01d30adbe941d/1436886208276/A+LETTER+TO+GROVER+CLEVELAND.pdf

11. Herbert, Auberon. Advocate of reason, individual rights, and limited government. The free library Website URL https://www.thefreelibrary.com/Auberon+Herbert%3A+Advocate+of+reason%2C+individual+rights%2C+and+limited...-a0472372933

12. Blackstone, Sir William.Commentaries 3 Right of revolution. Website URL. https://press-pubs.uchicago.edu/founders/documents/v1ch3s3.html

13, MacGregor, David, Self-Ownership: The Foundation of Freedom. Website URL. http://www.tolfa.us/arts/found.htm

14. Warren Josiah, Cincinnati Time Store. Wikipedia, Website URL https://en.wikipedia.org/wiki/Cincinnati_Time_Store

15. Rand, Ayn. New American Library; The Ayn Rand Lexicon; Human rights and property rights. Website URL http://aynrandlexicon.com/lexicon/human_rights_and_property_rights.html

16. Secrets of the Fed.com. "Spain is without a national government and the people are loving it." Web address, http://secretsofthefed.com/spain-is-without-a-national-government-and-the-people-are-loving-it/

Made in the USA
Monee, IL
04 November 2026

67383638R00144